AF658215

DISTRICT ADMINISTRATION

DISTRICT ADMINISTRATION

Redefining the Development Role

Edited by

Rakesh Hooja
Sunil Dutt

KANISHKA PUBLISHERS, DISTRIBUTORS
NEW DELHI-110 002

KANISHKA PUBLISHERS, DISTRIBUTORS
4697/5-21A, Ansari Road, Daryaganj
New Delhi-110 002
Phones : 2327 0497, 2328 8285
Fax : 011-2328 8285
e-mail: kanishka_publishing@yahoo.co.in

First Published 2008

© Indian Institute of Public Administration, New Delhi

ISBN 978-81-8457-068-7

PRINTED IN INDIA

Published by Madan Sachdeva for Kanishka Publishers, Distributors, 4697/5-21A, Ansari Road, Daryaganj, New Delhi-110 002; Typeset by Sunshine Graphics, Delhi, and Printed at Nice Printing Press, Delhi.

Foreword

The office of the district collector has undergone many structural changes ever since its inception in 1772 by Warren Hastings. Creation of institution of district collector as the representative of government is a model of outstanding innovation by the British. A district collector functioned as the most influential officer of the administration throughout the British period. But the term became so much a part of the colonial system that it was retained down to the end of British rule. In more than 150 years of British rule the office of collector witnessed considerable structural and functional changes. Besides revenue collection, the district collector exercised civil, judicial and military powers in districts during first twenty years of its inception. Later the judicial and magisterial powers were separated from him and transferred to the district judge. Up to early years of twentieth century, no native was eligible to become a district collector.

When India became independent in 1947 the office of the collector and district magistrate continued to be recognised as the most important official in the district. He had extensive jurisdiction over the administrative and revenue matters and was also vested with the most onerous task of implementing the planned development in the district under Five Year Plans. The District Administration became the hub of activity for development of the welfare state. With the passing of years, development administration has acquired deep roots, as opposed to the time-honoured administration. As this was happening all along, even the role of collector and district magistrate had also undergone a metamorphosis. With launching of schemes in various sectors there came a period when coordinating and monitoring role of district administration became more prominent. Following the 73rd Constitution Amendment there are over 65 departments in the district and their functional head is the district collector.

This transformation during the past four decades as a consequence of the introduction of planning process has brought the office into focus for development and welfare aspirations of people and policy-makers. When there is a consensus to recognize his supremacy in the district administration for its smooth sailing, aberrations have emerged here and there. It has come to be widely believed that the significance of Collector's position has eroded due to multifarious functions that she/he has been involved over time. It is the only contacting point both for the officer as well as the general public for understanding the effect of public policy pursued by the Government of the day. On the other hand, collector's position has become more cumbersome due to government's involvement in several different kinds of welfare activities for which he functions as an important channel.

Then there is a wider awareness and gradual process in the form of assertion of people's will which needed a greater reinforcement of democratic ethos and responsiveness among the civil servants, particularly at the district and sub-district. Another factor which adds to the demand on the district administrators' caliber and resources was the need felt for planning from below, in which the institutions at the grassroots have an important place.

This volume abounds in the scholarly and well-researched writings on the traditional and evolving role of the district administration in India since Independence. Put together these essays portray a comprehensive perspective of the office of the district collector and envisage its role in the changing administrative paradigm which is going to emerge with the new socio-economic realities in a globalized world.

18th June, 2007

S.P. Verma
Director
Indian Institution of
Public Administration
New Delhi

Contents

Introduction

Commentators have been ready to write obituaries about the demise of the institution of the Collector on a number of occasions starting from 1919 and the Montagu-Chelmsford Reforms which brought about provincial autonomy and dyarchy, to independence in 1947 and the advent of Parliamentary democracy, to 1959 and the introduction of statutory Panchayati Raj, to when the separation of judicial and executive functions as per the revised Criminal Procedure Code occurred at different times in different States, to the 73rd Amendment which Constitutionalized Panchayati Raj, to the impacts of political interference like the dramatic shortening of tenures of postings of Collectors, to the economic liberalization policies adopted by Governments in recent years. Somehow despite some decline in prestige, institutional role and efficacy, the office of Collector (also referred to as Deputy Commissioner or District Magistrate in some States) which was initially assigned a prime position in the local administration by the Court of Directors of the East India Company as far back as in 1786, has, despite ups and downs, by and large continued to remain pivotal in Indian administration. Of course, the role performed by the Collector has continually evolved and changed from time-to-time as the concerns of government have changed and, as technical changes have enabled modifications in the manner of governance and public administration, and as societies expectations from government have undergone transformation with the rising aspirations of the citizens.

This process of evolution and change in the role of the Collector is being chronicled in this volume through a selection of articles published in the *Indian Journal of Public Administration* over the last half century or so. The articles retain the flavour of the period in which they were written, but are relevant today as they throw light on the fascinating subject of district administration (which continues to be the fulcrum of field administration in India) with its stresses and strains during the last couple of centuries and especially after independence in 1947. The continuity as well as change in the texture of district administration where many old problems persist while new issues keep arising, is very well brought out in the articles chosen for inclusion in this book.

The role and level of importance of the Collector has not only differed during various phases of India's past, but also varies from State to State. However, broadly speaking, today's Collector is directly responsible for, or has a coordinating function at the district level, in the following spheres (not listed as per order of importance): (1) public order, law and order and criminal administration, (2) land record administration and land revenue court work, land reforms, as well as land acquisition, (3) supervision of the district treasury, (4) civil supplies and public distribution, (5) protocol, (6) disaster management and drought relief, (7) district development, (8) conduct of elections, (9) urban and municipal affairs, (10) social welfare and social security, (11) industries, (12) agriculture, (13) cooperatives, (14) district planning and district statistics, (15) registration and stamps, (16) excise, (17) consumer affairs, (18) removal of public grievances, (19) conduct of census — human, livestock, agricultural, industrial, etc., (20) coordination with bankers, (21) supervision of jails, (22) supervision of prosecution staff, (23) MP/MLAs Local Area Development Programmes, (24) procurement of agriculture produce, (25) conduct of special campaigns, (26) arms licensing, (27) cinema licensing, (28) regulation of fairs and festivals, (29) public relations, (30) e-governance, (31) various miscellaneous or residual matters which can be grouped under a category of general administration.

In fact, the Collector is the head of general administration as well as the agent and representative of the Government in the District. Thus, to slightly modify what someone wrote in the mid-1960s with reference to the office of the Collector in Uttar Pradesh, the Collector still represents the coordinated or unified (if not integrated) administration in the district, is directly in touch with Government departments in the State Secretariat, is consulted by Government in all controversial matters, has the resources of the revenue staff and district police at his disposal, has a faithful band of officers trained in the art of administration and subject to official discipline attached to him in the Collectorate, and has Government's full support in coordinating the working of all District Level Officers (DLOs) of various departments and agencies. In fact, various departments of Government often expect the Collector to supervise, coordinate and monitor at the district level important projects, schemes, programmes and campaigns being implemented by the department.

Thus, if not the direct boss, the Collector is certainly the captain of the team, supervising, funding, coordinating, interacting with, or controlling (as the case may be) the following and similar institutions to ensure that the district keeps functioning and developing in a satisfactory manner:

(*a*) Land revenue administration based district or revenue agency which also deals with many issues of general administration;
(*b*) The police setup;
(*c*) District Level Officers (DLOs) and staff of various State Government Departments and State Public Sector Enterprises;
(*d*) Development Agency the three tiers of Panchayati Raj including both elected representatives (who traditionally used to be called non-officials) and panchayat officers or functionaries;
(*e*) Municipal bodies and urban development agencies;
(*f*) Special project agencies created to implement specific projects/programmes to meet specific objectives;
(*g*) Officers of Central Government organizations at the district level;
(*h*) The district level judiciary;
(*i*) The Institutional Credit System;
(*j*) Cooperative institutions working in various sectors like dairy, agriculture, minor irrigation etc.;
(*k*) NGOs and Voluntary Agencies;
(*l*) Community Based Organizations (CBOs), Beneficiary Organizations or User Groups;
(*m*) District level associations of various professional, trade, industrialist, etc. bodies;
(*n*) Normal trade channels;
(*o*) Mass media network;

(*p*) Local level politicians, people's representatives and pressure groups; and
(*q*) Individual citizens.

The Collector and District Magistrate has been variously described as "the king-pin of district government", 'the fulcrum of Indian administration', '*Annadata*', '*Maai Baap*', 'agent of government', 'keystone of the arch of district administration', 'captain of the team', 'more than *primus inter pares*', 'eyes and ears of the government', 'voice and hands', or 'working arms of government', 'mainsoring of development', 'general manager of all government activities', ' the tortoise on whose back stands the elephant of government'— all of which attest to the importance with which the Collector is viewed—despite the fact that the office of Collector is under strain.

The actual working of Collectors in different parts of the country at different points of time, the problems and challenges faced by them, the various changes in their roles and functions and societies expectations from them, the efficacy of Collectors and the district administration, and the possible future of the institution of District Collector in India—all find mention and analysis in the articles that follow in this book.

It is hoped that the volume would be able to provide a systematic and many faceted view of the office of the Collector and of the district administration that he heads, and thus serve as a useful source of reference on this vital sector of governance in India, to administrators, scholars and all those interested in government, public administration and administrative reforms, local administration, development in general and the social sciences. It is also expected that they, and the intelligent lay reader, would be encouraged to ponder over, discuss and analyze various aspects of the evolving role and institution of the District Collector yesterday, today and tomorrow.

—Rakesh Hooja
—Sunil Dutt

1

The Collector, Today and Tomorrow

P.K. DAVE

Eighteen years after Independence, the Collector continues to be the principal functionary of the State Government in the district. But having said this, one must accept that for all the traditional trappings of his office, the continuity of his powers under the numerous major and minor statutes and his position in the district protocol, there have been changes of a fundamental nature in the role of the Collector and in the sphere of his power and influence both within the district and on major decisions and policy formulation at the State level. These changes are almost wholly related to two factors. The first is obviously the spread of democracy down from the national Parliament to the district, block and village panchayats with the peoples' representatives at all levels taking a progressively greater share in the making of decisions. And the second is the series of steps flowing from the Directive Principles of State Policy embodied in the Constitution which are "fundamental in the governance of the country".[1]

With the downward spread of democracy and with politicians gaining greater experience and, born out of that experience greater confidence in their capacity to administer the country, the interaction of the politician with the administrative apparatus has steadily gathered momentum. A direct result is the diminution of the authority of the Collector or, to put it differently, erosion of the finality of a Collector's decisions which marked the old concept of this office. This is quite apart from the transfer of certain functions, previously performed by the Collector, to the Panchayati Raj Institutions.

The Directive Principles of State Policy have affected the Collector's role in diverse ways. The most important effect flows from the preparation of national plans of development to translate into action the various Directive Principles concerning economic and social progress. With the implementation of those programmes not only has developmental activity grown in volume and pace but it has also resulted in a proliferation of the bureaucracy in all developmental fields with separate hierarchies of their own extending downwards into the districts. The various departmental heads and their regional deputies are more easily and more frequently available for advice, guidance and support to their District Officers. These hierarchies naturally wish to conduct their programmes according to their own technical requirements and tend to resent any institutional dependence on, and supervision and control of the Collector. The improvement of means of communication and telegraph and telephone facilities have assisted this centrifugal movement. The separation of the judiciary from the executive, which again is one of the Directive Principles, and which has now been implemented in the vast majority of States has also altered quite substantially the role of the Collector, who continues to be in-charge of law and order and the head of the police administration but ceases to control the criminal courts.

It may be useful to describe very briefly how, notwithstanding the far-reaching changes in his role, the Collector continues to be accepted, by and large, as the principal representative of the State Government in the district. The regulatory functions of the Collector in the fields of revenue and land records administration, general administration, criminal administration and law and order have remained more or less unaffected. His agencies in the field, which extend down to the village level, give him a position of pre-eminence not only for informing himself and the Government of the happenings in the district, the feelings of people on all matters of importance, their difficulties and their grievances, but also afford to the Government a machinery that can take on, virtually at a moment's notice, any added responsibility of a widespread nature. He also commands all the basic administrative intelligence in population statistics, land records, agricultural statistics, political trends, the law and order situation and so on; he is, therefore, the one authority towards whom every other agency can turn for guidance and assistance in its own programme. The public image of the Collector as the representative of Government also continues unchanged and difficulties and grievances are freely brought to him in his daily correspondence or when he is on tour. There is still confidence in the public mind that the Collector can be depended upon for an objective appraisal of a grievance and non-partisan executive action.

II

The Balwantrai Mehta Study Team on Community Development and National Extension Service, which in fact gave shape to the concept of Panchayati Raj envisaged the following role for the Collector:

> "At the district level, the Collector or the Deputy Commissioner should be the captain of the team of officers of all development departments and should be made fully responsible for securing the necessary co-ordination and co-operation in the preparation and execution of the district plans for community development. Where he is not already empowered to make the annual assessment of work of the departmental officers in regard to their cooperation with other departments, their speed in work, their dealings with the people and their reputation for integrity, he should be invested with such powers."[2]

This theme has prevailed over the last few years and has also found expression in various forms in the State legislations for the establishment of Panchayati Raj institutions in most States. In Madras, Mysore and Himachal Pradesh, the Collector is the Chairman of the District Development Council/Zilla Parishad, and in Andhra Pradesh he is a member of the Zilla Parishad and Chairman of its Standing Committees; in Assam, the Deputy Commissioner is a member of the Mahkuma Parishad; in Orissa, Punjab and Rajasthan, the Collector is a member of the Zilla Parishad with no right to vote; in Gujarat, he is an associate member, and in Bihar and Uttar Pradesh, he may attend meetings of the Parishad–in all these three cases, without the right to vote; in Madhya Pradesh, Maharashtra and West Bengal, the Collector is outside the Zilla Parishad. In practically all the States, the

Collector has certain emergency powers to suspend or prohibit any resolution of the Zilla Parishad and in certain States also to direct the execution of any work falling within the sphere of the Parishad which, in his opinion, is necessary for the implementation of development plans for the safety of the public, etc.[3]

It has to be admitted, however, that the implementation of Panchayati Raj in the various States has introduced the germ of diversity in district administration in contrast to the basic continuity and uniformity which has existed over almost a century. In Maharashtra and Gujarat, for example, apart from the emergency power to suspend the execution of any order or resolution of a Zilla Parishad, the Collector is not at all in the picture in regard to developmental administration. In Madhya Pradesh and West Bengal again, where the Zilla Parishads have not yet been established, he is likely to be outside the Parishad's activities. Planning at the national level over the first three Five Year Plans has more or less established what may be called centralized control in determining developmental policies and their execution through State Governments and the agencies subordinate to the Sate Government. Nation-wide activities like the Community Development programme afford an example. This necessarily implies a certain uniformity of institutions and procedures which the trend for diversity in the Panchayati Raj organization quite likely to disturb.

III

In recent years, there has been increasing emphasis on the role of the Collector in co-ordinating programmes of development within the district in general and the programmes for agricultural production in particular. The Working Group on Inter-Departmental and Institutional Co-ordination for Agricultural Production (Chairman—*Shri Ram Subhag Singh,* Union Minister for Agriculture)[4] recommended, in 1963, that the Collector should be the Chairman of the Agricultural Production Committee of the Zilla Parishad which should be responsible for co-ordination of the activities of all Departments concerned with agricultural production. The Working Group further stated that while "State heads of Departments will continue to deal directly with their District Officers as at present, but in matters relating to the working of Agricultural Production Committee, they should communicate through the District Collector". The Collector, it was also proposed, should record an annual assessment of the work of District Officers of the department concerned with agricultural production.

Addressing the tenth annual meeting of the Indian Institute of Public Administration on October 23, 1964, the Prime Minister, *Shri Lal Bahadur Shastri*, referred to the failure of co-ordination at the district level in the following words:

> "In regard to developmental activities, the difficulty at the present moment is that there is no proper co-ordination. Formerly the District Collector used to be the co-ordinating authority. He was in overall charge of every activity in the district."
>
> "The District Collector is there, but there are also, at the district level, officers of different departments, like P.W.D., agriculture, co-operation, education, etc. There is also someone in charge of the community development work. These different units function in a district, but they are not under the direct control or supervision of the District Collector. They have their direct connections with the respective Heads of Departments sitting in the State Secretariat, or in some cases with the departmental officers at the divisional level. The result is that there is no proper coordination."[5]

Addressing the National Development Council on 27th October, 1964, the Prime Minister spoke on the same subject as follows:

> "All too often we think of these things at the national level and the State level, while there is neglect and even confusion at the village level. The farmer has now to deal separately with representatives of different Government agencies, each owing allegiance to a Department of Ministry at the headquarters of the State or Central Government. The co-ordinating role which the District Officer used to play in the past has been lost. I would suggest to all the Chief Ministers present here today that they should restore to the District Officer, whether he is known as the Collector or the Deputy Commissioner, the status of a co-ordinator of all governmental activities in the district and confer upon him the responsibility for guiding all the efforts undertaken on behalf of Government, Central or State.

This may well mean splitting up the larger districts into more compact administrative units. This task should be faced as one of urgency. I would like to emphasise this point. Some of the districts, for instance, in Uttar Pradesh, Bihar and West Bengal are very large indeed. It would be advisable for better administration to break up these districts even if it means more expenditure which will be well worthwhile."

Again, in a broadcast to the nation on October 10, 1965, the Prime Minister, emphasizing the Collector's role in the drive to attain self-sufficiency in food production, said:

"The entire team in a district has to work with a sense of dedication in the same manner as a soldier on the battle front. The District Officer should regard himself in all humility as a commander who has to organize this drive and achieve the target which must be clearly laid down. He should delegate all his routine work to some other senior officer of the district administration, reserving his own attention and energies almost exclusively for work connected with agricultural production."[6]

It is interesting to note that whenever the country, a particular region or a district faces an emergency of any kind–war, tension caused by the belligerence of a foreign power, food scarcity, epidemic, floods and so on, the Collector immediately comes into his own and becomes the chief agency for tackling the multifarious problems that arise and is unhesitatingly given full powers of co-ordination extending to the requisitioning of all the governmental resources in the district. The Chinese attack on India in 1962, and recently, the hostilities started by Pakistan have demonstrated in ample measure that the one single agency available in the field for co-ordination of governmental action on a large scale is still to be found in the Collector. The implementation of all emergency measures is invariably entrusted to the Collector and his authority to co-ordinate is not disputed.

IV

It would be useful to consider certain specific aspects, such as, the size of Collector's charges, workload, and the proportion of officers of the Indian Administrative Service employed as Collectors, their age, seniorities and length of service to appreciate properly the implications of the changes that have occurred so far.

The average size of a district varies from 1,454 square miles in Kerala to 6,951 square miles in Rajasthan and the average population from about 5,17,000 in Assam to over 2.5 million for the districts of Kerala. Excluding Jammu Kashmir and the Union Territories, the size frequency of 303 districts based on the 1961 census was as follows:[7]

Area below 4,000 sq. miles and population below one million. 73
Area above 4,000 sq. miles and population below one million. 28
Area below 4,000 sq. miles and population above one million. 118
Area above 4,000 sq. miles and population above one million. 84

The States which have districts of an average size of over 4500 square miles are Rajasthan, Assam, Andhra Pradesh, Orissa and Madhya Pradesh; and the States with districts of an average population of over 1.5 million are Kerala (2.55 m.), Bihar (2.50 m.), West Bengal (2.41 m.), Madras (2.24 m.), Andhra Pradesh (1.81 m.), and Maharashtra (1.52 m.).

The optimum size of a district charge has been a matter of considerable speculation but no fixed formula for the ideal size of a district or for the population that should be covered by it has emerged so for—it also does not seem possible to lay down a dependable norm based on these criteria. The Bengal Administrative Enquiry Committee 1944-45, made the following observation:

> "104. There is clearly a limit, although there is no clear limit, to the size of a District."
> "Several witnesses tendered evidence to the effect that most of the districts in Bengal were too big for effective administration. Some of them thought a population of about a million represented as much as a District Officer could handle, others, that 1½ million was about right. Apart from the fact that it is impracticable to redraw the boundaries of all the Districts in the Province, it is not possible to find a formula which enables one to fix with precision the ideal size

of a district. So much depends on the density of the population, the topography of the area and the nature and state of its communications. If, for example, the network of roads in the Province is, as we expect, greatly extended and improved in the post-war period, Districts which are now difficult to administer satisfactorily will become perfectly manageable."

V.L.S. Prakasa Rao and S.L. Bhatt in their study on "Planning Regions in Mysore State—The Need for Readjustment of District Boundaries" suggested that a district with an area of more than 4,000 square miles and a population of 1 million and a taluka with more than 750 square miles and a population of 150 thousand are unfavourable for efficient administration and implementation of development programmes. However, any such empirical standards are neither likely to be acceptable nor quite rational and as Prakasa Rao and Bhatt themselves admit, "the character of regional factors should be also studied before delimiting regions for planning". As the Bengal Administrative Enquiry Committee Report has stated in the citation above, much depends on the density of the population, the topography of the area and the nature and state of its communications.

While this is so, it is apparent that the number of excessively heavy district charges has been growing at the Five Year Plans have grown in size an intensity, and State governments have found it necessary to appoint Additional Collectors and other assistants to reduce the burden of routine administration, revenue case work, etc. on the Collectors. In fact, successive Five Year Plans have commented upon the need for strengthening the hands of District Officer, and giving him adequate assistance to deal satisfactorily with the work of planning and development. It does not appear, however, that the mere addition of assistants would solve the problem and sooner rather than later the State governments will have to take a comprehensive look at the manageability of each district charge.

It is difficult to make an assessment of the workload of a Collector, for much depends on the size of the charge, the intensity of administration, the level of advancement attained by the local population and indeed the character of the people—litigious, assertive, caste-ridden, fractious and so on. In an analysis of the work of Collectors in the former Bombay State, the breakdown of a Collector's workload was shown as follows:[8]

		Per cent of his time
Correspondence	—	54
Case hearings	—	2
Official and other meetings	—	7
Very important persons	—	6
Daily visitors	—	5
Touring	—	26
		100

In an All India Survey of Collectors conducted by Gillespie[9] under the aegis of the Indian Institute of Public Administration, the all-India average of hours spent "on the job" by collectors in connection with their duties, including social activities directly connected with their official position was found to be 70 hours. The break-up of this time was as follows:

		Per cent
Paper work (including studying documents and reading material)	—	36
Touring and inspecting	—	18
Attending public functions	—	4
Attending meetings	—	7
Giving and receiving instructions and information orally	—	6
Receiving visitors in office hours	—	11
Presiding formally at courts	—	6
Time for thought and reflection	—	4
Receiving dignitaries and providing red carpet treatment	—	4
Job connected social activities	—	3
Other	—	1
		100

In Gillespie's survey, it was found that 20 per cent of the Collectors thought that their paper work was "excessive and burdensome" and 49 per cent thought that it was "excessive but not burdensome." Only 20 per cent thought the paper work "not execessive and not burdensome."

Even assuming that the figures of the time spent of paper work yielded by Gillespie's survey of 36 per cent are nearer the average, than the 54 per cent of the Bombay Report given earlier, it does appear that for a functionary who must make himself freely accessible to the people including the politicians of the district, who should find time to acquaint himself with developmental programmes of a large number of departments throughout the district, and spend a fair amount of time touring the villages where the bulk of the people he serves live, the time spent on paper work is excessive. It is also unlikely that an average workload of 70 hours per week, even if the figure is somewhat exaggerated, can leave the Collector time for keeping abreast of developments in the field of administration, for reflection and deep thinking on the problems of the district and for planning improvements in the district machinery. It is not strange, therefore, that Gillespie's survey indicated a large percentage of "job dissatisfaction". Thirty-four per cent of the Collectors felt that they had inadequate opportunities to advise Government on the making of major decisions which affect the district, 53 per cent characterized the opportunities to influence the sanctioning of funds for both capital and recurring expenses as "not very adequate" and "not adequate at all", and 30 per cent that opportunities to exercise control over what was happening in all the activities of Government in the district as "not very adequate" and "not adequate at all". Thirty-six per cent felt that in relation to their responsibilities the powers given to them by Government were "not very adequate" or "not adequate at all", and 44 per cent thought that the existing procedures of co-ordination among the various departments and agencies of Government were "not very adequate" or "not adequate at all".

Traditionally, the Indian Civil Service and after Independence, the Indian Administrative Service have both been considered as primarily meant for field administration and, therefore, it is somewhat loosely but frequently stated that the "career grade" of the Service is that of Collector. However, developments since Independence have been such as to change the very character of the "highest" Service in the country. As the following table will show, the proportion of senior posts which can be utilized for the posting of I.A.S. officers as Collectors has steadily fallen from 33.7 per cent in 1930, to 19 per cent in 1965. This is mainly because of the increase in the utilization of officers of the Service in the Secretariats at the Centre and in the States from 21.9 per cent in 1930, to 54.7 per cent in 1965.

	*1930**	*1942@*	*1950*	*1960*	*1965*
Number of Senior Duty Posts	764	722£	626	1297	1689
Number of Districts	257	215	293	320	321
	(33.7%)	(29.8%)	(46.7%)	(27.4%)	(19.0%)
Number of officers holding posts in State Secretariats	97 (12.7%)	180 (24.9%)	145 (23.2%)	409 (31.5%)	489 (28.9%)
Number of officers holding posts in the Central Secretariat	70 (9.2%)	163 (22.6%)	103 (16.4%)	208 (16.3%)	436 (25.8%)

Note: Figures within brackets indicate the percentage to the total number of senior duty posts.

* Includes Burma.

@ Undivided India.

£ This is the figure for 1940 but up to 1942 there does not appear to have been any change.

The effect of the changes noticed in the table above has been very far-reaching. Till recently, it has generally been believed that a direct recruit to the Indian Administrative Service becomes ripe for holding a district charge in the sixth year of his service. This position was reviewed in the "Report on Indian and State Administrative Services and Problems of District Administration" by V.T. Krishnamachari[10] and the following pattern was recommended:

Practical training	—	18 months
Charge of a sub-division	—	18-24 months
Under Secretary to the State Government and deputy to a head of department	—	18-24 months
Charge of a district	—	Towards the end of the sixth or in the seventh year of service.

With cadre strengths increasing to meet the growing demands for non-district requirements, there has been an increasing intake of direct recruits to the Indian Administrative Service, and one of the results has naturally been the quick turnover in the posts of Collectors—not only are officers with a certain minimum experience required for postings in the Secretariats and in various Departments, but district postings have also to be found for the newly recruited officers who complete their field training and become ripe for them. In Gillespie's survey referred to above, the frequency of transfer of Collectors was found to be alarming, the all-India average length of posting in a district charge being 1 year and 8 months. This is a feature which cannot but detract from the adequacy of the Collector's performance and may indeed require re-thinking of the structure and management of the Indian Administrative Service.

Another aspect, which has a bearing on the performance of Collectors particularly in the changed circumstances of the 1960s, is the age and experience of officers holding district charges. It will be seen from the table below that as against an average age of 47 years and 1 month and average length of service of 17 years and 3 months for direct recruits working as Collectors before the Second World War in 1939, the comparable figures in 1960 were 38 years and 9 months and 6 years and 11 months respectively; by 1965, the average age had fallen still further to 36 years and 5 months but the length of service had increased slightly to 8 years and 4 months.

As on 1st February of			*Age*		*Length of Service*	
			Direct Recruits		*Direct Recruits*	
			Years	*Month(s)*	*Years*	*Month(s)*
1939@	—	—	47	1	17	3
1960*	—	—	38	9	6	11
1961*	—	—	38	7	6	11
1962*	—	—	39	1	6	6
1963*	—	—	37	11	7	8
1964*	—	—	37	4	8	1
1965*	—	—	36	5	8	4

@ *Source*: The India Office and Burma Office List 1940.

**Source*: The Civil List of Indian Administrative Service, published by Ministry of Home Affairs, Government of India.

These developments in the cadre structure and utilization of the Indian Administrative Service, which is meant to provide the vast majority of Collectors, appear to be of great significance. The Collector today has far more to do than ever before and what is more important, a great deal is expected of him by the Government and the people. His responsibilities call for the ability to persuade, influence, convince and encourage not only his colleagues in the district but also the members of the Zilla Parishad, lack of adequate background experience and the resultant immaturity are likely to detract from the Collector's utility.

V

In the middle of 1960s, therefore, the position reached is that despite democratization of the administration and the transformation of his authoritarian image, the role of the Collector remains crucial to the governance of the country. There are obvious difficulties in ensuring that this crucial role is satisfactorily fulfilled: the departmentalization of development and other activities at the district, regional and State levels without at the same time adequate institutional arrangements for the performance of the role of co-ordinator by the Collector; the unwieldy nature of many district charges; the pressure of paper work; the changing character of officer utilization in the Indian Administrative Service and what is perhaps more important, the younger age groups and shorter experience which are both the result of this changing character. The office of Collector has survived all these pressures. There is no doubt whatever that the pressures will continue in the years to come; but the need for a co-ordinator at the district level will not disappear. The following two suggestions of Paul H. Appleby seem to give the right guidelines for the future.

> "First, and simplest, I am suggesting that in efforts to use local energies and capacities there should be care to maintain clear capacities for control at more broadly responsible levels of government, so that the communities will be firmly required to make the contributions they are said to be making, and so that what is done makes sense in terms of what is being done elsewhere whenever that matters. Secondly, I am suggesting that what is done in the communities be not unduly exaggerated,

be not misunderstood as constituting some transcendent kind of democratic achievement. In the long run, as India succeeds, the nature of an advancing, complicating civilization will require the transfer of a large part of this community activity into governmental bureaucracies with technical competence in knowledge and technical materials which will produce enormously more per man-hour".[11]

REFERENCES

1. India, *The Constitution of India*, Articles 36-50.
2. India, *Report of the Team for the Study of Community Projects and National Extension Service, Vol. 1*—Committee on Plan Projects, New Delhi, November, 1957, pp. 39-40.
3. India, *Panchayati Raj at a Glance* (as on 31st March 1964), Ministry of Community Development and Cooperation, New Delhi, Statemnt 9, pp. 92-93.
4. India, *Report of the Working Group on Inter-Departmental and Institutional Coordination for Agricultural Production*, Ministry of Food & Agriculture, New Delhi, pp. 6-7.
5. Indian Journal of Public Administration, New Delhi, Vol. X., No. 4, October-December 1964, pp. 595-596.
6. The Hindustan Times, New Delhi, October 11, 1965.
7. Based on a Study made in the Ministry of Home Affairs, Government of India, by Shri V.S. Bawa, I.A.S. on the "*Size of Districts in Relation to Plan Implementation at the District Level*" (unpublished).
8. Maharashtra, Report of the Reorganisation of District Revenue Offices, Government of Bombay, 1959, p. 24.
9. The author is grateful to the Indian Institute of Public Administration for allowing him access to some of the material of the Survey conducted by Mr. Jack Gillespie. The results of the Survey have not yet been published.
10. Planning Commission, *Report on Indian and State Administrative Services and Problems of District Administration*, New Delhi, August 1962, p. 18.
11. Pual, H. Appleby, "Some thoughts on decentralized Democracy", *The Indian Journal of Public Administration*, Vol. VIII, No. 4, p. 449.

2

The Emerging Role of the Collector

M.P. PAI

Philip Woodruff in *The Men Who Ruled India—The Guardians* quotes Lord Wavell, who in one of his farewell speeches remarked, that the British would be remembered not by this institution or by that, as by the ideal they left behind of what a District Officer should be. The conception of an officer of the State responsible for the overall good administration of a primary political unit has deep roots in India, going even beyond Akbar, who when he took over Bengal divided it into "Sarkars" with a single officer officiating as his agent.

However, the present system of district administration in India through a corps of select, trained and disciplined career officials is due to the work and thought of a brilliant group of administrators under Wellesley, including Munro, Malcolm, Elphinstone and Metcalfe whose names will find honoured places in any history of Public Administration. It is to this school of district administration that we owe the conception of a single high-powered agency to whom the ordinary citizen could look forward to, as the Government "represented simply and not by a multiplicity of officers, who would have powers to enquire, to judge and to punish, without the delay and the intricacies of the Western legal process". In practical terms, it meant a concentration of both wide authority and adequate power for all ordinary purposes. Macaulay observed in 1853 in the British Parliament that this was the most important assignment in the civil services of the Crown. The District Officer was described as "the sole consul of a great province, the district assigned to him being about the size of one of the four provinces of Ireland. In all that district there is not a single village—there is not a single hut—in which the difference between a good and bad Collector may not make the difference between happiness and misery."

The duties, functions and responsibilities of a District Officer have, however, varied from time to time. He has generally been the Head of the Revenue Administration, maintaining close personal contact with the agricultural population, which is the real India. He has also for over a century been the Head of the Magistracy and of the Police. Always he has been the local agent of the Government in the district with overall command of extraordinary situations in moments of crisis like flood, famine or civil commotion.

The need for such an officer had become apparent to the British during and immediately after the so-called "Mutiny" of 1857. Round about that time, opinions varied as to whether indirect control of the administrative machine by some sort of zamindari system would not (apart from considerations like the need to create a landed middle class) suit the country better and ease the burden of the British Power. The immediate response to the "Mutiny", however, was to bring the paternalist system to the height of favour in popular British estimation. The manner in which that outbreak occurred suggested to the British that they had lost touch with the people and public opinion, and led to a strong reaction in favour of a direct or personal system. As remarked by Sir Percival Griffiths "between Plassey and the Mutiny, the wheel turned full circle and the Company came back to the old Moghul view that all executive power must be concentrated in the hands of the local representative of the Government. Paternal if authoritarian rule was restored." Since then, the Collector or as he is called in some States the Deputy Commissioner—a term which came into usage when the supervisory powers of the Commissioner over the Superintendent of Police were transferred to the Collector—became the "eyes and ears" of the Government and functioned as their local agent. Indeed he is more than the "eyes and ears", since he is also the "voice" and the "hands".

As circumstances changed, the precise nature of the Collector's functions, responsibilities and powers also changed. His role altered continuously with the changing role of Government in the life of the people. The work of the Collector has in fact been a continuous expression of the growth in the range and complexity of the functions of the Government. For, no administrative post reflects the nature and purposes of the Government in India more completely than the post of the District Officer. The powers of this officer have changed not only because of the changes in the political system, but also as a consequence of the progressiveness of time itself. In India, as anywhere and everywhere, time has been more progressive than any individual is willing to be, and institutions, customs and the inertia of social habits have not stopped the earth from continuously spinning round itself and the sun. With the release of democratic forces, feudalism and paternal authority have gradually given way to modern representative systems of Government. A money-economy and industrialization have continuously encroached on the old patterns of life. No longer is perpetual homage paid to outworn institutions out of mere social inertia.

Since Independence, in particular, governmental activity has rapidly crept into spheres which under *laissez faire* ideologies, had previously been treated as of no primary consequence to the ruling power or the administrative machine. The role of Government in the life of the people has altered over the years as a consequence of four distinct factors—firstly, the influence of modernization of society and of a growing money-economy on the country-side; secondly, the increasing complexity of political and administrative organization; and thirdly, during the last fifteen years of greater governmental interference in all spheres of life due to the War and our present concepts of a Welfare State and planning for prosperity. Lastly, and perhaps most important of all, the natural extension of democratic institution from the National and State level to the district and the village has brought about changes in the forms of administrative organization, and the orientation of officers of the State, which are still in the making. With all these changes, the role of the District Collector has continuously changed. This article refers, however, to "The Emerging Role of the Collector", since the most revolutionary process of democratic decentralization is still in a state of flux. The ideal is roughly the same all over the country, but shapes and forms do not follow quite the same pattern and thoughts and ideas are still in the process of change and formation. Some aspects are still controversial.

II

Between the establishment of the Rule of the Crown in 1857 and the Transfer of Power in 1945-47, the Collector was virtually the Government. The objectives of Government hardly changed after the "Mutiny" from those which had been adopted after Plassey. The maintenance of law and order, the even-handed distribution of justice, construction, repair and control of irrigation works, land records, field surveys, the settlement of fair land taxes and their easy collection, some elementary attention to education, public health, roads, Railways, Posts and Telegraphs, these were then the content of good government. And for all these the Collector, with easy access to the poorest at all times, and particularly at his annual Jamabandy (or settlement of village accounts), was responsible. The administration of Civil Justice, and at certain levels of Criminal Administration also were no doubt placed in the hands of an independent Judiciary following the British tradition. But where speed was of the essence, even some aspects of Civil Justice were in the Collector's hands—rent and tenancy disputes, succession to Village Offices, and the like. Philip Woodruff quotes Mackay "To the people of India, the Collector is the Imperial Government. He watches over their welfare...... he establishes schools, dispensaries, goals and courts of justice. He levies the rent of their fields, he fixes the tariff, and he nominates to every appointment, from that of road-sweeper or constable to the great blood-sucking offices round the Courts and the Treasury." The Collector's start to or return from a tour is a public event, with horses and sometimes howdah and always a retinue of servants and clerks. His verandahs are crowded with bankers, shopkeepers, and landholders who have "come to pay their respects with ever so little a petition as a corollary." Visitors in waiting offer oblations of "brass dishes filled with pistachio nuts and candied sugar", which according to Mackay represent in "the profuse East the visiting cards of the meagre West". To check abuse and avoid embarrassment, Government orders issue on how heads should be politely inclined to receive a garland, and how if offerings exceed the two proverbial times, the brass dish should be returned with gracious thanks after abstracting just a handful of the nuts or a couple of the oranges.

Nevertheless, even in those Imperial days, development work was not unknown. It might have been secondary or sporadic or extracurricular. It might have been a personal fad or a hobby to ease boredom. But it was not uncommon for Collectors in their devotion to good Government to go beyond their book of words. The ideal set to the Collector and the powers invested in him made this inevitable. To quote Woodruff again "There was Brown, whose hobbies were tigers and embankments to store water in the rains; Smith who would go miles for a snipe and planted all the roads in every district he was ever in with double avenues of trees; and Jones who was building hospitals where he wasn't pigsticking.

'Why is my district death-rate low?'
Said Binks of Wezabad,
'Wells, drains, and sewage-outfalls are
My own peculiar fad'."

Years before Independence, F.L. Brayne, I.C.S. was to lay the foundation of the idea of development and extension in his famous Gurgaon experiment and Sir M. Darling, I.C.S., the roots of a co-operative movement. Even in the Police stage of the history of district administration, therefore, there were the seeds of a Welfare State and these grew here and there even if they did not rapidly multiply in a system which was flexible and could change as circumstances required.

With the passage of time, and the introduction of Constitutional Reforms, the Collector and the system of which he was the mainspring changed—as it was bound to do. His many-sided responsibilities increased in some directions and got reduced in others with the diversification of the Taxation System. Slowly some responsibilities were taken out of his hands either because they were becoming too technical as in the case of Income-tax and Sales Tax, or because full-time agencies could handle matters better as in the case of Education and Public Health. The Morley-Minto Reforms led to the sharing of his responsibilities for local administration with popularly elected bodies. As Chairman of the District Board, he assisted in crystallizing the needs of the people through the views of their representatives, and assumed extensive responsibilities for translating them into action. Later, with the inauguration of the Montagu-Chelmsford Reforms, he passed on his policy-making powers to elected non-officials whether members at the State Capitals or Mayors and Chairmen at local levels. His regulatory functions and has police responsibilities, however, remained. He still continued to be the head of the Land Revenue and Land Records Administration. Any difficult job, not the obvious assignment of another department was placed in his hands. He was the odd job man par excellence. With the transfer of power to Indian hands, he no longer retained his imperial position or his racial prestige. Nonofficial channels for contact between the people and the Government were also rapidly springing up either through elected legislators, or social workers. But he was still the accredited agent of the Government "the man on the spot", and on the whole, there was no fundamental change in his official role. The first main "shock" came with the Transfer of Power in 1945-47 and the second one more recently with the introduction of Panchayati Raj.

III

Democratic decentralization with its three-tier pattern of popular administration was the result of the recommendations made in 1959 by a Study Team of the Committee on Plan Projects headed by Shri Balvantray Mehta. It was soon to be called Panchayati Raj to show that its base went back to the democratic village communities of earlier eras. But objectives had started to take shape on the auspicious occasion of Gandhiji's birthday in 1952, when the Community Development programmes were initiated. These were a natural consequence to the Five Year Plans of national development and of a realization that for vitality and success, they had to be based in the life and thought of the villages and recognized to be primarily their responsibility. It was becoming clear that the eradication of poverty and the improvement of living standards which were the primary objectives of the Plans, could only be secured if each village co-operated with an "integrated multi-phased family and village plan", providing minimum essential health services, education facilities for children, adult education programme, recreational facilities, improvement of housing and family living conditions and programmes for village women and youth. The Balvantray Mehta Study Team pointed out that this could be done best, in fact done at all, not through

Government fiats worked through district officials, or charity offered by Government, but through the will and thought, initiative and planning of the village himself, Government agencies acting as friends, philosophers and guides. This gave a new twist to the work of the Collector: it made it complicated and difficult and practicable only if the Collector was imbued with a spirit of service and dedication to the country. It was now his duty even to create an urge for a better life, to suggest the means to it, to create local leadership, to channel to good purposes funds made available by taxation and sometimes to raise them. The Prime Minister, Shri Jawaharlal Nehru, once remarked: "Public servants must think of themselves as part of the people co-operating in this great adventure of building up India." No longer was he "*Ma-Baap*"; still less "*Annadata*". He was at best a "*Bada Bhai*". To quote Dr. Rajendra Prasad "the administration needs to have a human approach to all problems... That implies a spirit of service. Without this human approach and this spirit of service even the best trained administrator will fail.... They must conduct themselves in a manner which inspires people's confidence and co-operation."

The introduction of Panchayati Raj in 1959, therefore, gave a formal shape to a trend which had started well before 1929 and taken a recognizable shape in 1952. The varying forms of democratic decentralization adopted in the various States consequently made a call for re-orientation of a fundamental character. Where previously the Collector ordered, he now had to persuade and convince. Where previously he inspected and punished, he now led and encouraged. The younger officers could be moulded to the change but it involved a risk of loss of habits of independence and objectivity, which had been one of the strong qualities of the old I.C.S. Most of the older men were fortunately able to adjust themselves and play their new role reasonably well. Only the inelastic handful rued the blossoming of democracy. So far as the vast public were concerned, and excluding the few who hankered for personal power and confused this with the democratic process, the attitude towards the District Collector was, by and large, one of faith and confidence. In the new order in Andhra Pradesh, the Collector is a full member of the Zilla Parishad and Chairman of all its Standing Committees. In Madras, in a different pattern, he is Chairman of the District Development Council, which is a purely advisory body, but in this capacity he has powers to oversee and direct the development works of all State agencies. In Rajasthan, the Collector is a Member of the Zilla Parishad, a body which supervises, advises and co-ordinates the work of the main executive local bodies, which are the Panchayat Samitis and the Panchayats. He is also Chairman of the District Development Council. His position, however, continues to be focal in all the States. Everywhere the Governments apparently feel that only he could represent the Government and that administration will not function effectively unless he co-ordinates the various wings and unless his authority is felt by them. So also, to the non-official world (save for isolated viewpoints) he is the source of advice, guidance, assistance and finally of appeal. From a symbol of power, he is being transformed to a symbol of service and authority.

As we have noticed earlier in this article, despite the varying role which the Collector has played in the administration of the country and the many-sided and changing nature of his duties and responsibilities, he has always held a key position in the chain of authority. The importance of his position has depended on two contributing factors: Firstly, the trust and confidence that the Government have reposed in him as a consequence of his selection to his post on considerations of merit and experience have maintained his position as agent of the Government at district level. In this connection, it is relevant to make reference to the practice, for which the late Sardar Patel with his deep insight and vision was responsible, of allocating to each State at least one-half of its I.A.S. officers from residents of other States. This has not only been a factor in national integration, but also provided every State Government with a corps of officers with no local interests or attachments and on whose independence and objectivity the State and the people alike could count. This leads to the second factor of importance in the Collector's position, viz., the faith which the people of the district in his charge continue by and large to repose in him. On all controversial problems Government and people alike have always turned to the Collector for objective views and non-partisan executive action. The assurance that he will be objective and independent has fallen short if at all only of the confidence similarly reposed in the higher Judiciary. As in the past, his authority has not always depended so much on statutes or Government orders, as on his own ability to take a sound view and to act on it without fear or favour. There is some hope that this position will not change with recent political changes. For, competent Chief Ministers have always endeavoured to maintain the I.A.S. above political pressures. What then are the changes in prospect of the manner in which he will function?

In some fields and in some ways, it is clear that his position will be what it has always been. As the agent and representative of Government, he is likely to continue to be the "eyes and ears" of Government. He may not, in the future, be the only channel of communication between the Government and the people, but he will always be the most important channel and when controversies or conflicts arise the only dependable channel. So also in the second place, there will be a wide field of governmental activity in which he will assuredly have considerable authority. The regulatory functions of the Collector in the fields of Revenue and Land Records administration, criminal administration and law and order are likely to continue for many decades to come. Recently there has been some discussion as to whether his control over the Police which started after the "Mutiny" should continue. It is significant, however, that the recent Police Commissions appointed by the States, who have submitted their reports, have not recommended any change in the overall responsibility of the District Magistrate in regard to the maintenance of law and order. It cannot, of course, be gainsaid that with the present systems of recruitment and training of the Police force, our Superintendents of Police compare with the best in the world. Nevertheless, lower ranks leave much to be desired and for these and many other reasons which need not be gone into in this article, the public would hardly look with favour on any change in the Collector's role in the maintenance of law and order and the criminal administration. As head of the general administration, the Collector has given general satisfaction in the conduct of general and by-elections, the decennial census, the measures to tackle local crisis like flood or scarcity. For all these, no better or cheaper agency could be found. No local or elected functionaries can ever take full control over such situations, except in co-operation with or under the overall control of the Collector. It is in the field of developmental activity alone that his role is in some directions widening and in others changing into a new form now in emergence.

As already observed, developmental duties are nothing new to the Collector and were of importance even in the Company days, though the weight and sense of proportion were different. The Krishna and Cauvery Anicuts, the Godavari dam, thousands of tanks, wells, roads, schools, choultries, hospitals and dispensaries are due to the efforts of District Officers—whether under Government direction or on their own initiation. But these nation-building activities have become the normal functions of Government and with changes of political forms, the Collector's role can no longer remain the same. The responsibility for these has been placed in the hands of the elected representatives of the people in varying forms and to differing extents in the various States. One common pattern, however, in all the States is that the executive agencies are directly or eventually controlled by the Government and with increased decentralization and delegation of powers the need for an agency to co-ordinate the work of these agencies has increased. In all the States, it has been accepted that the necessary powers of co-ordination can best be exercised only by the Collector. This is not only because this is the sphere of a trained and experienced administrator, but also because such co-ordination is possible only if the co-ordinator is respected by those whom he deals with. At present, the Collector has no alternate in such a choice.

IV

There have been differences of view on the executive agency which can best deal with the programmes of democratic institutions at the base. Many presidents of Zilla Parishads have chafed under the idea that these powers do not vest with them. They have confused responsibility for formulation of programmes and policies with the direct operation of machinery for putting them on the field. They have assumed that democracy involves the assumption of executive powers by an elected representative of the people. The have overlooked how, as a result of the long experience of municipal bodies in all States, the formulation of programmes and the settlement of budgets and taxation and general supervision only have been left to an elected body through its non-official Chairman or Mayor, but responsibility for execution placed with a permanent official. Recent history has shown the soundness of such a division of functions not only because a permanent trained agency will attend to the execution of plans and programmes better, but also because an elected representative will face embarrassment particularly in the fields of location of amenities, collection of taxes, and so forth, if execution of details is made his responsibility. Quite recently, in answer to a question in Parliament, the Union Home Minister, Shri Lal Bahadur Shastri, made it clear that the Central Government had no intention of vesting executive powers in the hands of Mayors or Chairmen of Municipal Councils and that any such move would be retrograde. There is not much doubt, therefore, that the Collector is likely to continue to be the principal executive, besides being the chief co-ordinator between those responsible for the work of the various agencies in the district.

It is in the field of the working of democratic institutions, however, that the Collector will have to play a new and difficult role. For success in the development field, whose importance far outweighs the regulatory functions, close liaison between the Government and democratic institutions at the village and district level are of great importance. The channel of communication will obviously be the Collector, but for the satisfactory working of development programmes, mere communication will not do. Our new local bodies are young and inexperienced with a tendency to regard their new powers either as so much patronage to be distributed or sometimes worse still to be distributed on a group or regional basis, so as to secure future election support. Such feelings are human and often times due to the youth of these institutions. For, the experienced political leader is as short in the country as the trained administrator. The party system which should not really obtain at the village and district level has unfortunately let to pressure groups. This calls for an agency of Government endowed with the ability to persuade, convince and encourage. Much will depend on the respect commanded by the person who constitutes such an agency and his personal qualities. This agency, which must be the Collector, can no longer rely merely on the past or recent prestige of his office. Success will only be guaranteed by his ability to bring groups together and to secure decisions on the basis of merit alone.

Finally, it will be the duty of the Collector to secure the efficient and co-ordinated working of the various departments charged with the execution of programmes set by local elected bodies and also to see that these departments work without interruption or fear of improper pressures. The role will be a very difficult one, since the smallest mistake might damage him either in the eyes of local political leaders or of the services and may also bring him into disfavour with the Government. It would follow that the Collector of the future will have more considerations to weigh, and factors to allow for, than a Collector of the past. In consequence, the recent tendency to post junior officers to these posts in some States will have to be reversed. Equally the reluctance of senior officials to accept district assignments is to be deplored and discountenanced. Quite clearly the time has come to recognize the importance of these posts and render them more attractive than posts in the Secretariat or in the Heads of Departments where isolation from pressures of politics add to the attractions of the special pays which these posts carry from the days when officers had to be induced to give up posts in the districts (which they generally preferred) and work in the cities.

The emerging role of the Collector underlines once again the great need for careful choice, and patient training of the officer who will have to fill this important assignment. His position is as much of a key position today as the one visualized by Lord Wavell in the sentence which started this article. As observed by Shri V.T. Krishnamachari:

> " The Collector's role has changed but not diminished, for he now has the function of guiding democratic bodies. Often he has to carry conviction with members of democratic institutions".

A sound education, a good background, careful training, some years of experience, broad views, an elastic mind, tact, the ability to get on with all types of people, openness to conviction and the power to convince, capacity to take a sound view on relevant evidence, and to act on it firmly, freely, and without fear or favour—all these are needed by a Collector to be successful. In essence, he is the type of man the British administration produced with a large measure of success. Only his orientation has to be very different today. Need we doubt, however, that he can be produced if the educated youth of the country are infused with a sense of integrity, a sense of patriotism, and a concern for the common good? And if ministers, political leaders and legislators will encourage these qualities, promote objectivity and independence and not allow the administrative services to be exposed to improper pressures because of parochial, temporary or party needs?

> "Nothing appears more surprising, to those who consider human affairs with a philosophical eye, than the easiness with which the many are governed by the few, and the implicit submission with which men resign their own sentiments and passions to those of their rulers".
>
> —HUME
>
> (In 'theory of Politics'
> edited by Frederick Watkins)

3

District Officer in India: Agent for Change

EDWIN EAMES AND PARMATAMA SARAN

Despite the change in government that took place in India after independence, the structure of district level administration has remained relatively unchanged. What is most surprising about this continuity is that the administrative system, which initially was established as an essential element of colonialism; remains almost intact. The only difference is that the old Indian Civil Service (ICS) has been replaced by the indigenous Indian Administrative Service (IAS). In the words of Sardar Patel:

> When the British left in 1947, members of the Indian Civil Service were the force that helped, under the leadership of the new government, to maintain or to re-establish order, to integrate the princely states, apportion the Indian Army between the two successor States [sic.] and carried on the services necessary for the larger society.[1]

Interestingly enough, an arm of the colonial power whose major objective was to maintain the *status quo,* even if it had to be repressive, remained unchanged in the new system which proclaimed development, social and economic change as its goals. The question then is: "Can the administrative structure established by the British for maintenance of colonial rule be converted to the goals of social and economic development?"

In a field study conducted in India, we explored the changing role of the District Officer[2] as an agent of change in the context of India's drive toward modernisation.

HISTORICAL BACKGROUND

One view of the development of the British District Administration in India sees it as nothing more than an extension of the system established by the Mughal rulers of North India. The Mughal rulers divided their kingdoms into bounded geographic units for the purpose of taxation. Tax collection in a particular district was assigned to an individual who had complete control over the collection of revenue. However, the British added two major functions to the duties of tax collection: maintenance of law and order, and handling of general administration.[3] General administration included looking after the well-being of the people of the district as well as providing assistance in times of need and crisis. Thus, District Officers became the arm of government residing in the district under his jurisdiction.

Relatively early in the history of district level administration, a controversy developed about the fundamental nature of the role of the District Officer. Two alternative models were tried out. One, followed in Bengal, projected the District Officer as a coordinator of the activities of other district level officials. The second model, followed in Madras, established the District Officer as a strong individual with total power over sub-ordinates as well as over those living in the district.[4] Eventually the Madras pattern prevailed and fiscal, police and judicial powers became centralised in the hands of the District Officer in all regions of what essentially became known as British India.

Recruitment into the service that administered British India was originally through nomination by members of the Board of Governors that was responsible, for the well-being of the East India Company. However, within a short time, recruitment became open to British young men who could compete successfully in a series of examinations developed and graded by members of the academic community.[5]

At one point in the development of the colonial administrative system that became known as the Indian Civil Service (ICS), a special training institute was introduced. However, this scheme was soon abandoned and the training of recruits to the service took place in the major universities of England. Such training was primarily academic, although some emphasis on knowledge of India was required.

Exposure to district administration for new recruits subordinate to the District Officer was designed essentially as on-the-job training. The District Officer was responsible for training the new recruits in addition to acting as a role model. The newcomer was assigned a variety of tasks at the district level before being given charge of a segment of the district called a sub-division. He was required to serve in this capacity for several years before being given charge of a full district. At this time, he became the focal point of local level administration; he had almost absolute control over the lives of hundreds of thousands of people. Unless a District Officer was unable to maintain peace in his district or deliver the required revenues that ran the government, he had complete autonomy. His district superior, the Divisional Commissioner, would visit the district on a regular but infrequent basis. It was unthinkable that the commissioner would interfere in the actual administration of the district. Divisional Commissioners as well as other high ranking officials, followed a policy of non-interference because they knew from their own experience that the District Officer was the one who had to be in control of the district.[6]

In most early accounts of life in the district, the District Officer is described as being at the apex of a triumvirate consisting of the Superintendent of Police, the Civil Surgeon, and himself. Since the District Officer was the Chief Magistrate of the District, all other district officials were clearly in a subordinate position.

Once an individual gained membership in the ICS, he was virtually assured a District Officer was part of the career pattern, but there were no objective criteria for satisfactory performance. Unless some very unusual circumstances came up, an individual served his first 15 years in the district. Initially, he was a trainee, then he moved on to the position of a Sub-Divisional Officer. After serving in the sub-division and the district, he went to an administrative position in one of the provincial capitals or in the Central Secretariat.

The British monopoly of the ICS was broken in the last quarter of the nineteenth century. Since the first Indian recruit, Devendra Nath Tagore, a brother of Nobel Laureate Rabindra Nath Tagore, many Indians joined the service.[7] However, the Indianisation of the ICS did not fundamentally change the role of the District Officer. His main goals remained collection of revenue, maintenance of law and order, and general administration of the area under his control.

SOURCE OF INFORMATION

Data for this article are derived from a larger study, *Changing Role of the District Officer in India,* for which the authors conducted fieldwork in India, especially in the state of Bihar, in 1980-1981.[8] We divided our fieldwork into four phases. In the first phase, we interviewed former District Magistrates who were then posted in senior positions at the State Secretariat, Patna, capital of the state of Bihar. In the second phase, we went out to the districts and interviewed the District Magistrates posted there. Whenever possible, we also interviewed Divisional Commissioners. In a few cases, we had the opportunity to talk to the Superintendent of Police, who is head of the police force at the district level. In the third phase, we travelled outside Bihar to meet former ICS officers who had served in the districts before India's independence and had since retired. In the fourth phase, we interviewed senior government officers, including some who had retired. Others interviewed for this project were political leaders, including ministers, senior lawyers as well as common citizens, to get their view of the role of the District Officers. In addition, we visited three major institutions responsible for the training of IAS (Indian Administrative Service) officers. These were located at Mussoorie, New Delhi and Ranchi.[9]

In our interviews with 20 officers, who had served as District Magistrates during the last 10 to 15 years, we placed emphasis on their activities during the time they served in the district and the changes they have seen taking place in the role of District Officer since leaving that office. Each interview lasted from two to four hours. In some cases, we had to sit in two or three sessions with the same respondent.

In our interviews with 22 District Magistrates presently serving in the districts, we explored issues concerning allocation of time and effort, political and other pressures, and the relationship of magisterial regulatory, and developmental functions to one another. We had to go directly to the districts for these interviews. In some cases, we revisited districts and in others we had second interviews with officers while they were visiting Patna. In a number of cases, we had the opportunity to carry on interviews and conversations with District Officers over a period of two to three consecutive days. We were also able to observe a number of the District Officers as they interacted with elected officials and subordinate officers, presided over courts, and granted personal interviews to citizens. We accompanied some of these officers on their tours for several days, to help us better understand their inspecting duties, their involvement in developmental projects, and contacts with the public.

In interviews with 20 retired ICS officers, we placed major emphasis upon their activities during the time they had served in the districts, and upon changes that have taken place since then. The interviews with retired officers were shorter than those with current officers, and took no more than two to three hours each.

During the course of the interviews, especially with current District Officers, it became clear that increased political pressure in district administration and the growing power of the Superintendent of Police at the district level were of much concern to the District Magistrates. We, therefore, interviewed a number of political leaders and police officers (serving as well as retired) to hear their side of the story.

In course of informal conversations with friends and colleagues, we were advised that in order to get a full picture of district administration we should interview non-officials in addition to those who were responsible for supervising the District Officer's activities. We interviewed six Divisional Commissioners in the course of our visits to those districts which were also divisional headquarters. We interviewed a number of political leaders, judges and lawyers, both presently working and retired senior government officers at Patna, and scholars and journalists. In addition to formal interviews, we spoke to scores of people in Bihar and elsewhere concerning the changing role of the District Magistrate and the future of that office. With the help of a research assistant, we collected news items concerning the working of District Magistrates in Bihar.

PROFILES AND ATTITUDES OF DISTRICT OFFICERS

There were clear differences of socio-economic background between those District Officers who had served in the British administration (the ICS) and those in the new administration (the IAS).

Because of the then recruitment practices, only members of the elite classes could join the ICS. A possible important motivation for joining the ICS was the ability to identify with the British as much as possible. This meant that those Indians who joined the ICS came from the upper castes, had high social and economic status to begin with, and to fit into the British scheme of things. Among the Indian population, they were commonly known as "Brown Sahibs", implying that other than their brown skins, they were like *sahibs,* a term used in India for Britishers as well as for Indians of very high status. The 20 former ICS officers, whom we interviewed, all came from elite backgrounds and conformed to the characteristics mentioned above.

At the initial stage of recruitment into the IAS, the old elite image and background of the defunct ICS were maintained to a great extent, with many District appointments being made without competitive examinations. A majority if the senior IAS officers, whom we interviewed, conformed to this pattern. When the IAS was expanded and recruitment was based on an all-India examination, merit alone rather than other considerations prevailed. This shift is reflected clearly in our IAS respondents, a group of them came from very modest social backgrounds, including members of the lower castes, scheduled castes and tribes.[10]

Our sample of respondents from the older ICS clearly represented an elite sector of Indian society, while the set of IAS respondents was a mixture of upper, middle, and lower class segments of contemporary Indian society. Determining to what extent the latter's social and economic backgrounds have influenced their attitudes as civil servants and as District Officers was an important objective of our study.

One of the major changes that has taken place since the ICS was replaced by the IAS has been a recognition of the true notion of a "public servant". Members of the ICS worked on behalf of an alien rule, so their main responsibility was to maintain law and order. They were the symbol of supreme authority and power, and as such they could be repressive. On the other hand, members of the IAS were supposed to serve a duly elected government in independent India, and could not be repressive. No doubt IAS members too symbolise power and authority, but the major change that supposedly should have taken place was the inculcation of the notion of a true public servant; priority should have shifted from the maintenance of law and order to developmental activities.

In our interviews and observations, we found a number of changes in the attitudes and behaviours of the IAS officers. However, many of these ostensive changes seemed superficial. Athough our respondents verbally, and to some extent behaviourally, expressed agreement with the emergent role of public servant, their overall behaviour still conformed to the norms of a master, not those of a public servant. We obviously had no opportunity to observe ICS officers acting in their official capacity as they are all long since retired; hence we have no empirical basis for a true comparison between the two groups on this point. However, as indicated earlier, IAS officers do come from varied social and economic backgrounds, and thus there is lack of uniformity in their attitudes and values. While some IAS officers had accepted their status as public servant, and were highly motivated to bring about social and economic change in their districts, the majority lacked such a goal, and still interpreted their role only as that of keeper of peace.

From comments of those who have witnessed the functioning of both the ICS and the IAS, we gathered that there really is no qualitative difference in terms of attitudes and behaviour between the two groups. Some informants even suggested that the IAS officers are more arrogant and discourteous to the public than had been their ICS predecessors. One thing that does come out clearly is that more modest social and economic backgrounds of the IAS officers has not necessarily resulted in greater sympathy and sensitivity in their dealings with the public. Occasionally officers with modest social backgrounds were considered to be even more arrogant and less sympathetic to the public than were their social and economic superiors.

Despite some structural changes that have taken place in the role of the District Officer since the British days, these changes have not fundamentally altered the attitudes and behaviours of those presently serving in the districts.

Many young IAS officers told us that their attempts to work in a more democratic way, with a sense of commitment to the social and economic well-being of the people, did not work because the public took them lightly. As a result, they changed their style, and started acting more like "*Bara Sahibs*" (big masters). Finally, it seems safe to say that changes in the class, caste, and tribal distribution of ICS and IAS officers has not resulted' in any significant changes in the attitudes', values, and behaviour patterns of these officers. Their socialisation has been in terms of the older system of governance.

ROLE OF THE DISTRICT OFFICER: THEN AND NOW

We have previously noted that the major functions of the District Officer under colonial rule were general administration, maintenance of law and order, and revenue collection. These functions have been maintained in the transition from colonial rule to independent status. However, the structure and context within which these functions are performed has changed.

Since the data base of District Officers who served during the final days of colonial rule is derived from interviews with only Indian members of the ICS, the information about district administration in the old colonial regime will be somewhat skewed. However, we believe that many of the problems the Indian ICS officers faced were shared by their European counterparts.

During the final days of the British rule, the major thrust of all aspects of district administration was to contain the independence movement. Many of our informants had had to deal with the leaders of the movement who visited their districts or were residents of the district under their jurisdiction. As Indians, most indicated their sympathy had been with the movement, but as members of the ICS, they all agreed that their major commitment had been to the maintenance of law and order. They had been caught in the middle. They felt that they had to satisfy the demands of their imperial supervisors, but they also wanted to maintain some kind of amiable relations with those who eventually would become their masters.[11]

For those who served in the districts during the World War II, the war events influenced their entire view of district administration. Scarcity of supplies, war bond rallies, mobilisation of defence league, were all enumerated as major events occupying their time during this tenure. The District Officers, who served in Bengal during the 1944 famine, indicated their extreme displeasure with the way this crisis was handled by those higher up in the administrative hierarchy. From several accounts, it appears that the British fear of a Japanese invasion superseded their concern for the welfare of the local inhabitants. The result was a large number of needless casualties.

Although World War II and the struggle for India's independence were the major national issues in the two-and-a-half decades before independence, many local issues were also mentioned. Crop failures resulting from droughts and occasional floods brought into action the formidable array of relief measures available to a District Officer. Periodically, communal disturbances between Hindus and Muslims had to be dealt with, and part of the District Officer's time was devoted to curbing localised criminal activities, such as dacoitics and other forms of lawlessness.

As a number of ICS informants noted, they faced many problems in the districts, but they had the power to deal with them. The police were under the control of the District Officer, who was still the major judicial figure in the district.

Those serving in the districts during the post-independence period faced a host of new problems. The partition of the country created not only the serious problem of immediate nature, *i.e.*, controlling communal rioting, but also the long-range problem of refugee resettlement and rehabilitation. Scarcity of supplies, a phenomenon that had become acute during the World War II, continued. It is still cited as an important problem by those serving in the districts today. In addition, some forms of political unrest threatened all the major functions of the District Magistrate.

For those who served in the districts during the period of transition, however, the major event was the redefinition of their role rather than allocation of any specific problems to them for solution. Many of the judicial and magisterial functions were excised from their role as District Officer. During this period, the covert tension between District Magistrate and Superintendent of Police became overt. Local politicians found it advantageous to enlist the support of police authority in matters of arrest and detention rather than go to the District Magistrate. As a result, police officials became more powerful and a threat to the authority of the District Magistrate.

While the transitional District Officers saw their powers eroded, they also felt that their responsibilities were increased. In addition to health, education, maintenance of supplies, crisis intervention and control, and revenue collection, the District Officer now became responsible for economic and social development in the area covered by his district.

At the present time, District Officers see themselves as overburdened, relatively powerless, and inadequately compensated. Some still find time for recreational and culturally creative activities. However, most said that they had almost no time for leisure. In our visits to the districts, we observed the validity of this assertion. The District Officer not only puts in 12 to 14 hours a day, but is on call at all times. Because of the massive growth of technical departments at the district level, the District Officer no longer is in direct control over many of the departments and their activities. He has moved from the position of an executor to that of a coordinator.

A constant theme and area of contention throughout our interviews was the following question: "Who is/was closer to the people, the old ICS District Officer or the current IAS District Officer?"

As might be anticipated, two opposing positions were taken. Many older ICS officers suggested that they had been closer to the people of the district because they visited the villagers on horseback or by bullock cart and made themselves available to the people. As one former ICS officer said, "When we were camped in the mango groove near a village, anyone could approach us with any problem or complaint." Touring was an activity mentioned by every ICS respondent as a major, and pleasurable aspect of the job. This also gave them a better opportunity to meet and interact with the people in the district. The present-day District Officers, with the multiplicity of responsibilities entrusted to them, find it impossible to engage in such 'luxuries' as did their ICS predecessors.

Despite this recognition of the time limitations faced by present day District Officers, all of the IAS respondents felt that they were closer to the people. They claimed they had to take into account the desires of local politicians, such as members of the State Assembly and Council, as well as officials elected to local *Panchayats* (village councils) and *Zilla Parishads* (district assemblies).

Some ICS respondents felt that they had, indeed, been very far removed from the people of their districts. This may have been because, as we noted earlier, they were "Brown Sahibs." In such cases, other than handling of subordinate district officials, their official contact was limited to local *Zamindars* (big landholders).

Unlike the ICS District Officers, who served under colonial rule, the present IAS officers were being pressured by political bosses. Their tenure in the district was largely dependent upon the pleasure of influential politicians, especially those from their area. This has resulted in a much shorter tenure for the District Officer, especially in the states of Bihar and Uttar Pradesh. During the time this study was in progress, the average tenure of a District Officer in our district was only nine months, compared to at least three years for ICS officers.

Almost every respondent mentioned political interference or the pressure of politicians in the district administration as one of the most obstructive and negative elements of the job. This ranged from demands for favours such as giving a license, a cement or sugar permit, to making appointments to minor government jobs or transferring to and from such jobs.

Perhaps the shift in the role of the District Officer can best be summarised in the words of an officer who had served during the transitional period. He observed:

> In the old days, ICS District Officers were rulers; at the present time, IAS District Officers are those who would like to rule, but cannot.

DISTRICT OFFICER AS AN AGENT OF CHANGE: MYTH OR REALITY

Traditionally, the governmental attitude toward the role of the District Officer is that he is ultimately responsible for everything that occurs in his district. However, the thrust of the government since independence has shifted from law and order to developmental activities. In directive after directive, the District Officer is exhorted to take the lead in bringing about social and economic change.

Economic development is measured by increasing production in both the agricultural and industrial sectors. There are a number of factors related to increased productivity, including extension of electrical power, better roads, increased irrigational facilities as well as availability of fertilisers. An important element in economic development is availability of credit for rural population. With nationalisation, the government has put pressure on bankers to open branches in rural areas. These branches are extending credit to small farmers for all kinds of agricultural improvements.

With the adoption of a constitution that contains many sections dealing with to a programme of social and economic change. This pledge has been translated into programmes of redistribution of land to the landless, housing for *harijans*, education for all, medical assistance to the poor, and protecting the civil and political rights of all minority groups.

From the perspective of the state and federal governments, it is the District Officer who is responsible for implementation of all programmes of economic and social change. How have District Officers performed in relation to these expectations? The answer to this question is complex, and will be explored in the remainder of this article.

SOME CONSTRAINTS

Political Interference

With only one or two exceptions, District Officers complained about the impact of political interference on their activities. In many cases, this took the form of politicians interference on behalf of big landowners who did not want their land to be acquired by the Government. Another frequently cited measure of political interference was in the area of criminal cases. District Magistrates were often asked to use their remaining judicial powers to help the politician's supporters in the district. Since the residual power of the District Magistrate is to dismiss any case against an individual in his district, many District Officers reported that they were under constant pressure to use this power. In addition to such interference, they were called upon to issue gun licences, permits for scarce supplies, such as sugar and cement, and to give preferential treatment in transfers and postings to minor government officials within their jurisdictions.

Why do District Officers succumb to these pressures? They do so because politicians have influence on their tenure in the district. Appointments and transfers of District Officers have been politicised. The Chief Minister and his Cabinet, in consultation with the Chief Secretary, determines who will serve in a district. The Chief Minister is the leader of the majority party in the State Assembly; by virtue of that position, he is the *de facto* head of the state, whereas the Chief Secretary is a senior member of the IAS. The latter is the highest ranking executive in the state appointed by the cabinet. The cabinet ministers are full ministers in the State Government, in-charge of various departments. The cabinet has the power to appoint and transfer District Officers. As a result, District Officers are constantly under the pressure of these ministers, their close associates as well as their political allies.

This climate of uncertainty of tenure in a district, created by political reality, has not only demoralised the District Officer, but is also seen as having an adverse effect on the performance of his duties as an agent of change. In the past, a District Officer stayed in the district for at least three years. This was sufficient to establish himself in the district as well as to plan his actions during his tenure. At the present time, the District Officer is so uncertain of his stay in any district that he has no motivation to organise activities on a long-term basis. As noted above, most District Officers complained of political interference as a major impediment.

District Officers might be transferred and have their lives disrupted, but they cannot be dismissed from the IAS. They are either shifted from one district to another or sent to the state secretariat. Some individuals mentioned that during the President's Rule, when the state political apparatus was not functioning actively, little was done at the district level related to developmental work. Another District Officer told us that when a cabinet level minister visited his district, a large number of his constituents came to see him with a variety of demands. The minister instructed the District Officer to look into these matters. Some of the demands were genuine and the District Officer was able to redress them, while others were not, so he did nothing about them. This District Officer, saw the positive impact of political interference. Had the minister not visited his district then, some of the legitimate demands would not have come to the District

Officer's attention and he would not have done anything about them. Another tactic frequently used by ministers is to make public demands on the District Officer and then privately ask him to ignore them.

Our sense of the situation is that while unpredictability of tenure in a district that is politically influenced has a negative impact on the District Officer's role as an agent of change, political interference often does help in terms of expediting developmental activities within the jurisdiction of the District Officer.

As previously noted, the role and responsibilities of the District Officer in post-independence India has expanded while his power base has been eroded. At the district level, departments responsible for specific functions, such as irrigation, education, road construction, etc., have either been expanded or newly created. Most department heads at the district level deal directly with their superiors at the state secretariat. Furthermore, planning is done in the state secretariat and passed on to those functioning at the district level. In this departmental process, the District Officer has very little to do or say. He is expected to aid in the implementation of plans even though he is not consulted in their formulation. As onc irrigation secretary at the state secretarial pointed out, "The District Officer is needed to acquire land and make sure that there is no interference in the construction of irrigation canals." When asked if any District Officer were consulted about the need for such canals in the district or where they should be placed, the answer was 'No'. This type of situation is a source of complaint to many District Officers. They claim that they are not consulted, but are told what they have to do to make the centrally developed programme work. Others confess that they lack the technical knowledge and expertise to be included in the formulation of plans.

It should be noted that from the very beginning of district administration under British rule, a debate has been going on about the merits of specialist versus generalist as District Officer.[12] The present policy continues to select the generalist rather than the specialist, although some District Officers have been recruited from specialised branches of government, such as engineering and finance. To what extent the lack of collaboration with District Officers by secretariat officials is the result of the lack of technical knowledge by the District Officers is difficult to determine. In some cases, District Officers are overlooked in the centralised planning process, which is characteristic of most developmental activities at the state level.

Ad Hoc Nature of the Office

To become an effective agent of change, the District Officer must be able to plan and execute schemes for social and economic development. In addition to the brief tenure, a number of other factors work against his becoming an agent of change.

When we were getting ready to go out into the districts for our interviews, we were advised that because of the potential threat of Hindu-Muslim riots, because both Hindu and Muslim festivals were due soon, we should delay our visits to the districts. After these festivals were over, we were told that the District Magistrates were currently very busy supervising the forthcoming census. We realised then that soon something else might be coming up; therefore, instead of waiting any longer, we went to the field about the same time as the census operation was starting.

A daily schedule of work activities that includes presiding over courts, granting personal interviews, supervising the work of subordinate staff, holding meetings, and going on inspection tours consumes most of the time available to a District Officer. The wife of a District Officer complained that she rarely got to see her husband. Another District Officer whose wife lived with their children in Patna for their education, said that it would have been impossible for him to devote enough time to his work if his family lived with him.

The lack of free time at the District Officer's disposal became evident to us in the course of our field work. Rarely could an interview be completed without some interruption by telephone or personal intervention by the staff or a visitor.

A frequent source of interruption is visiting dignitaries, which most often includes ministers. Protocol requires the District Officer to receive, be available to, and see off ministers. Such interruptions of their developmental work are common and time consuming.

Another related strain on the developmental capability of the District Officer is the necessity of responding to crises. Such crises include communal disturbances, floods, dacoity, rail or road accidents, and disturbances on educational campuses. When we asked District Officers about major problems in their districts, responses were along the lines indicated above. No District Officer said that the major problem was inability to produce change. Most District Officers who gain a reputation for being effective do so through crisis intervention, not as agents of change.

In some cases, where District Officers were inclined to do developmental work, they felt that no recognition was given for those activities. In yet other cases, where District Officers really tried to serve as catalysts of change, as a result of their actions they either were openly ridiculed or were removed from the district. This is suggestive of the fact that District Officers are still seen as those who are responsible for the maintenance of law and order; their main contribution is to respond to crisis, rather than to work as agents of change. This sentiment was echoed by a District Officer who said, "When the government policy forces us to fire at a disorderly mob, it is in the headlines, but there is hardly any mention or appreciation anywhere of our developmental activities."[13]

The *ad hoc* nature of the job is even more apparent in urban districts than in rural districts. In urban areas, the demands on the District Officer's time and the number of crises that can occur are increased tremendously. However, balancing these negative aspects is the fact that those appointed to urban districts, such as Ranchi and Patna, in Bihar had already proven themselves in rural districts and remain in the district for a longer period of time. These experienced officers were expected to carry out the same kind of activities in urban areas and had earned a reputation in rural districts for crisis intervention and time management. Once again, it should be noted that there is little opportunity or emphasis on developmental activities in urban areas. If anything, the District Officer in a rural area has a greater potential of becoming a catalyst of change. One of the former District Officer said, "Any District Officer who is posted in an urban area and claims that he is doing developmental work is simply lying."

Differences in Individual Orientation

Despite the multiplicity of factors that oppose commitment to the development aspect of district administration, some District Officers do attempt to become actively involved in changing the lives of the public at large. We believe this commitment derives from a personal orientation rather than governmental policy or training or a reward system. Some former District Officers, who had been really committed to change, found their tenure in the district short-lived. Usually they did not last there for more than six months. As one former District Officer said, "When I tried to break the hold of money lenders and implement (a) minimum wage in my district. I found myself immediately transferred to the secretariat."

Some individuals begin with a commitment to improving the welfare of the people but soon learn that translating this commitment into reality not only requires time and energy, but also invites opposition from vested interests. In several cases, District Officers went into great detail describing their attempts to obtain land from the larger landowners to be distributed to the landless. Not only did the large landowners oppose them in every way possible, but when finally forced to sell some of their surplus land, they attempted to cheat by turning over unusable land.

When District Officers remain committed to change, they are relatively free to select the areas of their preference. Some District Officers focused on health issues, others fostered the extension of banking facilities into rural areas, while still others, despite local opposition, remained committed to land reform.

Another aspect of individual differences that influences developmental activities is in time management. While many District Officers complained that they had little time for activities other than general administration, some stated that once the minimal requirements of the job were met, such as maintaining law and order, holding courts, etc., the District Officer was free to spend time on any project he deemed worthwhile. What seemed to be emerging was a dual view of the position: one saw it as totally time consuming and *ad hoc* in nature; the other saw it as manageable if proper managerial techniques were used. If the latter position were adopted, change could become an important part of the activities of the District Officer, if he managed his time well and was committed to change.

In almost any job, individual psychological factors do influence actual performance. However, based upon our research, we would suggest that the job of the District Officer provides greater freedom for individual choice than most other jobs. There are obvious limits, most of which have been discussed above. A District Officer who tries to alter the structure of the district radically would probably have a short tenure because of the opposition of local power brokers. However, within the limits discussed, there does seem to be considerable leeway for the District Officer to promote developmental activities. He can be placid and let the district run by itself or he can be an activist and take a leadership position.

NEW DEVELOPMENTS

Two major developments occurred at the time of our study which indicate the nature of the reorganisation of district administration taking place at that time. These were the introduction of the post of Deputy Development Commissioner (DDC) and the *Zilla Parishad* (district assembly).

Traditionally, a senior level state civil servant, called the District Development Officer (DDO), was in-charge of all developmental activity in the district. He was under the direct control and supervision of the District Officer. In creating a new position, the DDC, an additional IAS officer was posted in the district with complete authority and responsibility in the area of development. The justification for this change was based upon the view that the District Officer had so many responsibilities that he had little time to devote to development. On the other hand, the DDO was too subordinate in rank to become an agent of change. It was hoped that an IAS officer, although junior in seniority and rank to the District Officer, would become a more effective agent of change.

This system had already been tried in the State of Maharashtra and the Bihar Government was modelling its programme after that of Maharashtra. Most of the District Officers, who commented to us on this move, were extremely negative. They pointed out that some years ago a similar programme had been established in a number of districts in Bihar with disastrous results. They also claimed that the state of Maharashtra was moving away from this system of dual control, apparently as a response to its ineffectiveness.

At the time of our study, no DDC had been posted to the districts we visited. Therefore, it is not possible for us to comment on their impact. It is evident, however, that the Government of Bihar has recognised that the District Officer has not been and cannot become an effective agent of change.

In conjuction with the introduction of the DDC, the Government of Bihar also established *Zilla Parishad* (district assembly). District Boards have existed in the past, but the newly created bodies are supposed to have considerable power within the district in the sphere of development. The district assembly will be a totally elected body with elected chairpersons. The DDC will act as Secretary of the body. Between the DDC and the district assembly, it is hoped that a new more rational and effective programme of change can be implemented at the district level. The district assemblies would no longer be rubber stamps to approve all governmental programmes. They would become partners in the planning and implementation of developmental schemes. The DDC, however, will still be responsible for the actual implementation of the programmes.

This attempt to democratise planning and developmental programmes was approved of by most of the District Officers we interviewed; however, it must be noted that those bodies were not operational at the time of our study. Some critics have questioned the appointment of the DDC as secretary of these elected bodies. They claimed that the State Government wanted to give some power in the field of planning to elected representatives in the district, but not too much. However, on the whole, this measure was seen as a demoralisation of the developmental process. If successful, these bodies could become major factors in economic and social change at the district level.

CONCLUDING REMARKS

It is apparent that significant shifts have taken place in the role of the District Officer from colonial times to the present. Much of the power formerly associated with this position has declined, whereas a major addition to the role has been the responsibility for economic and social development.

In most cases, while District Officers recognised development as a major goal, they failed to carry it out effectively because of their preoccupation with maintenance of law and order. There are a number of additional reasons for their failure—the lack of commitment being the most important. Other obstacles are short tenure in a district, political interference, the *ad hoc* nature of the office, and individual differences in ability and motivation.

We noted that the Government of Bihar had implicitly recognised the inability of District Officers to deal with developmental issues, so they created *Zilla Parishads* (district assemblies) and introduced the new position of Deputy Development Commissioner (DDC). Despite these changes, it is still questionable whether development at the district level will proceed smoothly.

There are two alternative assumptions with regard to the role of the District Officer. One projects the District Officer as a catalyst of change and the other rejects it. A criticism of the former assumption is that the present policy of the introduction of the DDC is not likely to succeed because it creates dual authority in district administration, especially in the sphere of development. In our view, the major barrier to carrying out developmental activity on the part of the District Officer is his preoccupation with maintenance of law and order. Of course, there are other constraints, but they are manageable. We would suggest that if the District Officers were completely relieved of his law and order responsibility, he could serve as a catalyst of change. We would further suggest that law and order responsibility be given entirely to the police head of the district. This, of course, is based on the assumption that the District Officer should be the catalyst of change in the district.

An alternative assumption is that the District Officer, who is a carryover from the colonial administration, cannot be an agent of change in independent India. This perspective places major emphasis on decentralisation and the inculcation of democratic values. If this assumption is followed, as seems to be the case in Bihar at the time of our fieldwork, then all responsibility for developmental activity should be taken away from the District Officer and/or any other government agent. If the government wants to decentralise and democratise the planning process, then it should stimulate the growth of the *Zilla Parishads* as well as other locally elected bodies such as *Panchayats* (village councils).

The creation of the new position of the DDC does not seem to be a practical or effective solution to the problems of development. From our point of view, establishing *Zilla Parishads* as independent bodies without any government officer overseeing their activities and giving them full power in the sphere of development will be a more welcome and effective way of accelerating the process of change in India, especially in its rural sectors.

REFERENCES

1. Dwaine Marvick, *Political Decision-Makers,* Now York, Free Press, 1967, p. 34. Also see II. J. Pandya, "Sardar Patel and the Indian Administrative System—A Note", *Administrative Change,* Vol. 3, No. l, July-December 1975, pp. 87-91. Pandya deals at length with Sardar's role in reorganising Indian administrative system after independence.
2. All of the provinces of British India were divided into basic administrative units or districts. During the latter days of the British empire, there were some 250 of these administrative units each under the control of a District Officer, who was usually called Collector or District Magistrate (DM) or Deputy Commissioner (DC). These titles also suggest his major functions: collection of land revenue and other taxes and maintenance of law and order within the district. In joint role as Collector and DM, he combined both executive and judicial functions; he was responsible for the well-being of his wards. Blunt suggests that he was there to serve the people of the district [Sir Edward Blunt, The I.C.S., London, Faber and Faber, 1937], and Woodruff, another British historian of the ICS, describes the attitudes of a number of District Officers, who clearly perceived the primacy of their obligation to the population of the district [Philip Woodruff, *The Men who Ruled India,* Vol. 11, *The Guardians,* New York, Schocken Books, 1964]. In this article, we will use the terms 'District Officer' and 'District Magistrate' (DM) interchangeably.
3. G. P. Srivastava has dealt with this issue at length in his book, *The Indian Civil Service,* Delhi, S. Chand, 1965.
4. See II. Rai, "Dual Control of Law and Order Administration in India: A Study in Magistracy and Police Relationship", *Indian Journal of Public Administration,* Vol. 13, No. 1, January-March 1968, pp. 43-64.
5. See Sir Edward Blunt, *The I.C.S.,* London, Faber and Faber, 1937.
6. This sentiment was also echoed by the present Divisional Commissioners whom we interviewed. Even in those districts which are also divisional headquarters. Divisional Commissioners maintained low profile and let the District Officer have full control. They would give advice only when consulted by the District Officer and interfere only in extreme situations only.
7. See introduction of Kewal L. Punjabi (ed.). *The Civil Servant in India,* Bombay, Bharatiya Vidya Bhavan, 1965.

8. Edwin Eames and Parmatma Saran did this project jointly during their sabbatical year, however, funding was received separately by Indo-American Sub-commission for Eames, and Smithsonian Institution for Saran. For interviewing retired Indian ICS officers, we visited many Indian cities, but all present District Officers and most former IAS District Officers come from the state of Bihar. State of Bihar was the chief venue of our study.
9. The main training centre for IAS is Lal Bahadur Shastri National Academy of Administration at Mussoorie. However, the Indian Institute of Public Administration in New Delhi is actively involved in the in-service training of IAS officers. The Institute at Ranchi basically caters to members of the State Civil Service but IAS members posted in Bihar also go to the Institute for short orientation courses in order to familiarise themselves with the conditions in the state.
10. See Om Prakash's "Socio-Economic Background of Regular Recruits to the IAS–A Study", *Journal of Constitutional and Parliamentary Studies,* Vol. 12, No. 1, January-March, 1970, pp. 43-59; and also Om Prakash, "Socio-Economic Background of Schedule Castes/Tribes Regular Recruits to the IAS", *Administrator,* Vol. 22, Nos. 2 and 3, 1977. In many of our conversations with the IAS officers, it was confirmed that such a shift had actually taken place.
11. Our ICS respondents took time to explain their individual position with regard to India's independence movement. Many felt that despite their best efforts, they remained suspect both in the eyes of the British officers and the leaders of the independence movement.
12. See H. Rai, "Dual Control of Law and Order Administration in India: A Study in Magistracy and Police Relationship", *Op. cit.*
13. This sentiment was expressed by many respondents. They also suggested that while on paper development has the priority, in reality it is the maintenance of law and order.

4

District and State Administration: A New Leadership Role for the IAS

G.C. SINGHVI

The two operationally significant forces dominating district executive administration in our country could unmistakably be identified as the District Officer, on the one hand, and various district heads of the State Government's executive departments, like PWD, irrigation, agriculture, animal husbandry, cooperation, education, forests, police, prisons, excise, taxation, industries, fisheries, social welfare, public health engineering, medical and health, etc., on the other. Both are forces to be reckoned with. The former is the chief representative of the State Government in the district and has variously been described as *'Annadata'*, *'Maabap'*, 'representative and agent of government', 'general manager of all government activities', 'eyes and ears (and sometimes arm) of government', 'the kingpin of administration', 'the key-stone of the arch of district administration', 'the captain (some time non-playing) of the team', 'the man on the spot', 'the area specialist', *'primus inter pares'*, 'the first citizen in the district', 'the supreme head of the district administration' and more recently and in more benevolent terms, like 'friend, philosopher and guide', 'adviser, educator and helper', 'the fulcrum of grassroot democracy', 'the main spring of development', and 'the director of the Rath of Lord Jagannath (the Rath of Panchayati Raj)'.[1] The District Officer also holds the key posts of district collector, deputy commissioner, district magistrate, district development officer and district election officer. The District Officer is supposed to play the leadership role in district administration as he is the leader of all the departments' (other than judiciary's) district level officers. Besides, the district level officers have their own departmental, divisional or regional level officers and heads of the departments who too exercise supervision and control over them. This clearly underscores the fact that the State Government Departments' district level officers are subject to a duality of control, one of the District Officer and the other one of their departmental superiors. The latter is a well-defined overall control whereas the former is a loosely defined general control. That is, perhaps, why the District Officer occupies a unique position in the country's administration and it is said that there is not and never has been an official quite like the District Officer anywhere else.[2]

SOME PROBLEMS OF THE EXISTING SYSTEM

Financial administration, personnel administration, technical administration and day-to-day routine administration of the departments are in the domain of the departmental officers, the district level officers and their superiors, the heads of the departments and their divisional level officers. The latter exercise full administrative and operational control over the district level officers. Thus, the departmental superiors are the bosses in the real sense of the term insofar as departmental district level officers are concerned and the District Officer's control assumes a form similar to that of the control of an overseer and a coordinator. The District Officer, in one form or the other, writes the annual confidential reports of the district level officers. Moreover, they have to concede the supremacy of the District Officer since he is an officer of the Indian Administrative Service and is nearer the State Government and its secretaries than the heads of the departments. The district level officers are aware of his pivotal position. They also know that their District Officer may be the secretary to the government in their department some day. Thus, this broad conceptual framework serves as a constant reminder to the district level officers that they have two bosses to serve, namely, the departmental superiors and the District Officer, respectively. They are expected to accomplish the seemingly difficult task of keeping both of them on their right side.

As a result of this duality of control, neither the district level officers nor the District Officers seem to be fully satisfied with the existing arrangement. The district level officers lament over the fact that the District Officers treat land revenue, executive magistracy, supply, elections and developmental work as their 'own' while they accord a stepmotherly treatment to the functioning of the other district departments. Moreover, they feel that the District Officer's control over them is rather superfluous since he is unable to help them genuinely in case of need. Despite having powers over them, he does not show sufficient responsibility towards the district departments. Instead of sitting in the driver's seat, he resorts to what is called back-seat driving. When the district level officers want anything to be done for their department, the District Officer, more often than not, asks them to contact their departmental superiors for the purpose. It is also contended that the District Officers are, by and large, young and not so mature as to impart real guidance to the experienced district level officers. The District Officers then are hard pressed for time since they are already overburdened with their 'own' work. They have thus no time to perform the role of a 'co-ordinator'. The district level officers, therefore, argue that this inept duality of control should go and they should have only one boss out of the two to serve. But this constitutes only one side of the picture.

The other side of the picture constitutes the District Officers' complaint to the effect that the district level officers look more towards their departmental superiors and do not keep them (District Officers) fully posted with the activities of their departments. What they feel is that even in the writing of the annual confidential reports of the district level officers, the District Officer has not been of much avail.[3] Thus, they regretfully conclude that they are only nominal heads of the districts and superfluous kingpins of district administration, that they do not wield real authority and that they are more the drudges than the masters of the various departments functioning in the district.[4] Therefore, they feel that unless the District Officers are made the real executive chiefs and administrators of the district and supreme over everyone and everything except the proceedings of the courts of justice (that is the district level officers are placed under the subordination of the District Officers) they will not be able to play their leadership role effectively and stimulatingly. Moreover, the district administration may not be able to achieve a breakthrough in such an unnourishing atmosphere.[5]

It is unfortunate that as a result of this growing dissatisfaction generated amongst the district level officers and District Officers, the district administration suffers from a depression which defies description in precise terms. We find that some district level officers bother more for their departmental superiors than for the District Officer and some others bother more for the District Officer than for their departmental superiors. There are others who try to please all and end up either in miserable failure or in astounding success. There are still others who do not bother for anybody and are indifferent towards their work. All this hampers the creation of a climate conducive to meaningful and purposive administration in the district. The cumulative impact of this process extending over several years has been that the credibility of the District Officer as a leader of the district team has considerably eroded.[6] In the ultimate analysis, in the present set-up, it is the State on which incalculable damage is inflicted.

Addressing the tenth annual meeting of the Indian Institute of Public Administration on October 23, 1964, the Prime Minister, Shri Lal Bahadur Shastri, referred to the failure of coordination at the district level in the following words:

> In regard to developmental activities, the difficulty at the present moment is that there is no proper co-ordination. Formerly the District Collector used to be the co-ordinating authority...
>
> The District Collector is there, but there are also, at the district level officers of different departments, like PWD, agriculture, cooperation, education, etc. ... These different units function in a district, but they are not under the direct control or supervision of the District Collector. They have their direct connections with the respective Heads of Departments sitting in the State Secretariat, or in some cases with the departmental officers at the divisional level. The result is that there is no proper co-ordination.[7]

It is, therefore, perhaps high time to consider and recognise how much of the traditional basis is worth preserving and what new role the district level officers or the District Officer should undertake. This is a reality which must be confronted.

DEVISING A NEW SYSTEM

Without indulging in any methodological fanfare, I would now highlight what constitutes a reasonable course of action in order to find a way out of this imbroglio. That there is a need for coordination in the working of different government departments in a district is an indisputable fact. As long as this will continue to be paramount and in the foreseeable future, it seems it will, the way out would seem to lie in relieving the District Officer of his responsibilities as district collector, district magistrate, district development officer, district election officer, etc., and then vesting in him the powers of deputy head of all the departments operating in the district.[8]

Role of District Officer

To illustrate, it may be suggested that the District Officer could be vested with the powers of a divisional commissioner for the land revenue and executive magistracy work, of a deputy inspector-general of police[9] and prisons departments, of a deputy director for functions pertaining to agriculture, industries, transport, medical and health, college education and mines and geology departments, of a deputy registrar for cooperatives department of a conservator of forests, of deputy commissioner for labour, excise and taxation and that of superintending engineer for public works (building and roads), irrigation and public health and engineering departments, so far as his district is concerned. This list is not exhaustive and is merely illustrative of the various regional and divisional level functionaries whose functions could be merged with those of the District Officer.

The duties of the district collector, district magistrate and district election officer could be accomplished by the incumbents of the existing posts of additional collector and additional district magistrate, by designating them as full-fledged district collector, district magistrate and district election officer. Incidentally, this change will be compatible with the change brought about by the Code of Criminal Procedure, 1973, under which the district magistrate is merely the chief executive magistrate of the district and as such his status is analogous to the status of the chief judicial magistrate of the district. The posts of district development officers could similarly be held by the deputy district development officers who are invariably officers of the existing provincial civil services (State Administrative Services), drawing their pay in the senior scale.

Apart from the autonomous corporations and bodies and the judiciary operating in the district, there would be no government department which will be out of the purview of super-ordination and control of the District Officer. At the same time, the District Officer will not be holding charge of any department directly as is the case at present. Instead, his role will be of an overseer, supervisor and coordinator for all the departments alike. In short, his role would be that of a leader and head of the team of all district level officials.[10]

Abolition of Posts of Heads of Departments

Under this new pattern, there will unquestionably be no place for independent heads of the departments. Their posts will have to be abolished. Instead, the secretary to the State Government dealing with a department shall be the *ex officio* head of the department. For each one of the major departments, there shall be an independent secretary-cum-head of the department, whereas two or more than two minor departments may be grouped together and one secretary-cum-head of the department be appointed for each such group. For assisting this functionary, there will be specialist officers equivalent in rank and status to the present-day divisional level officers. Some of them will be posted as deputy secretaries to the government, while others can do jobs dealing with training, research and other specific functions. The senior-most departmental officer will serve as advisor to the Government (minister and secretary). Obviously, the number of advisors will conform to the number of departments.

In the office of the District Officer, there will be only personal staff of the District Officer, such as personal assistant, accounts clerk and receipt and despatch clerk in addition to a staff officer to assist him in his work. This staff officer should, in the fitness of things, be a generalist. As far as the remaining staff is concerned, the District Officer will have at his disposal the services of that staff which is posted with the district level officers. Thus, it will enable the office of the District Officer to be officer-oriented.

The district level officers will send their office files to the District Officer for those cases where the papers are to be perused or orders are to be issued by the latter in his capacity as deputy head of the department. There will be a frequency of discussions in person or on telephone, conferences, visits and inspections of the offices of the district level officers and visits to tehsil headquarters and sub-divisional headquarters on the part of the District Officer. Monthly meetings of district level officers presided over by the District Officer should then prove more fruitful and rewarding than what their present versions show. In the proposed set-up, a substantial District Annual Administration Report could be published with advantage and expedition. Tours and use of government vehicles by district level officers could also be controlled and coordinated with greater circumspection. Not only that the writing of annual confidential reports of the district level officers by the District Officer too would be more meaningful than the present-day reports because he could then watch the functioning of the district level officers from much closer quarters. This will be in contrast to the present-day District Officers and divisional level officers as the latter in most of the cases sit hundreds of miles away from the point of actual policy-implementation.

Justification for the Proposed System

It may be pointed out that the action-proposals put forward in this article are not the products of fancy; they are conceptually sound and structurally feasible. As discussed earlier, in the proposed set-up, the District Officer will be relieved of his functions as district collector, district magistrate and district development officer, and will assume the role of a super-ordinate, supervisor and coordinator as far as the government departments operating in the district are concerned.

It is almost certain (and when precise details are worked out, it may also be confirmed) that these proposals would stand the test of economy and provide a prospect which should be welcome, particularly at a time when pressures of acute inflation and consequent worse financial stringency are weighing heavily on the administration. Then, the abolition of the offices of the divisional level officers of all departments by merging them with the office of the District Officer will predictably result in a lot of saving to the state exchequer. Similarly, the merger of the offices of the secretaries to the State governments and heads of departments is most likely to cause reduction in governmental expenditure to a considerable extent. This will happen as both these offices have at the moment almost similar sections and branches, maintenance of which involve duplication of expenditure and endeavour.

The proposed set-up would, thus, be economical and at the same time conducive to increasing efficiency and efficacy. It will inescapably cause an inextricable, deep and all-round involvement of the District Officer in the affairs of the district which will have a direct and decisive impact on district administration as a whole. It would also eventually cause rationalisation of administration at various levels since the proposals emanating from specialist district level officers would be processed by the generalist District Officers. They would also be scrutinised by a specialist in the secretariat before the generalist secretary puts it up to the popular minister who, in turn, will have the benefit of mature advice of the specialist advisor. There will, thus, be a happy combination of endeavours made by the generalists and the specialists and that is what is needed today.

It is neither the generalist nor the specialist who can do everything by himself alone. The reason is that the scientific expert is a narrow specialist who cannot even acquire the general knowledge necessary to grasp the social and philosophical implications of those technical matters on which he is an acknowledged expert. The knowledge of the generalist, as far as any one speciality is concerned, is not thorough enough for him to master the complex problems now associated with science and technology. Thus, both of them administratively and operationally need each other.

One inherent danger in the scheme which could undoubtedly be apprehended is that, in course of time, the office of District Officer might so expand as to have sections in his office corresponding to all the departments of the government existing in the district. This might be a sinister development which has to be guarded against right from the inception. This is because once this development takes place, the proposed new pattern would become an easy prey to Parkinson's law and render district administration as deficient as it is today.

As far as the secretariat level is concerned, the secretary to the government (and *ex officio* head of the department) will also have a generalist staff officer to assist him. All other officers, whether of the rank of deputy secretary or assistant secretary, will be either the departmental (specialist) officers or the secretariat service officers.

ONLY ONE ALL-INDIA ADMINISTRATIVE SERVICE

There will be certain natural corollaries to this proposal. In this set-up, there would be no place for any All-India Service other than the IAS.[11] The other two All-India Services, namely, the Indian Forest Service and the Indian Police Service, will have to be abolished and officers of these services replaced by officers of the appropriate state services.

In this context, in the states, there will be no generalist administrative service other than the IAS operating at any level. The existing provincial civil service (State Administrative Service) shall have to be broken up into different specialist administrative services, such as excise, taxation, transport, land revenue (including executive magistracy), supply, etc.

Training of the New Service

A point crucial to the emergence of this set-up will be the broad-basing of training of officers of the Indian Administrative Service by increasing the content of professionalism in training attuned and harnessed to the goals of the new activity charter of the IAS. The foundation for this professionalism edifice could be laid if the young entrants are made to acquire a 'basic literacy' in certain areas of study which could precisely be identified as follows:

1. Science and technology;
2. Social and behavioural science;
3. Law (Principles of Legislation, Constitution of India, Administrative Law, the Civil Code and the Criminal Code);

4. International Affairs (International Politics, International Economics, International Law and International Organisation);
5. Economics in government;
6. Management in government (and all that goes to make administration management-oriented); modern tools of management and other numeric aids (or quantitative techniques) to decision-making with particular accent on economic analysis;
7. Human relations in management;
8. Administration in action (Governments at the Union and State levels, and departmental and local administration);
9. Impact of 'people' on the policy and programmes for change, nature of group dynamics, and public relations; and
10. Research and development.

This can be achieved by devising a two-year Master of Governmental Administration (MGA) course which could be undergone by those candidates who qualify for entry to the IAS at the UPSC's IAS and other services combined competitive examination. The curriculum to be devised for the MGA course should emphasise the multi-dimensional aspects of administrative problems and comprise the ten fields enumerated above. Every candidate selected for doing MGA should, on joining the course, get a stipend and not regular salary. The stipendiary system will facilitate the achievement of educational targets by the young learner. He should start getting regular salary only after completion of MGA, final selection for appointment to the IAS and actually joining the IAS in pursuance thereof.

Structuring the Cadre

Closely associated with this proposition is the reconstitution of the cadre of the IAS. Comparatively speaking, in this set-up, more weightage will have to be given to the specialist and secretariat services for gaining entry into the IAS by promotion. For example, the proposition of percentage would have to be kept as follows: 50 per cent for direct recruitment, 40 per cent for promotion from specialist services of the state (4% out of this 40% will have to be earmarked for State Secretariat Services) and remaining 10 per cent for promotion from Central Secretariat Services (this last mentioned percentage incidentally is conspicuous by its absence at present).

Chances of promotion in the specialist services of the state will not at all adversely suffer in the proposed set-up because apart from most of them getting promotion to the IAS, they will be getting posts of deputy secretaries and equivalent specialist posts at the state headquarters. It may be reiterated that all such posts will be equal in status and pay to the existing divisional level officers in the departments.

The posts of heads of departments will also not be lost to the specialist services as there will be an advisor to the government for the department of that very status and drawing his salary in the same pay scale as admissible to the present-day heads of the departments. Even then, if it appears that some specialist services are being deprived of a few senior posts because of the proposed set-up, then their cadre strength could be so readjusted that there may be less of direct recruitment and more of promotions which would tend considerably to lessen frustration in the specialist services. Even as things stand today, in many departments, superior posts are created not because they are really needed but they are created just to open up avenues of promotion to the members of the services concerned and thereby avert stagnation and consequent demoralisation. However, in this process the state exchequer suffers adversely.

The concept of the IAS—a focal general purpose service—as an all-India oriented service, emanates from the Constitution of India as being common to the Union and the States. The principal warranty of the concept, to borrow the phrase from the second Hoover Commission, comprises "experience in more than one charge, experience in both staff and line operating work and experience in both the departmental and field services".[12] It, thus, presupposes the existence at the base of a scientific and rational method of 'rotation, tenures and transfers' and arrangement of posts in line and staff functions at the 'district, regional and central levels' all knit into a comprehensive system. In simple words, the assumption is that there is a regular, systematic and steady two-way flow of IAS officers between the States and the

Union, between the districts and the state headquarters and between line and staff jobs, which infuses broadness of outlook in administrators and in the administration of the Union, the states and the districts. And this can be achieved by setting up hierarchies with a sufficient number of levels of relatively slight differentiations in pay and responsibility in such a manner as would make it obligatory on every IAS officer, stage by stage, to man line jobs and staff jobs in the state as well as State Government jobs and Union Government jobs by rotation, and in the process earn over a dozen promotions throughout his service career.

This 'concept' could easily be translated in terms of 'structure' by enunciating an innovational position-classification and compensation plan for the IAS somewhat on the following lines:

Post	*Pay Scale (1983 standard)* Rs.
IAS Probationer under training	700-800
Sub-Divisional Officer (State)	800-1100
Staff Officer to District Officer (State)	1100-1400
Under Secretary (Union Government)	1400-1600
Deputy Secretary (Union Government)	1600-1800
Staff Officer to Secretary to Government-cum-Head of Department (State)	1800-2000
Director in a Ministry (Union Government)	2000-2250
District Officer (State)	2250-2500
Joint Secretary (Union Government)	2500-2750
Member, Board of Revenue (State)	2875 fixed
Secretary to Government-cum-Head of Department (State)	3000 fixed
Additional Secretary (Union Government)	3250 fixed
Chairman, Board of Revenue (State)	3500 fixed
Chief Secretary (State Government)	3750 fixed
Special Secretary (Union Government)	3875 fixed
Secretary (Union Government)	4000 fixed[1]

There can be no doubt that once the District Officers are drawn from the IAS officers drawing their pay in the scale of Rs.

2250-2500, the incumbents will obviously be quite senior persons who, by virtue of their maturity and experience, could certainly impart tangible guidance to the district level officers of all departments.

Advantages of the New System

The district level officers will agree in their hearts; though debate in minds, with the fact that the present duality of control over them will get terminated under the new system and they will be required to look towards only one man, i.e., the District Officer. As a result, the entire gamut of relationship between the District Officer and the district level officers will assume an altogether new complexion conducive to growth and development.

Collaboration between the government and the district administration will also be closer than what it is at present because whenever the District Officer will go to the state headquarters, he could meet all his bosses—the secretaries to the government-cum-heads of departments—and get things done for his district. From the point of view of political bosses also, this proposal should prove to be a boon because at the district level they will virtually have to contact only one man, and at the state level too, they will have to contact only one man for each department.

Most pertinently, it may be pointed out at this juncture that the proposed set-up will not at all interfere with the working of the Panchayati Raj Institutions, particularly the Zilla Parishad, because the Zilla Parishads are concerned with the district level officers whereas the District Officer will be their super-ordinates. As such, if any district level officer does not function to the satisfaction of the Zilla Parishad, then it could complain against him to the District Officer to make him work. In this manner, the contemplated administrative changes are likely to serve as morale booster to Panchayati Raj.[14]

The tax-paying and, more than that, the non-tax-paying citizens should also welcome the change. For, instead of going to the divisional headquarters for so many errands, in the proposed set-up they will be required to go to the district headquarters only and there too they may hope to get redressal of their grievances under one roof and from one man. It will mean and entail less botheration and expense to the citizen.

Induction of this new pattern in district administration is likely to bring into sharp focus the fact that in this set-up the powers, duties and responsibilities of the deputy heads of departments, vesting in the District Officer, will have to be rationally revised keeping the feasibility angle in full view. These shall have to be so devised that the District Officer, as deputy head of all the departments, may be able to cope up with and do full justice to these. In other words, many powers, duties and responsibilities of the deputy heads of the departments, as existing today, shall have to be delegated down the line to the departmental district level officers. Then, we may have instances of some districts which may be adjudged to be too big and too unwieldy to be controlled by one District Officer. The obvious answer in such cases would lie in breaking up such districts into two or more, as the case may be. We are aware of the need for such breaking up being felt under the present set-up in case of several districts.[15]

Finally, it may be asserted that when a balance sheet of this current proposal—which envisages an arrangement by which executive authority is concentrated in one man at the territorial district level and also in one man at the functional state level–is drawn, it will show that the balance is heavily weighing in favour of gains and that the proposal should inevitably usher in a new era in the annals of the history of district and state administration in the country. It can confidently be anticipated that the emerging new pattern of district and state administration, attuned to making the District Officer and the secretary to the state government omnipotent and omniscient administrators, would enable them to make a balanced and distinctive contribution to the total administrative endeavour at the district and the state levels.

REFERENCES

1. P.R. Dubhashi, "Leadership Role of ihe Collector", *The Indian Journal of Public Administration*, Vol. XI, No. 3 (July-September 1965), p. 615.
2. Over a century ago, Macauley explained to the House of Commons: "Such a power as that which Collectors in India have over the people is not found in any other part of the world possessed by any class of functionaries." R.N. Chopra, "The Collector in the Nineteen-Sixties", *The Indian Journal of Public Administration*, Vol. XI, No. 3 (July-September), 1965, p. 482.

3. "He is expected to see that nothing goes wrong in his district, but he has little power outside the Magistrate and Collector field to see that things go right... He can cajole and persuade: he cannot compel." *Report of the Bengal Administration Enquiry Committee* 1944-45), para 65. Sir Archibald Rowlands was the chairman of the committee.
4. "Another serious drawback... the Collector-Magistrate had continued to be immediately responsible for the administration of other departments operating in the district under the control of their departmental chiefs at the provincial headquarters. All these departmental chiefs...acted as so many masters of Collector...The District Officers were in fact acting as 'drudges of so many departments and masters of none'." B.B. Misra, "The Evolution of the Office of Collector", *The Indian Journal of Public Administration*, Vol. XI, No. 3 (July-September), 1965, p. 359.
5. "The position of the Collector is under strain... A simple 'unity of command' no longer obtains... Thus while the responsibilities have grown, the prestige of the District Collector has declined, and function without power has become the privilege of the District Collector." Dubhashi, *Op. cit.*, p. 620.
6. "Even after Independence, the Collector remains the first official in the district though it is a moot point whether much of the glamour attached to the post has dimmed." A.N. Kidwai, "The Collector in the Nineteen-Sixties—Assam", *The Indian Journal of Public Administration*, Vol. XI, No. 3 (July-September), 1965, p. 414.
7. Quoted by P.K. Dave in "The Collector Today and Tomorrow", *The Indian Journal of Public Administration*, Vol. XI, No. 3 (July-September), 1965, p. 379.
8. Sir George Campbell (Lt. Governor of Bengal between 1871-1874), had he been alive, would certainly have been happy with this proposal because he felt even then that the District Officers were not what they were and that their power and influence had gone from them.
9. "In 1947, it was often said that the Police State was ended and the Welfare State had come. In this was involved a double misconception. The Police State cannot be abolished, it must always remain; indeed the Welfare State is a superstructure built on the Police State; the superstructure would collapse if the foundation disappeared." J.D. Shukla, "The Collector in the Nineteen-Sixties—Uttar Pradesh", *The Indian Journal of Public Administration*, Vol. XI, No. 3 (July-September), 1965, p. 587.
10. "It would be much more convenient if the Collector is officially recognised as the head of the team of the District Level Officers and is given full powers to set about his task in any manner that he

considers appropriate... .the District Level Officers would necessarily have to function according to the orders of the Collector and the Collector for his part will have to take the full responsibility for the actions of the District Level Officers". N. Narasimha Rau, "The Collector in the Nineteen-Sixties—Mysore", *The Indian Journal of Public Administration,* Vol. XI, No. 3 (July-September), 1965, pp. 531-32.

11. "...the Union will go, you will not have a United India, if you have not a good All-India Service, which has independence to speak out its mind, which has a sense of security that you will stand by your word... if you do not adopt this course, then do not follow the present Constitution. Substitute something else," Sardar Vallabhbhai Patel (speaking in the Constituent Assembly Debates).
12. USA, Commission for Organisation of the Executive Branch of the Government, *Report of the Task Force on Personnel and Civil Service,* Washington, 1955.
13. "... a tendency has also sprung up for officers to avoid the field posts, if possible, and that too mainly in the districts. So more and more the period as a Collector may be looked upon as a necessary evil to be got through somehow. What we expect of a Collector is certainly much more than this. The situation can certainly be remedied." B. Sivaraman, "The Collector of the Seventies", *The Indian Journal of Public Administration,* Vol. XI, No. 3 (July-September), 1965, p. 635.
14. "...since a spirit of mutual understanding and psychological readjustment is still lacking on the part of both the District Officer and the elected representatives of society, the dichotomy between the two continues. While history favours the former, politics lends support to the latter. If democracy is to survive, both must learn to live together in peace and harmony." B.B. Misra, *Op. cit.,* pp. 366-67.
15. Addressing the National Development Council on October 27, 1964, the Prime Minister pleaded for restoration to the District Officer of the status of a co-ordinator of all governmental activities in the district and in the context said: "This may well mean splitting up larger districts into more compact administrative units. The task should be faced as one of urgency." Quoted by P.K. Dave, *Op. cit.,* p. 380.

5

Administering a District in India: Reviewing Collector's Institution

D.S. MISHRA

The role and responsibilities of the office of District Collector (DC) have undergone considerable change since the Independence. From enforcement of law and order, and collection of revenue for his administrative unit the office has grown as an important arm for implementing national and state policies on welfare and planned development. Being the chief executive at he district, his status is like a mini-government—all in one at the district level. The enhancement of responsibilities and span of functions over the years has also witnessed a substantial deterioration for the institution of DC. Politicisation of administration, corruption and political interference have largely contributed in bringing disrepute to once famed and sacrosanct office. Sincere efforts are called for from all concerned to restore moral authority and inviolability of this important institution.

INTRODUCTION

Institution of an office with territorial jurisdictions found in the Indian history during the Mughal period as *Subedar*. The East India Company, which came to India for trade and business were given the responsibility of collection of revenue as Diwan of Bengal, Bihar and Orissa. Warren Hastings, the Governor-General of the Company instituted the office of Collector for this purpose with territorial jurisdiction. The term was retained during the British Rule. It was through this office that the colonial rulers used to execute there command and retain local control. The expanse of Collector's control was the lowest administered unit, which was called the District, during the British Rule. Besides revenue collection, the District Collector (DC) exercised civil, judicial and military powers within his territory. In the year 1792, the judicial powers were separated from the DC and a new office of District Judge (DJ) was created to administer justice in the District. During the period of Governor-General Lord William Bentinck from 1828-35, the magisterial duties were segregated from the DJ and annexed to the DC and therefore, the new nomenclature assigned to this officer was Collector and District Magistrate. An office of Deputy Collector to assist DC in discharging his responsibilities was instituted during this period.

Initially, DCs were appointed from Covenanted Civil Service (CCS), which was recruited through patronage system consisting exclusively of whites from the Great Britain. These officers were trained in Haileybury College in England regarding Indian polity, law, economy, history, administration etc. Later, with the recommendation of Macaulay Committee, a competitive examination to recruit members of CCS, which was by then known as Indian Civil Services (ICS), was introduced in 1855.[1] Even though there was no formal bar to Indians to participate and get selected in ICS on the basis of merit, no local/indigenous person could hold the office of DC until the later part of the 19th century. This was because there was only one centre of examination in London; the test was based on the English education with the age limit being 18 to 23 years. Later Indians started getting selected in the competitive examination and the number rose after the age group was changed and centres were located in India as well.

During the British Rule, DC was mainly responsible for collection of land revenue and maintenance of law and order in his territorial jurisdiction. He represented the crown at the district level for all other official responsibilities. The DCs maintained high quality of devotion, dedication, loyalty, integrity and professionalism towards their duties and the Rule. District Collectors played very important role in implementation of Lord Cornwallis' permanent settlement of land records. This was a major landmark in the history of land management in India. As head of police administration of the district, she/he played significant role in containing any disturbances and maintaining peace and order.[2] What can be boldly asserted is that the (ICS) officer class was like Ceasers wife—above suspicion and the highest level of integrity was maintained.[3] When, for instance, Surendra Nath Banerjee, then an Assistant Magistrate in *Sylhet* (now in Bangladesh), was found lying, the higher civil service was shocked and he had to pay the price—he was dismissed from the coveted Indian Civil Service.[4] This service and the office of DC were incorruptible during the Raj. It is said that no other service in the world was better officered than the Indian Civil Service. Leslie Palmier writes about ICS: "...it was recruitment of a class of persons educated and shaped into a particular code of behaviour, together with subsequent indoctrination into the values of the Indian Civil Service (ICS). These seem to be the factors making for the great prestige held by the ICS from the early 19th century to the Independence of India in 1947."[5]

II

OFFICE OF COLLECTOR AFTER INDEPENDENCE

After Independence in 1947, Government of India debated whether to retain the ICS or to discontinue the service as that represented the oppressive and aggressive regime of the British and was therefore despised by the national leaders during the freedom movement. The views of first Indian Home Minister Sardar Vallabhbhai Patel prevailed and the service was retained as a steel frame of Indian governance system with the new nomenclature of Indian Administrative Service (IAS). It was expected that the service would provide continuity in administration and be a bridge of balance between Centre and States in the federal set-up. Such officers, who are selected through an all India level competitive examination conducted every year by the Union Public Service Commission (UPSC) with minimum qualification of undergraduate degree in any discipline from an university or equivalent and are in a specific age group, become the member of this premier administrative service in the country. To retain the federal character of governance, these officers are allocated to their own home state and other States/Union Territories (UTs) on the basis of their merit and preference in the competitive examination. After initial institutional and field training as lower level functionaries in the district, an IAS officer is posted as Collector and DM after around six to eight years of service and remains in such positions or equivalent posts in the State Secretariat she/he or parastatal bodies or Central Government Secretariat till she/he completes about 16 years of service.[6] Officers from State Civil Services are also promoted to IAS after putting in minimum 12 years of service on the basis of their merit against one-third quota reserved for such services.

The office of DC is also known as District Officer or Deputy Commissioner in some parts of India. The role and responsibility of DC has undergone considerable change since Independence. With the adoption of Indian Constitution on January 26, 1950, the country became a welfare state and assumed the role of social benefactor and nation-builder apart from regulator of peace and order and collector of revenue, as was the case during the colonial rule. Further, with the introduction of Five Year Plans in 1951, National Extension Programme in 1952 and PRIs in 1957, an era of planned development and public participation in governance was initiated. The representative form of democratic government required holding of free and fair elections at regular intervals for Central and State Legislatures and political executives. All these led to wide ranging structural and functional changes in the tasks performed by the DC.

III

ADMINISTERING A DISTRICT

The district is the lowest administered unit of the Union. The area and population of a district varies from state to state and even within the States/UTs. Some of the districts are bigger than many countries in the world in terms of geographical size or population. For the purpose of effective administration, the district is divided into revenue sub-divisions, developmental blocks and police stations. These three sub-units are generally not co-terminus. Lowest populated unit in a rural area is called village. Over 80 per cent of Indian population lives in these villages. Administration of the present day district in India is quite a complex affair. The revenue administration directly reports to the DC. The development functions are performed by plethora of district level functionaries who report to DC as well as to their departmental heads in the Division or State Headquarters. The DC controls the police through District Superintendent of Police (DSP) to maintain law and order in the district. With the 73rd and 74th Amendments to the Constitution, which have strengthened PRIs and ULBs respectively in the states, the role of DC in performance of developmental functions has been significantly reduced.

Various statutes of the Central/State Governments give wide-ranging powers to the office of DC. These vary from maintenance and management of land records, collection of land and other government revenues, acquisition of land, maintenance of peace and order, preventive detention and other such measures, implementation of social legislations, conduct of elections, regulation of essential commodities or services etc. With the Amendment of Criminal Procedure Code in 1973, the magisterial functions of DC were reduced to preventive actions only. The power of committal of accused criminals to the Sessions Courts was transferred to the Judicial Officers. Further, she/he derives various powers under the rules, regulations, standing instructions and official orders of the Central/State Governments. It may be observed that the activities and roles of DC are vast, unrelated and many a times not well-defined by law or delegated legislation or government orders. Since she/he represents the Central/State Government at the district level she/he is expected to watch the interests of the governments and function as their eyes, ears and working arms.

In the public parlance DC is considered as *'Mai Baap'*, i.e., parents of the people in the district. For any type of the grievances or injustice, related to all kinds of offices of the Central/State Government, DC is approached by the public. It seems as if she/he has the panacea for all ailments in district level governance. This is continuing as the legacy of the British Raj even though the powers of DC have been significantly pruned down over the years after Independence. Civil Society Organizations (CSOs), Non-Governmental Organizations (NGOs), public leaders or any other agitating groups submit their memoranda addressed to the Central/State Government to the DC so that their prayers or causes of agitation could be forwarded to the concerned for expedious necessary action. All types of problems, whether related to essential services like electricity, drinking water, health, education, sanitation etc., or infrastructure like road, irrigation, agricultural inputs supply or purchase of agricultural produce etc., everything comes under the domain of DC and so different groups demonstrate and agitate for unsatisfied demands. Sometime this leads to serious law and order problem.

IV

TASKS AND RESPONSIBILITIES OF DC

The tasks and responsibilities of the present day DC varies from Sate to State. However, major functions common to many states are as under:

Public Security, Law and Order and Preventive Action

Under the Police Regulations, Collector and District Magistrate is the head of Criminal Administration of the district. With the assistance of DSP, she/he maintains law and order in the district. With the prudent application of the powers conferred under various statutes, she/he takes preventive actions to ensure public peace and tranquillity in the district. She/he has powers to bound down miscreants for good behaviour and peaceful conduct, make the preventive arrests under Criminal Procedure Code, impose restrictions on unlawful assembly or impose even curfew that restricts free movement in the declared area, get the risk to public life removed, order for externment of hardened criminals from the district boundaries with directions for regular intimation to the local police about the actual whereabouts, issue/suspend/cancel arms licenses, order for preventive arrests under National Security Act if there is threat to public security, grant parole to under-trials/convicted criminals etc. District Magistrate (DM) is the head of the Jail Administration as well in the district.

Additional District Magistrates (ADMs) and Sub-Divisional Magistrates (SDMs) assist the DM in carrying out these responsibilities. With the growing discontent among the public regarding provision of civic amenities, caste and communal tensions, student and labour union agitations, farmers' movement and political instability over the last two decades, tasks of DM to maintain law and order has become more difficult. She/he has to bank upon the Central Police Forces *e.g.* Rapid Action Force (RAF), which has expertise in controlling riot or riot like situations and Central Reserve Police Force (CRPF) apart from the State Armed Police and district police to contain serious law and order deterioration in the district.

With the present day scenario of terrorism, militancy, naxalism and separatism going on in some parts of the country, which are major threats to public peace and order, the role of DM further enhances to ensure coordination among intelligence agencies and State as well as Central Police/Armed Forces. This is necessary to ensure effective action against those who disturb the law and order and instill confidence among the public to have their normal day-to-day activities.

As head of criminal administration in the district, DM monitors the progress of prosecutions/acquittals in the district and allows filing of appeal in the criminal cases acquitted by the judicial courts. She/he also coordinates with the District Judge and District Superintendent of Police to facilitate disposal of criminal cases and serve the interest of the State by ensuring that the judicial courts penalize the guilty.

Land Record Administration

Under Land Record Manual, DC is the custodian of all land in the district. The Revenue Administration, functioning directly under him is responsible to maintain periodic records of right (*Khatauni*), records of possession (*Khasara*), records of crops production, records of mutation of rights on the land through succession or otherwise, collection of land revenue and other government dues etc. Various statutes empower DC and/or his designated officials to acquire land for the government, consolidate fragmented land holdings, declare surplus land under land ceiling legislations, allotment of land to landless/poor etc. Powers to mutate land rights, apportion land among family members, change the usage pattern of the land, settle the land rights in the areas where such settlements have not taken so far, hear and resolve all types of disputes related to the land as Revenue Courts etc. are also conferred to such authorities.

India is primarily an agrarian society, where land holds highest esteem in the public perception. Land disputes lead to fight and even murder in the rural areas. Therefore, a systematic land record keeping is of utmost importance in Indian governance system. With the advent of Information Technology, governments have assisted district administration to computerize the land records for efficient data management and quick retrieval. Farmers require the extracts of their land holdings for seeking any bank loans or various other purposes. With the active interests and hard work, some of the DCs have done pioneer work in this field with the assistance of District Informatics Centre (DIC). The model is available for rest of the districts to utilize the power of information technology to provide more client-friendly services of land records to the farmers.

District Planning

DC heads the District Planning Council (DPC). In some States, Chairman of Zilla Panchayat (District Board), who is an elected public representative, chairs the DPC. In such cases, DC is the vice-chairman of the Council. This body is responsible to prepare five-years and annual district plans for the amount allocated to the district by the State Planning Board. Inputs from all the line departments are taken and considering the allocations for committed expenditures on ongoing schemes and projects, fresh amounts are allocated for the programmes specific to the district that can utilize the strengths of the district to generate employment, assets and infrastructure. As head/deputy head of the Council, DC monitors the progress of implementation of approved schemes/projects and anticipated expenditures by the line departments at regular intervals. As a resource mobilization major, DC heads the Co-ordination Cell of the banks in the district. This body prepares annual plan for public lending under all sectors by different banks operating in the district and monitors the progress on periodic basis.

District Development and Coordination

DC, being the executive head of the district, is the Chief Co-ordinator for all kinds of government functioning at the district level. The government is organized in line departments with district level officers in most of the departments to carry out their mandate in the territory. Examples of such departments are public works department to carry out roads and buildings constructions and maintenance; irrigation department to provide irrigation facilities through canal system or deep bore tubewell system; electricity department for rural electrification and upkeep of the electrical facilities; rural engineering services to implement minor road/drainage or other engineering works in the rural areas; health department to run preventive and promotive healthcare schemes including immunization and family welfare programmes and provide medical facilities through district and subordinate hospitals and also keep a tab on quality provision of food and drugs in the district; social welfare department to assist poor, old aged, disabled and widows through social security schemes and run special schemes for education and economic upliftment of members of Scheduled Castes/Tribes and OBC (other backwards classes); Panchayati Raj department to ensure smooth functioning of PRIs i.e., grassroots level democratic institutions for local self-governance; District Rural Development Agency (DRDA) to administer Central Government sponsored/assisted rural development programmes; District Urban Development Agency (DUDA) to execute urban development/employment generation schemes in the urban areas; minor irrigation department to assist farmers to set up their own minor irrigation projects; agriculture department to promote agricultural extension and support services; cooperative department to help banking and other consumer/agricultural services through village/urban cooperatives; dairy development department for improving milk production in the district; animal husbandry department to encourage improvement of cattle breeds, piggery and poultry and provide veterinary health care services; fisheries department to facilitate fisheries cultivation; District Industry Centre (DIC) to help establishment of small and cottage industries and attend to the entrepreneurs' grievances; women and child welfare department to run schemes for supplementary nutrition and preprimary education of children and preventive/promotive healthcare facilities for pregnant and lactating women; education department for primary and secondary education in the district; district economics and statistics department to prepare and update various statistical informations regarding the district; district informatics office to facilitate district level computerization etc.

The above departments can be categorized into infrastructure, agriculture, social development, and economic development departments. Even though the district departmental officers report to their line authorities at Division/State headquarters, they report to DC for preparation of annual plans, their execution and monitoring and mid-term modifications, if necessary. Various committees have been set up by the State/Central Governments under the chairmanship of DC to facilitate effective inter-departmental coordination and close monitoring. Chief Development Officer (CDO) or Chief Executive Officer (CEO) of Zilla Panchayat assists DC in carrying out inter-departmental coordination functions.

With the growing welfare and developmental role of the state, these responsibilities of DC are likely to increase in future. New departments have been added over last two decades or existing departments have expanded their reach to the districts. In the areas with tribal population, the Central/State Governments are running special schemes for the welfare and economic upliftment of these groups. DC coordinates these programmes as well. Central Government has started granting Rs. 2.5 crore to each Members of Parliament (MPs) and State Governments Rs. 0.50 crore to the Members of Legislative Assemblies/Councils for area development programmes in the respective constituencies. DCs have been made responsible to get the schemes/projects prepared in accordance with the government guidelines in consultation with the concerned public representatives and get them executed on the ground. This casts a major control and coordination responsibility to DC.

Disaster Management

Various types of natural disasters like flood, drought, forest fire, earthquake and manmade disasters like fire, major accidents, riots etc., pose big threat to the lives and properties of the people in the districts. Some districts are more prone to specific type of disasters than the others and those will require preventive measures. DC chairs the District Disaster Management Committee (DDMC), which is responsible for making advance plan to mitigate the effect of impending disasters and provide assistances for protection, relief and rehabilitation in the face of such disasters. She/he is authorized to grant gratuitous relief to affected families to attend to immediate hardships caused by the disaster. DC also monitors distribution of social security/insurance schemes to the poor in the district.

Some of the DCs have played very important role in attending to the challenges posed by the natural disasters like cyclone of Orissa, major floods in different areas, or earthquake in Uttarkashi (erstwhile UP and present Uttaranchal) or Bhuj (Gujarat) etc. DC heads the civil defence organization in the district. This organization has enlightened and motivated citizens as members, who give their time voluntarily to attend to public grievances. Also, the district has *Nehru Yuva Kendra* (NYK) and Rural Youth Clubs (RYC), with volunteer youth (men and women) to provide support services in the wake of any public emergency. The district level officers of these organizations report to the DC.

District Civil Supplies

The DC is responsible to oversee the arrangements for provision of essential commodities to the citizens through Public Distribution System (PDS). The PDS operates through chain of fair price shops that issue rationed quantities of essential commodities like wheat, rice, sugar, kerosene etc. at subsidized rates to the economically weak section of the society. The District Supply Officer who manages these shops works directly under the DC. The distribution is assured through ration cards issued to the eligible families through the district supply office. This department has been authorized under law and government instructions to penalise the hoarders of essential commodities, ensure proper usage of weights and measures, deal severely with adulteration in diesel/petrol etc. For this purpose, DC gets raids conducted at regular/random intervals in different business premises.

District Excise Department

Income from the auction of liquor and other intoxicants' shops is a major source of income to the exchequer of the States, which are not following dry strategy. District Excise Officer directly reports to the DM and organizes annual auction under her/his chairmanship. Various liquor mafia are operating in different parts of the country and therefore, these auctions become a challenging task to ensure that the State gets maximum revenue and at the same time the auction is not grabbed by such mafia elements. A prior thorough checkup of the antecedents of auctioneers is ensured. After the confirmation of the auction, DM oversees through the departmental officers that monthly rentals are paid regularly and the quality of liquor is not deteriorated by adulteration or imitation (me-too) products.

Fair Prices to the Agricultural Products

District and sub-division level agricultural markets have been set up to ensure that the farmers are able to auction their products at reasonable price. To save the farmers from distress selling after the harvest, government announces minimum assured prices for major agricultural products and DC sets up a chain of such procurement shops under the auspices of marketing department, cooperative department etc. to purchase the farmers' products at these prices and supply the same to Food Corporation of India (FCI), which maintains very large regional warehouses to ensure supply through FPS or market, if there is any kind of scarcity of such products, to control the market prices. This onerous task is performed in the district under direct supervision and control of the DC.

Entertainment Taxation

The District Entertainment Tax Officer reports to the DC. She/he is responsible to ensure that there is no pilferage of entertainment tax in the district. The DC grants permission to hold public entertainment events after ascertaining the sensitivities of local population and levying relevant tax. She/he supervises cinema halls and disc TV from the point of view of compliance of government instructions and guidelines and timely deposition of due taxes.

Supervision of the District Treasury

The DC is incharge of district treasury. Chief Treasury Officer and other Treasury Officers work under her/his supervision and guidance. This calls for not only guarding the public money and government property but also ensuring strict compliance of government instructions on financial prudence. Any slip may cause major trouble in terms of monetary embezzlement or misappropriation, which is viewed very seriously by the government. Now-a-days most treasuries have been computerized and that makes accounting much simpler. The treasuries store not only the cash and revenue stamps but are also engaged in disbursing pensions to retired government servants, salaries and other benefits to government employees, finances for government schemes/projects/programmes etc. The level of transactions is colossal for each district and daily statements on receipt and disbursal under various heads/sub-heads of the budget with full details are sent to the government.

Registration of Transactions and Stamp Duty Collection

State laws require payment of stamp duty as certain fixed percentage of the amount or some fixed amount for registering different types of transaction e.g. sale deed, transfer deed, gift deed etc. For the purchase and sale of properties DC is authorized to notify circle/area rates so that transactions do not take place at lower rate to avoid government tax. Registrar/Sub-Registrars who report to DC manage all business related to payment of or regulation of stamp tax. Additional District Collector (Finance and Revenue) assists DC to ensure strict compliance of government instructions on the subject. The DC/Additional DC hears the appeals to the orders of Registrar. Also, stamps are sold through District Treasury, which is controlled by the DC.

Conduct of Elections

Holding of regular free and fair elections is *sine qua non* of representative form of democracy like India. Election Commission of India has been entrusted with the task of holding elections for Central/State legislatures whereas the responsibility to hold elections for PRIs and ULBs devolves on State Election Commissions. The DC is designated as District Election Officer (DEO) and he is responsible for preparation/updation of electoral roles and holding of free and fair elections in her/his district. She/he assumes the responsibility of Returning Officer (RO) for Parliamentary Elections, whereas in all other cases concerned ROs function under her/his superintendence and control. She/he mobilizes the resources within the district and sometimes from outside as well to meet this challenging responsibility. Every election is a major event for the district, especially with diverse interests controlled by caste/religion or other considerations leading to violent clashes, at times. She/he also conducts election to various cooperative institutions in the district.

Protocol Functions

This has assumed a very important role with the proliferation of political executives. The DC oversees all protocol functions in the district as per standing instructions/guidelines issued by the Government. This responsibility includes receiving and seeing off apart from organizing stay, conveyance and security to the dignitary. In some of the frequently visited districts because of religious/oblique tourist business importance, a senior Addl DC is posted for this purpose only, whereas in all other districts DC deputes one of the Deputy Collectors to perform the requisite tasks and responsibilities. In case of certain dignitaries like President/ Vice-President/Prime Minister of India and Governor/Chief Minister of the State, she/he has to be personally present and supervise the duty. Protocol duty is a very sensitive matter and any lapse on part of the district administration is blown out of proportion to embarrass the DC and sometime get her/him transferred.

Public Relations and Publicity

The State Government posts District Information Officer (DIO), reporting directly to DC, to promote and popularize government's schemes, programmes and priorities. She/he does this through distribution of published material received from state headquarters or printed in the district, organization of puppet/road shows, cultural evens, cinema or video film/documentary shows etc. in rural/urban areas. She/he also liaises with local newspapers and representatives of national news agencies/electronic media to project a positive image of the government. Any campaign of the government *e.g.* awareness regarding health and sanitation or ill effects of drug abuse etc. is organized by this officer. These efforts consume significant time of the DC.

Residual Functions

Apart from the above, any function of the government in the district, which is not allocated to any line department automatically, comes within the jurisdiction of the DC. Being the chief executive of the district, his status is like a mini government—all in one—at the district level. This casts a very big responsibility on her/him and requires quick decision-making and high coordination skill. Her/his limitation is that she/he has no authority to mobilize resources and yet she/he is expected to perform the duties with available budget and with all the constraints imposed under government order/instructions. She/he has to keep in line with the government priorities and be sensitive to the local needs as well. For example, if the district has high potential for tourism promotion, she/he can seek instructions of the government to initiate specific programmes and cannot start things on her/his own. That too, if the government of the day has different priorities, she/he will have to keep her/his tourism promotion programme on the back seat and concentrate on government's directions.

Some of the Examples of Residual Functions

These are campaign for encouraging small savings by public; distribution of scholarships to the students belonging to SC/ST/OBC/handicapped categories; overseeing district armoury, which includes ceased arms/ammunitions and reserved arms; organization of tourism/sports events; forced removal of encroachments on the public way; overseeing collection of trade tax; security arrangements for religious processions/congregations/fairs/festivals/big cultural events; conduct of decadal census etc.

E-Governance in the District

With the advent of Information and Communication Technology (ICT), e-governance has become an important agenda in all Indian districts. Central Government has opened offices of National

Informatics Centres (NIC) with experts on ICT in every district. Varying degree of work has been done in application of technology in management of land records, criminal records, arms records, development projects and schemes etc. Some states have attempted developing prototypes but actual applications on ground are based on the interest taken by individual officers. Specially state of Andhra Pradesh has done pioneering work in providing public services through IT kiosks.

V

CHALLENGES BEING FACED BY THE DC

From the above description it may be observed that the DC is burdened with immense responsibilities and even though she/he has district level officers reporting to her/him for performance of line tasks, mere coordination, supervision and control may eat out all her/his time of 365 days of the year not leaving anything for the family or self-contemplation. Somebody has aptly commented with concept drawn from Greek mythology that the Collector is the tortoise on whose back stands the elephant of the government. The elephant has grown considerably both in volume and dead weight, with more sporadic and temperamental behaviour, perhaps more demanding in devotion and less forgiving of error, and consequently a more formidable burden to carry. It is logical that in such a situation, the tortoise should have expected added nutrition, indulgent care and touch of cheer, to prove equal to his increased load. The irony is that she/he is desired to grow lean, to shed her/his drown posture (which is no small asset in holding the weight) and to bear injury philosophically, on one hand; to show better strength, display keener attachment and develop thicker skin, on the other.[7] She/he is expected to be very careful and vigilant in performance as even the smallest failure is a dereliction for which she/he is accountable and may have to face reprobation and sometimes injury to the career. Any achievement on the part of DC is merely seen as discharge of the duty for which she/he is being paid by the Government. There is no other way of appreciation or acknowledgement.

If DC is sincere towards her/his duties, she/he will require more than 24 hours in a day. A typical day of the DC is filled with meeting with public to listen to their variety of grievances and direct the concerned authorities to do the needful, attending to the court work related to revenue and criminal (preventive) matters, chairing standing departmental coordination committee meetings to plan, monitor or review progress of different schemes/ projects/programmes, carrying out scheduled inspections, attending public functions (maintaining good public relations is very essential to cultivate intelligence sources and have people to bank on during any kind of riots or flare ups!), issuing local instructions on government orders/other correspondences/VIP (very important person) references, dictations on court and other files after going through the records, attending to protocol matters etc. At the time of any crisis like riots, accidents, disasters, special campaigns of the government, DC becomes further busy or has to prioritise his functions by postponing certain tasks for the future. Despite tough routine, the pleasure of serving the public especially the downtrodden that do not have voice of their own is so high that DCs enjoy this public service and attend to their work with utmost sincerity. This is why office of DC has emerged not as a mere government post but an institution in the Indian scenario.

The position of DC is not uniform all over the country. This institution commands more respect, status and prestige in feudal and backward states like UP, Bihar, Tamil Nadu etc. In comparatively developed States like Gujarat, Kerala or Punjab, DC does not have the same status. Because of high level of awareness, prosperity, urbanization and changed professional composition with more dependence on industry, business and service sector, common men are least dependent on the government institutions. Enterprise and entrepreneurship is growing among the people of these states and that keeps them away from the dependency syndrome. Moreover, even in the predominantly feudal, rural and agrarian states, there has been substantial deterioration in the institution of DC over the years. The causes for such decline have been discussed as under:

Prevalence of Corruption

There has been substantial fall in moral/ethical values of the government servants. It is said that bureaucracy can only mirror the morality of the society at large.[8] Not many years back austerity, penance and simple living and high thinking were revered in the

Indian society. With the growing commercialization, such values have given way to respect for individuals on the basis of what she/he possesses and not her/his virtues. Earlier people were despised or seen with suspicion if they made quick progress in material possession but such values have taken back seat now.[9] DCs are no exceptions. Once upon a time ICS officers were known for highest standards of honesty, integrity and commitment to work. These virtues remained with IAS till 1960s but slowly so-called pragmatism replaced the intrinsic worth of the service. Now, officers with age-old traditional values are rarity and corruption has become institutionalized and 'accepted' thing.

Undoubtedly, a DC who is corrupt will not have moral force to face the criminals or bad elements of the society. For obvious reasons, she/he will not side her/his justice towards the poor. Shri M.K. Gandhi, who is known as the father of the nation, coined the word *'Daridranarain'* for the poor, which means seeing the image of God in the poor. She/he is urged to keep the interest of *'Daridranarain'* at the top of his priorities and concerns in the public service. The government policies are skewed towards the benefit of the last man in the row, which is called 'Antyodaya' in the words of Acharya Binoba Bhave, a reverent freedom fighter and leader of 'Bhudan Yajna' *i.e.* donation of land movement. But growing corruption has engulfed these virtues from the premier service of the country. Making fast buck rather than commitment to public service has given birth to dangerous trend where the public good is compromised to private good. This is a bad omen for the office of DC, who is the principal representative of the State at district level. Others may emulate her/his conduct and behaviour and that may put the district administration in the evil trap of corruption.

Short Tenure

It is being observed that over the last decade, tenure of DC in the district has reduced significantly. The instability in political executives has been reflected on this important institution very adversely. The situation has become so bad that some of the DCs have had less than three months' tenure and definitely the average tenure is less than a year. Considering the variety of tasks and responsibilities of DC, it is an injustice to the local population to appoint their chief executive for such short tenures. It takes few months before one is able to understand the peculiar features and characteristics of the district and gets familiar with the policies/ priorities/programmes and men on ground. By the time she/he is on the grip of the situation and is prepared to make positive contribution, she/he is transferred to a new district or secretarial/ parastatal assignment. The district is, therefore, deprived of getting benefits from her/his skills. Moreover, frequent transfers demoralize officers whereby motivation and commitment level drops down unfortunately. After all, the officer has to sustain a family and everyone including husband/wife or children are adversely affected by unscheduled transfers.

Political/Administrative Interference

Present-day DC faces many challenges in discharging his/her duties through independent decisions based on equity, fairness and rule of law. Their decisions are often influenced by the agenda of their political and administrative bosses who in turn may be under pressure from others. In this age of coalition government the demands and preferences of a range of political leaders have to be adjusted by the chief political executive so as to be able to continue in power. Not surprisingly, this often comes at the cost of sacrificing the greater public good. Bureaucrats are pulled in opposite directions and often make compromises in order to be able to survive in the system.

Role of the Local Political Leaders

Large-scale unemployment and the increasing glamour of politics have led to a spurt in the number of local leaders or politicians. With no particular ideological base but with a strong control over local communities, these small time politicians are co-opted by various political parties to mobilize local support during and after elections. Coalition governments have contributed in making the local leaders rather powerful and important players in the governance process. By virtue of their access to senior party leaders they are able to exercise much control over local decision-making processes, including the work of the DC. Untimely transfer of government officials is used as a threat to ensure compliance. It is a common practice that rumour of her/his transfer out of the district floats everyday and she/he has to be on her/his guards to face any eventuality if she/he performs the duties sincerely without any fear or favour.

Sycophancy

The reasons stated above have given birth to sycophancy in DCs. They are turning out to be 'yes women/men' to survive in the system. This is another dangerous trend as this takes one away from the reality—good or bad. If the chief executive does not muster courage to state the truth and take appropriate and effective action, what can be expected of subordinate district level officers who desire protection and patronage from the DC for their fearless action in the public interest and under their provisions of the government instructions? Sycophancy could be cancerous to the state as well. The criminals and evil perpetrators will not be brought to the book and may harbinger irrevocable damage to the society because of this tendency in senior administrators like DC.

Anonymous Complaints

Even though government has issued instructions to ignore routine anonymous complaints, the concerned officer is asked to explain charges of very serious nature. Something, which may appear extremely grave on papers, may be totally false and unsubstantiated. If there was any truth in the complaint, the concerned person should put up his name, address and signature on the paper so that evidence could be adduced with her/his assistance. Seeking explanation on such presumably false complaints, whose status is like hearsay, is demoralizing and demotivating to a well-meaning and sincere officer.

Departmentalism

Assumption of role of development administration by the government has given birth to large number of the line departments. The departmental heads who are sitting in the state headquarters or regional heads in the divisional headquarters do no want to part away with their authority *vis-à-vis* district level officers or field cutting edge level functionaries. This makes the job of DC very difficult and complicated. There is a growing tendency on part of state/divisional officers to tour the districts without informing DC and issue oral instructions on the spot without having complete data/knowledge on the subject. Sometimes, this complicates matter, as the compliance of such orders could be embarrassing to the government as well as the public. Also, district level officers have started bypassing the DCs institution and apprising the matters to their higher departmental bosses until they find themselves in some soup. Departmentalism leads to poor coordination at the district level and sometimes the outcome is so much alarming that unscrupulous elements are able to muster benefits from multiple sources at the cost of genuine and needy persons. This is why, DC's role in bringing in synergy in the system is extremely important specially for a resource starved country like India.

Low Plan Funds

The annual planning exercise has become more of a ritual than a meaningful objective exercise. The allocated funds are barely sufficient to cater to the requirements of ongoing schemes/projects and major portion is eaten away by the commitment on salary and other benefits to government employees. This does not leave enough resources to plan for district specific schemes/projects. Earlier system of united funds, which allowed discretion, has also been done away with. A motivated DC finds herself/himself at a loss in absence of financial support. Therefore, there is a need to look into district level resource mobilization strategy, may be with public participation.

Emphasis on Evidentiary Materials

Government departments have multiplied their work many times by prescribing long proformas for collection of periodic/random collection of data. Most of these are not based on prudent management principles, and are not even compiled, collated and analysed as decision-making tools at headquarter level. Lot of garbage is collected at the cost of time of officers that could have been spent in the field. Earlier DCs were known for their extensive tours, which helped them in understanding the pulse of the public to avert any impending danger. Now-a-days, with so much of evidentiary workload, she/he does not find time to carry out such extensive tours. This makes her/him more of paper-based officer and distances her/him from the common public or field realities.

Role of Mass Media

Mass media plays a very important role in making public opinion on any issue. They could be very effective in routing out corruption or other malaise from the system but at the same time they could be dangerous through yellow journalism. The strength of the press could be exploited in intimidating, blackmailing or extracting the administrative machinery. Even though there is Press Council of India (PCI) which could be approached to derecognize journalists engaged in such evil, hardly anyone approaches PCI with such complaints. Unfortunately, the local press takes sides and has vested interest in promoting/damaging personalities. This is a serious constraint and challenge to any DC to manage mass media effectively without falling into their trap.

VI

CONCLUDING OBSERVATIONS

To conclude, DC enjoys immense power to do justice to the poor and needy, ensure an environment of peace and order to provide opportunity to public for social and economic development, help create necessary infrastructure and promote all-round growth in the district. This is a very honourable position in the government, which requires strong sense of commitment, accountability, ethical and moral standards, honesty and integrity, hard work and fair judgement.[10] Certain aberrations have come to this institution and they need to be taken care of by the political executives to make the tortoise stronger and more responsive under the present-day job pressures. Even though PRIs have been invigorated taking away some of the developmental responsibilities of DC, the institution is still extremely important from the point of view of revenue, development and welfare administration and maintainer of law and order in the district and has the distinction of being the principal representative of the government at district level. In fact, in all times of crisis, it is the DC who is maximally depended on by all government bodies.

In words of Macaulay, "such a power as that which Collectors of India have over the people in India is not found in any other part of the world possessed by any class of functionaries".[11] Now, the powers have further grown under the welfare and development regime in post-independence era making the office of District Collector unparallel in any part of the world and enviable. Rather than making it weak and therefore ineffective, holders of the position should be exposed to modern day management techniques and learn to make best use of latest developments in information and communication technology to become more effective in delivering the constitutional mandate to the public and lead to good governance in the district. The team of district level officials, whom she/he leads should also be given such expositions and instill the significance of public service with high level of ethical/moral standards to live upto the expectations.[12]

REFERENCES

1. S.R. Maheshwari, *Public Administration in India,* New Delhi, McMillan India, 2000.
2. O.P. Dwivedi, R.B. Jain and B.D. Dua, "Imperial Legacy, Bureaucracy and Administrative Changes", *Public Administration and Development,* Vol. 9, No. 3, 1989, pp. 253-269.
3. David C. Potter, *India's Political Administrators: From ICS to IAS,* Delhi, Oxford University Press, 1986.
4. S.R. Maheshwari, *Op. Cit.*
5. Palmier, Leslie, "Corruption and Probity", *Asian Journal of Political Science,* Vol. 8, No. 1, 2000, pp. 1-12.
6. T.N. Dhar, "Indian Administrative Service in Uttar Pradesh", *Indian Journal of Public Administration,* Vol. 48, No. 3, July-Sept, 1997, pp. 638-61.
7. Chaturvedi, M.K, "The Elephant and the Tortoise", *Indian Political System: Trends and Challenges,* Grover (ed.), Verinder, New Delhi, Deep and Deep Publications, 1997, pp. 282-83.
8. Gerald E. Caiden, Dwivedi O.P. and Joseph G. Jabbra, (eds), *Where Competition Lives,* Bloomfield, Connecticut, USA, Kumarian Press, 2001.
9. R.B. Jain, (ed.), *Corruption-free Sustainable Development,* New Delhi, Mittal Publications, 2004.

10. R.K. Trivedi, "Whither Indian Administrative Service?", *Governing India*, O.P. Dwivedi, R.B. Jain and Dhirendra Bajpeyi, (eds.), Delhi: BR Publishing, 1997, pp. 97-118.
11. M.K. Chaturvedi. *Op. cit.*
12. O.P. Dwivedi, "On Common Good and Good Governance: An Alternative Approach", *Better Governance and Public Policy*, Dele Olowu and S. Sako, Bloomfield, CT.(eds.), USA: Kumarian Press, pp. 35-52.

6

Whither District Government?*

ABHIJIT DATTA

In a thought-provoking paper, Nirmal Mukarji has pleaded for devolution of political powers to directly elect district governments in the country.[1] In an earlier paper, Mukarji sketched out the structure of his proposed district government in India's federal polity.[2]

THE MUKARJI PROPOSAL

The Mukarji proposal on district government may be stated in terms of the following attributes:[3]

1. District government should form a third-tier of India's federal polity, with proper constitutional backing.
2. Its powers should be constitutionally specified and, in the domain so marked out, it should have functional autonomy.
3. Its representative character should be ensured by a system of direct elections, to be held at regular intervals, under the overall supervision of the Election Commission.
4. Supersession should be constitutionally barred.

---

* An earlier version of the paper was presented at a UGC National Seminar on: "Changing Perspectives on District Administration", at Tirupati, March 28-30, 1989. The author would like to express his gratitude to Shri Nirmal Mukarji for helpful comments on the earlier paper, while assuming full responsibility for the views expressed here.

5. Finances to match functions should be assured, through state finance commissions or other means.
6. District government should replace the Collector pattern, the district bureaucracy coming squarely under its control.

Alternative Forms of District'government

Mukarji suggests that replacement of the District Collector and the Zilla Parishad by an elected district government is necessary from three angles: (*i*) democratic, (*ii*) federal, and (*iii*) local control.[4] However, it is possible to show that an 'independent'[5] system of local government could also substantially meet requirements of the Mukarji proposal. Table 6.1 brings out the basic structural characteristics of three alternative models of district government—coordinate, independent and autonomous.

Table 6.1: Three Models of District Government

Sl. No.	*Structural Aspects*	*Coordinate*	*Independent*	*Autonomous*
(1)	*(2)*	*(3)*	*(4)*	*(5)*
1.	Constitutional placement	7th Schedule (separate list)	7th Schedule (List III)	6lh Schedule (generalised)
2.	Nature of powers	Plenary	Delegated	Devolved
3.	Election	Direct	Indirect	Direct
4.	Supersession	Barred	Subject to judicial review	State discretion
5.	Finance and functions	Finance to be earmarked in the national tax-pool and awarded by the state finance commission; functions to be reallocated from Lists I & II in the 7th Schedule	Taxes and functions to be delegated from Lists I-III in the 7th Schedule	Taxes and functions as provided in List II in the 7th Schedule
6.	Personnel system	Separate	Various (except all-India)	Various (including all-India)
7.	Executive functionary	Political	Political	Bureaucratic

CONSTITUTIONAL STATUS

All the three models of district government indicated in Table 6.1 would require constitutional changes to bring them about—substantial in the case of a coordinate, somewhat for the independent, and least for the autonomous districts.

Among the three models, only the independent district government is organically linked with a system of sub-district local government. While there may not be a need for additional units of local government along with the autonomous district, creation of local government in a system of coordinate district would presumably be the responsibility of the State Government and these two sub-state government—district and local—would operate in parallel to each other.

A coordinate district government would exercise the plenary powers of the State while the other two forms would subsist under the delegated or devolved powers of the Union and the States. Therefore, the success of the coordinate district government would depend on the fine-tuning of the 7th Schedule items in the Constitution in a manner that all the three levels of government may be distinct and separate from each other.

Election and Supersession

Both the coordinate and the autonomous district governments would be directly elected/while the independent district government would be a federation of unitary local governments and concerned only with trans-local functions—mandal panchayats in the large rural districts; and the mandals, towns and cities in the metropolitan districts. Smaller independent rural districts would have a unitary structure. The independent district government is, therefore, more flexible in terms of local and area-wide functional responsibilities with variations in terms of methods of electoral representation.

As for supersession Mukarji would like to ban supersession of the coordinate district government. This is unrealistic as long as the State Governments are allowed to be superseded for "breakdown of constitutional machinery". What Mukarji perhaps has in mind is to debar unprincipled and prolonged supersession by the State Government. These could be effectively controlled if supersession is permissible under extraordinary circumstances or when these are subjected to judicial review of the substantive reasons therefor. This is envisaged under the independent district government model, where the courts could go beyond the procedural and motivational angles of supersession to judge the reasonableness of the supersession itself.

Mukarji suggests the Election Commission to supervise district elections; the same plea could be made to enable the Comptroller and Auditor-General to oversee the functioning of the co-ordinate districts. Similar provisions could be made for the independent districts as well.

Finance and Functions

Mukarji's plan for financing coordinate district government hinges on a "new financial regime" where all the public revenues are pooled together for subsequent distribution among the various levels of government in accordance with constitutionally fixed percentages.[7] Similarly his plan for delineating the functional jurisdiction of the coordinate district government is contingent on a *de novo* functional redistribution among the three levels of government.[8] An alternative and less drastic method would be to use the existing Union and State powers through the use of the Concurrent List of the 7th Schedule in the Constitution, as has been proposed for the independent district government. The autonomous district governments are limited to the ambit of the State List of the 7th Schedule.

A related issue is the role of the Central and State Finance Commissions to bridge the fiscal gap of the district governments. Under the Mukarji proposal, one would expect a crucial role for the Central Finance Commission; strangely enough, he talks only of the state finance commission to underwrite the possible deficits of the concurrent district government.[9] It needs to be emphasised that a finance commission assumes an initial tax-function mix, and that it cannot recommend functional readjustment to suit financial allocations to the recipient governments.

It is possible to devise methods of central and state revenue sharing plans through statutory means and their allocation to the district government through a constitutional machinery, like the central and state finance commissions, even where specified taxes and functions are assigned to the district governments.

Personnel and the Executive

While it is easy to agree with the Mukarji proposal that the district bureaucracy should function under the district council and its political executive, one has to be aware of the problems of placing an all-India cadre officer as the chief secretary of a concurrent district government. On the other hand, it is possible to devise a combination of personnel systems for the independent and autonomous models of district government, depending on the degrees of state control exercised on them.

Induction of a political executive and bureaucratic accountability to it is inherent in a concurrent district; this may be desirable elsewhere as well, particularly for the independent model. A unified personnel system for the independent area-wide (district) and local governments could be created and controlled through voluntary arrangements, but creation of integrated state cadres to serve them would be somewhat difficult. This is easiest for the autonomous district governments, but is fraught with role conflicts when the elected members would demand executive powers.

The issue of political executive is, therefore, central to the choice of personnel systems in the district government and where this is conceded, as under the independent or autonomous models, the exact mix of personnel system, therein would vary depending on the extent of state power delegated or devolved to them. In any case, it would not be possible for the existing district collector belonging to an all-India cadre to be posted under a concurrent district government whether or not he acts as the district chief secretary, as per the Mukarji proposal.

DISTRICTS AS UNITS OF REGIONAL GOVERNMENT

The District Fixation

The existing districts as units of the state's field administration are regarded as the starting point of sub-state decentralisation of governments in India. However, the following two points are overlooked in the process: (a) this is a top-down approach from the point of view of delivery of public services under the State Government, and (b) a locally-based public services approach cannot be easily accommodated in the normal districts, barring a population size of more than a million. Even the smaller districts with a population of more than 20,000 may not be locally-based. Therefore, it is necessary to be clear whether the districts are to be viewed as units of area-wide, or locally-based governments. The Mukarji proposal, while allowing for size variation of the existing districts, does not recognise its basic trans-local orientation.[10]

The Balwantray Mehta report resolved the dilemma by combining the district administration and the Zilla Parishad (with indirect election from the Anchal Parishads) in which the regulatory powers vested in the Collector, and the development responsibilities were assigned to the Panchayati Raj (topped by the Zilla Parishad). Mukarji is rightly dissatisfied with this hybrid arrangement of district governance; at the same time, by retaining the unitary structure of district government Mukarji perpetuates the existing service delivery and regional orientations of the district set-up. The Asoka Mehta report also adopted the same district-centred view of the Panchayati Raj.[11]

An alternative method of harmonising district and local governments would be to: (*a*) retain the present size of the normal districts and view them as units of area-wide local governments under a federative arrangement, and (*b*) reduce the present size of the smaller districts with a population of less than 20,000 to create unitary authorities for their governance. These two conditions can be met only under the independent model of local and area-wide governments.

Nature of Regional Governments

Doubts have been expressed about the justification of regional governments as being "redundant and dangerous" in the English context in the following vein:[12]

Regional government is a threat to good government both nationally and locally. Its menace arises from the functions it is intended to perform:

(*i*) Functions that should be carried out nationally;
(*ii*) Supervising, controlling and resource allocation functions over local authorities, which will limit local government;

(*iii*) Functions that are at present carried out by local government; and

(*iv*) Functions that could be carried out by local government, *e.g.*, health, training, further and higher education, and economic development.

Regional government, thus, weakens strong central government and lessens the actuality and the potential of local government.

In order to be successful, regional governments should: (*i*) undertake only trans-local functions, (*ii*) depend on precepting of local taxes, (*iii*) represent local interests through indirect local electoral constituencies, and (*iv*) act as agents of the constituent local authorities. While the first-two conditions were met in England, the last two were not; this may have created the jurisdictional confusion between the English regional and local governments, leading to their eventual abolition. On the other hand, the Canadian regional governments may have succeeded primarily due to their federative organisational set-up.

The fears expressed about the English regional governments have added force in India with an 'attached' system of rural local government, a dependent array of municipal governments, and the special authority-dominance in the metropolitan areas. A total restructuring of local government is, therefore, a condition precedent to the success of regional district governments.

LINKING DISTRICTS WITH LOCAL GOVERNMENTS

Unitary Authorities

The primary units of local government will have to be unitary: in the rural areas a viable population size could be around 20,000, while in the urban areas this could start at 50,000 for the towns and 5,00,000 for the cities. It is necessary to have a uniform pattern of political executive, *e.g.*, the cabinet system, like the mayor-in-council in the Calcutta municipal corporation, consisting of varying number of executive councillors (say, 3 to 9) depending on the size of the council. The tax-function mix could be the same, but their actual utilisation may be subjected to state approval. This would mean unification of local governments for both the rural and urban areas for a 'detached' system of local government in the country. This itself would revolutionise the present Panchayati Raj pattern of rural local government.

Decentralised Units

Under the unitary structure, there could be provision for functional decentralisation to the smaller units of settlements: for the rural areas, with a village population of around 5000; and for the cities, with a neighbourhood population of around 50,000. There may not be a pressing need for a decentralised set-up in the towns, except for specific tasks or for a limited period. In other words, the existing electoral linkage between the village and mandal/ anchal councils could be done away with due to the envisaged unitary structure of local government. The reasons for doing it are two: (*a*) the electoral system would not be prone to manipulations by the power-brokers of the State Government (both political and executive), and (*b*) direct election is relevant at a level where there is a matching of taxes and functions. The Gandhian notion of village government could be sustained in terms of its mobilisation potential, but without its operational shortcomings.

Metropolitan Areas

The metropolitan areas (with a population exceeding 10 million) would need trans-local functions to be discharged very much in the same manner as for a district government. Therefore, it is possible to create metropolitan district governments and linking them to their constituent rural and urban unitary authorities. Where a metropolitan government is concerned with a limited range of functions, alternative organisational arrangements, such as, inter-local contracts or special authorities, could also be explored. Essentially, creation of metropolitan governments needs to be viewed in terms of enhancing the capabilities of the constituent local governments, rather than substituting their allotted roles. In other words, the metropolitan governments are supposed to be discharging area-wide local government functions, rather than act as decentralised units of the State Government having all the trappings of state control.

In any metropolitan area, there would be a core city area (with a population of up to five million) which needs to be specially catered to both for representation purposes, as also for the sake of retention of its civic identity. Outside the core city, the rest of the metropolitan area would consist of a medley of local authorities, *viz.*, smaller cities, towns and rural mandals. The peri-urban areas would be included either in the mandals or in the smaller townships. All the peripheral local authorities need to be represented in the metropolitan authority, both in terms of their population and for the type of authorities involved.

If the metropolitan authority is seen essentially as agents of the local governments within the metropolitan area, then metropolitan functions and finances are to be settled in that light: specific functional delegation and precepting of local taxation would be the mainstay of its working arrangement. Allocation of Plan funds to the metropolitan authority has to follow the same logic. Also, it has to be ensured that the metropolitan authorities do not emerge as a multi-purpose variant of the states' special authorities or a corporate form of district administration in metropolitan area.

An Assessment

It is clear that a 'concurrent' district government is inimical to the strengthening of local government where voter-proximity and administrative viability coincide to the maximum. It only attempts to relate the activities of the State Government to an artificial area which is too small for exercising plenary powers and too large to discharge local responsibilities. The 'autonomous' districts, on the other hand, represent only a single variant of local government for too large an area. Only the 'independent' form of local and area-wide governments can effectively harmonise the differential needs of the local governance, while accommodating its area-wide needs as well.

A variant of the metropolitan area could be a special area with unique tribal, cultural, linguistic or geographical characteristics: small enough for conferring separate state-hood, but large enough for trans-local responsibilities. It is possible to adopt this variant of area-wide local government to meet the needs of the special areas, as was sought to be met through the device of autonomous districts under the 6th Schedule of the Constitution.

RESTRUCTURING THE STATE MACHINERY

Future of the Collector

The fundamental issue concerning district government revolves round the future of the Collector (or District Officer). Mukarji is quite right in saying that since the colonial times, there is no alternative thinking of district administration except through the Collector. Even the two Mehtas were somewhat ambivalent on this issue, while the Dantwala and Hanumantha Rao reports were politically retrograde in their views on district planning.[14] Therefore, the issue is: whether the states' (and central) leadership would give up their primary instrument of control of rural affairs by conceding to district government?

Changes in Field Administration

Assuming a predisposition towards democratic decentralisation through the creation of district government and corresponding strengthening of local governments, the future point of co-ordination of the states' field administration could be shifted above the district, *i.e.*, at the divisional-level in the larger districts/states. For the smaller districts/states and also for the metropolitan districts, the concept of field administration becomes redundant.

Apart from the residuary (coordination?) responsibilities of the Collector, two other functions need to be relocated: (*i*) law and order, and (*ii*) management of land records. It is possible to bifurcate the law and order responsibilities between the state and district (including local) levels, so that state police could function under a divisional police commissioner, as in the case of metropolitan police. Management of land records could be either transferred to the state registrar of land records or devolved to the district (and local) governments.

There is a case for making political appointees to act as the state government agents (Chief Commissioner?) in the divisions of the larger states. The danger of future political conflicts at the district (and local) level being accentuated through the process needs to be balanced against the advantages for assigning the essentially political role of coordination to a political appointee.

Obviously, this will have its own implications for sustaining the generalist civil service (*i.e.*, the IAS) in the country.

Control of Special Authorities

The future of the states' special authorities would also be affected in the process of reorganisation of the state administration in the wake of creating multi-purpose elected authorities in the districts and below. Many of the special authorities are discharging essentially local functions, with a poor track record of cost recovery of services. Handing them over to the district and local governments would ensure inter-functional coordination and cost recovery compulsions. Where expedient, some of the ad hoc authorities could be privatised—either wholly or partially—so that potentially marketable services are not handled at tax-payers' expense. Some of the local services may also be reviewed for similar treatment. In any case, creation of general purpose elected authorities would encourage political accountability and coordination of locally-based public services, which are missing under the existing trend of proliferation of private estates of entrenched functional departments of the state government in the form of special authorities. The net result of creation of elected district governments, of any variety, would be abolition of a large body of the states' special authorities and their ad hoc agencies.

CONCLUSION

We have seen that the Mukarji proposal, as formulated, leaves a number of questions unanswered about the design of district government. Also, the implications of such a proposal are far-reaching from the angles of future pattern of local government and the machinery of state administration. Many of these questions are basically political in nature and, without a broad political consensus at the national-level about the desirability of district government, it is not possible to hazard any guess about its feasibility.

One thing, however, is clear: any future discussion on the reform of rural local government cannot ignore the Mukarji proposal. For the first time in free India, such a bold proposal of democratic decentralisation has been made which promises to completely break-away from the inherited colonial tradition of governance and administration in India.

Along with the choice of form of district government, it is also necessary to think of an appropriate structure of unified local government in the country. An effort in this direction could be initiated by a national commission on decentralisation to update the thinking of the erstwhile Royal Commission upon Decentralisation (1907-09) initiated in the early years of the colonial raj. The Mukarji proposal is the first tentative attempt in this direction for creating a national debate on democratic decentralisation in free India relevant for the 21st century.

REFERENCES

1. Nirmal Mukarji, "Decentralisation Below the State Level: Need for a New System of Governance", *Economic and Political Weekly,* March 4, 1989, pp. 467-72.
2. Ninnal Mukarji, "The Alternative: District Government?", in M.L. Dantwala, Ranjit Gupta and Keith C. D'Souza, (eds.), *Asian Seminar on Rural Development: The Indian Experience,* New Delhi, Oxford and IBH, 1986, pp. 235-61.
3. *Ibid.,* p. 257.
4. *Ibid.,* pp. 255-57.
5. An 'independent' system of local government was suggested by the author by transferring the relevant entry from the State List to the Concurrent List. *C.f.,* Abhijit Datta "Constitutional Status of Local Government in India", *Indian Journal of Public Administration,* Vol. 33, No. 2, April-June 1987, pp. 309-17.
6. An 'autonomous' system of district government exists for the tribal areas of the North-East under the sixth Schedule of the Constitution.
7. Nirmal Mukarji, "Decentralisation Below the State Level: Need for a New System of Governance", *Op. Cit,* p. 471.
8. Nirmal Mukarji, "The Alternative: District Government?", *Op. Cit,* p. 258.
9. *Ibid.,* p. 257.
10. Nirmal Mukarji, "Decentralisation Below the State Level: Need for a New System of Governance", *Op. cit.,* (Tables 2 and 3), pp. 469-70.
11. *Ibid.*
12. G.W. Jones, "Against Regional Government", *Local Government Studies,* September-October, 1988, pp. 10-11.
13. Nirmal Mukarji, "The Alternative: District Government?", *Op. cit.,* p. 253.
14. *Ibid.*

7

The Changing Role of the District Officer* (1860-1960)

HARIDWAR RAI

INTRODUCTION

The head of an Indian district is variously described as the District Magistrate, the Collector or the Deputy Commissioner. He is also referred to, rather loosely from the point of view of law but accurately from the point of view of the responsibilities that he discharges, as the District Officer. In fact, the official designations applied to this officer–Collector, Deputy Commissioner, or District Magistrate–convey but a very imperfect conception of his duties and responsibilities.

When any duty devolves on him by statute, he is referred to as Collector or District Magistrate, but many of these duties have nothing to do with the magisterial or revenue administration. The collection of revenue and the maintenance of law and order were the chief duties of the Magistrate-Collector. They still continue to be his important concern. They form, however, only a fraction of the sum-total of his work. With Independence and the commencement of the Five Year Plans, his responsibilities as a Development Officer have taken precedence over his traditional functions. In the present article an attempt has been made to describe and discuss some important issues that have come up during the last one hundred years of the history of the office.

---

* This is an abridged version of the essay which won the second prize in the IIPA Essay Competition, 1962.

I

THE EVOLUTION OF THE OFFICE

The seventy years preceding the Mutiny were 'strongly formative' in experiments in district administration. They witnessed a struggle for recognition and acceptance between the two schools of district administration–the Cornwallis school and the Munro school. The Cornwallis school of district administration was based on a principle of 'checks and balances' and division of powers. It was opposed to concentration of too much authority in the hands of the Collector, and believed in anglicizing the indigenous administrative system. The Munro school, on the contrary was impressed by the Mughal tradition of concentration of powers in the hands of one man making him the real ruler of the area in his charge.[1]

In 1786, all the elements that were to constitute "the administrative mosaic of British India"[2] were present, though a coherent administrative pattern had yet to emerge. However, by an important decision made that year, the Court of Directors of the East India Company came to the conclusion that "the Collector should be retained as a permanent feature or local administration,"[3] and ordered the Supreme Council "to combine in the person of the Collector, the offices of Revenue Administrator, Civil Judge and Magistrate." It was felt that the new administrative arrangement would strengthen the sovereignty of the country and the power of the executive.[4]

Cornwallis was, in principle, opposed to the concentration of revenue and judicial functions. He, therefore, broke with "the personal, authoritarian tradition of Indian Government, and based his work explicitly on the principles of the English political tradition"[5] with which he was well-acquainted.

The Magistrate and Collector in the Provinces following the Munro pattern of district administration, such as Bombay, Madras and North Western Provinces during the period 1818 to 1858, was an effective and powerful ruler of the area in his charge and exercised wide discretionary powers. He was "practically a local governor, exercising a wide-ranging superintendence over his district".[6] The Province of Bengal, on the other hand, did not have such a representative of government in its districts who could occupy a position of pre-eminence and primacy and "watch over and promote the general welfare, from every point of view, of the people committed to his charge."[7]

But the Bengal system of district administration under which the District Officer was a mere revenue collector underwent a change in 1859. On the recommendations of Halliday, the first Lieutenant-Governor of Bengal, of Dalhousie, and of Canning, it was decided, immediately after the Mutiny, to bring Bengal in line with other Provinces by having its districts under a District Magistrate and Collector. The effect of the Mutiny, though subtle, was decisive on the role of the District Officer. It brought the paternalist system to the height of favour in British estimation. "The Punjab" say Thompson and Garrat, "which had been recently settled in a very direct and personal manner, had shown a very remarkable loyalty to the Company, and the appointment of Sir John Lawrence as Viceroy, in 1864, completed the triumph of this school of though."[8] From 1860, the general policy was to build up a strong cadre of British officials, encouraging them to tour as much as possible.

II

THE DISTRICT OFFICER IN AN ERA OF TRIUMPHANT BUREAUCRACY (1859-1919)

Growth of Special Department

An important result of the assumption by the Crown of the governance of India was "a widespread belief that the Company's former actions had often been illegal" and, therefore, "must be regularized."[9] The Indian Council's Act of 1861 was followed by the passing of land revenue, and tenancy laws and by the three codes–the Penal Code, the Criminal Procedure Code, and the Civil Procedure Code. All this legislative activity curtailed the executive and discretionary authority of the District Officer. The Collector, however, continued to be the chief agent of government in his district; he continued to be responsible for its laws and order and well-being. But as time passed, his duties came to be discharged in a different manner and by changed methods.

The elaboration of public business led to the division of administration among a number of new departments, usually of a highly specialized nature, tending to absorb part of the duties for which the District Officer had been exclusively responsible. These new activities demanded a technical knowledge which could be acquired only by special training, and so the control which the Collector had formerly exercised over them in his district was in part replaced by that of departmental chiefs represented in each district by their officials. There developed, as a consequence, right through the system, "a growing rigidity, hardening of arteries, an increasing uniformity, a sense of superiority and a lack of human sympathy, more red-tape, more office work, loss of the old direct human rule of one man..."[10] The District Officer gradually came to pass more of his time at headquarters, less on tour. The telegraph cut down his discretion, just as it cut down the local Governor's and even the Governor-General's, and the closer touch between Government and local officers made it increasingly necessary for the latter "to solicit sanction before taking action and not to act in anticipation of it."[11]

It was at such a time that Sir George Campbell, one of the staunchest of the paternal school, was appointed Lieutenant-Governor of Bengal. He intended "to govern actively",[12] by which he meant "to use the power and influence of the executive more actively and decidedly in promoting...the honest performance by each class of the obligations which undoubtedly attach to it by law or otherwise..."[13] His important official move to this end was to strengthen the position of the District Officer in the district so that the latter as Government representative could help him in governing more actively. He was, therefore, anxious to see that "district level officers of specialized departments should not have too many masters and that the District Officer should control the local departments".[14] He accordingly introduced changes to make the Heads of Departments the agents and inspectors on the part of Government, bound to aid, counsel and guide their local officers, each in his own department, without exercising local authority over them. He desired to make "the Magistrate-Collectors, no longer the drudges of many departments and masters of none but in fact the general controlling authority over all departments in each district",[15] and "the real executive chief and administrator of the tract of country committed to him, and supreme over everyone and everything, except the proceedings of the Court of Justice".[16]

However, this clear and unequivocal primacy of the District Officer was confined to his dealings with the police in the district.

Other district level heads could not be so clearly brought under his direct control. In purely technical aspects of their operations they continued to be guided and supervised by their superiors at the Provincial headquarters, through even here plenty of vagueness persisted. Though this did not greatly affect his pre-eminence within the area of his authority, it enormously increased his office work and also reduced his capacity to deal directly and personally with the affairs of his district. Towards the close of the Viceroyalty of Lord Curzon it became increasingly apparent that civil servants in districts "were generally tied to their desks and found little time for informal contact with the people of their districts".[17]

The Beginning of the Present Century

The Royal Commission upon Decentralization (1907-1909) which studied the position of the District Officer very carefully found that his position had been materially reduced and recommended that "his position as administrative head of the district should be recognized by officers of all special departments".[18] The Commission underlined the unifying influence of the District Officer over the various branches of Government work in a district and recommended that he should "be entitled to call for any information which he thinks fit from them (officers of special departments), and to have such information given to him spontaneously in matters of importance, while any views he may express should receive the fullest consideration".[19]

The changes that came in the wake of the reforms of 1909 were not intended to affect district administration, though in the secretariats "men wondered how it would be possible to carry on Government at all. Indeed, all through the reforms period, the District Officer took things less tragically than his masters".[20] The District Officer, however, came to be more overburdened with office work and he could not be "reasonably expected either to become well-acquainted with the people of his district or to exercise over his subordinates that watchful and sympathetic control that is essential to good administration".[21]

It must, however, be noted that even towards the close of this period, the District Officer, in spite of considerable weakening in his position vis-à-vis other officers of special departments, continued to be the general representative of Government in his district and in varying degrees influenced the policy in all these matters. "He is always there in the background to lend his support or, if need be, to mediate between a specialized service and the people."[22] He was still much more than a *primus inter pares* and acted as "a direct representative of Government to whom complaints on every conceivable subject can be addressed, and through whom the Government can act".[23]

III

THE DISTRICT OFFICER IN A PERIOD OF CONSTITUTIONAL REFORMS (1919-47)

The Effect of the 1919 Reforms on the Position of the District Officer

Up to 1909 at all events, and even in some measure up to 1919, Government had been, in its essentials, at one with the civil service. The I.C.S. had been a great ruling corporation and had not been a civil service in the English sense. The I.C.S. man had been mainly responsible to men in his own service, and ultimately to the Secretary of State for India. He had wielded administrative, executive, judicial and political power. He had been the system of Government, and, in the ultimate analysis, the Government itself. But under the Montagu-Chelmsford reforms of 1919 all this had to go. The I.C.S. were to work in the context of a new power-structure which had come into existence with the implementation of the reforms in the form of "a Legislative Council in which the majority of the members are elected".[24] The new power affected district administration in various ways.

The influence of the new Legislative Council accentuated the tendency to make departmental activities independent of District Officer, especially in the transferred departments, such as Education, Excise, Agriculture, Co-operative Credit and Industries. Under the old set-up, the advice of the District Officer was sought on questions of policy, and reliance was placed on the advice he gave. Under the new system, although the District Officer was still consulted, the views of the Legislative Council and local politicians came to carry more weight than before, and the decisions on both questions of policy and matters of local importance came to be governed by considerations of political expediency.[25] The result was a contraction of the influence of the District Officer both in relation to Government and in local affairs and a reduction of the scope of his initiative. The District Officer was left ordinarily with the duties of enforcing law and order through his control of the magistracy and police, and of collecting the land revenue and other public demands. His were the duties, says a report, "of maintaining the fabric of Government and securing a good part of the revenue needed for such maintenance as well as for the benevolent activities of Government in which he has no longer much share."[26]

The duties of the District Officer in his capacity as Collector did not alter appreciably as a result of the reforms. But as District Magistrate, the District Officer, in most of the Provinces, had, for the most part, a much more anxious time during the reforms period than before. It was his duty to combat the non-cooperation movement and in a great many districts the possibility of serious clashes between the Hindus and the Muhammedans had to be faced on a growing number of occasions.

A basic change that came about in the position of the District Officer as a result of the reforms was a change in respect of his relation with local bodies. This change was "by far the greatest".[27] His function vis-à-vis the local bodies, particularly the District Board, became limited to the right to intervene, to prevent action calculated to lead to a breach of the peace or to grave injustice to sections of the population, and to the duty of inspecting the local bodies and reporting his views to the Ministry. It was an extension of the principle of dyarchy into the districts.[28]

The introduction of the reforms was not looked upon with approval by a large number of District Officers who were all members of the I.C.S. Even a small measure of popular control, considerably diluted though it was, appeared to them to undermine the whole administrative structure built up assiduously by their predecessors. The Report of the Government of Bihar and Orissa on the Working of the Reformed Constitution (1923-26) is representative of the views of such a critical and hostile section of the members of the I.C.S. It says, "The position of the District Officer has definitely changed for the worse...the new system has inevitably diminished his efficiency."[29] But the Report of a committee appointed by the U.P. Legislative Council to co-operate with the Indian Statutory Commission struck a significantly different note probably because it was presided over by a non-official and consisted of members of the Council. "It is true", the Report admitted, "that there is a tendency on the part of Government which has to justify its actions before a legislature, not to leave entire discretion in the hands of their local officers. This may have resulted in some curtailment of the exercise of the powers vested in the District Officer, but no concrete cases have been cited to show that the District Officer has found himself hampered in the discharge of his burden of responsibility under the existing system of Government."[30] But the fact remained that the I.C.S. disliked the Montagu-Chelmsford reforms and looked upon the Act of 1919 "as a fatuous, foolish and premature measure which was doomed to failure".[31] "It had, therefore to be proved a failure", remark Wilson, "regardless of the fact that in proving it a failure, the flames of a wider and much more ambitious movement were being fanned by these bureaucratic and wrecking Bourbons..."[32]

The working of the reforms, however, did not affect the dual capacity of the District Officer and he still remained "the principal executive agent of government, the one man who can get things done, whether it be the repression on the outbreak of disorder...or...the initiative of a child welfare movement..."[33] He had still very great prestige among the inhabitants of the district. He was the embodiment of Government to most of them. He wielded large powers of patronage and was responsible for making a large number of appointments. His recommendations for honorary magistrateships and nominated memberships of all local bodies were ordinarily accepted. He granted seats at ceremonial functions such as "durbars" and the coveted Indians titled and honours and other rewards were conferred at his suggestion.

The Simon Commission which was not in favour of any further weakening of the position of the District Officer opined that in spite of changes or adjustments of the District Officer must remain a very important person in the district, "the embodiment of effective authority, and the resource to whom the country-wide turns in time of difficulty or crisis."[34] The Commission, therefore, defined the relations between the District Officer and the district heads of technical departments and the Superintendent of Police in such a way as to ensure the primacy of the former as the head of the district and recommended that "except in matters of the pure routine the Collectors must be informed of almost every activity in all these departments".[35]

The Impact of Provincial Autonomy on the Office

The working of the Reformed Constitution of 1919 over a period of time had obliged the District Officer to adjust himself, even if with reluctance and sometimes cynical disdain, to new demands and changed conditions. The new change under the scheme of Provincial autonomy came to be viewed by the District Officer "with feelings resigned and wary. On the whole, however, the change proved less startling than might have been expected".[36] He had now to work in juxtaposition with the district organization of the party running the Provincial administration.

The change brought about by the inauguration of the Provincial autonomy was a change in emphasis as to the functions of Government. It had been the basic assumption in earlier days that the District Officer "must concentrate on the first essentials–public order, the swift administration of justice, the prompt payment of taxes moderately assessed, the maintenance of accurate and up to date land records which would prevent disputes. Those had been the four first things".[37] But popular governments, particularly Congress Governments, chalked out ambitious programmes of reconstruction and rural development. By 1939, the year the Indian National Congress laid down the reins of Government, the emphasis had changed, and rural upliftment, co-operative banks and village panchayats had come to be regarded as the first concern of the Government.

The District Officer was in charge of these schemes in villages. In addition, he had to add to his already countless duties "the maddening and infructuous business of answering questions, whether put down for formal answer in the House or sent informally direct, the host of subjects included under the head Rural Development, and the labour of persuading where he had been used to command".[38] Consequently, his office work increased, he became more circumspect, he did not always find it possible to check land records, and cases took longer and longer to be settled.

IV

THE DISTRICT OFFICER AFTER INDEPENDENCE

The District Officer and Democracy

After Independence, one of the major problems that faced the country was the relationship between the civil servant and the newly created organs of the Government. The initial reaction of the democratically constituted governments and legislatures to civil servants was one of distrust and even hostility, for an important plank of the national struggle against the British was the denunciation of the Civil Service which was, in the beginning, mostly British. It was, however, soon overcome because of a deep sense of patriotism and loyalty to the Constitution displayed by the Civil Servants.

The District Officer and Technical or Development Departments

An important thing which was discovered on the eve of and immediately after Independence was that the feeling of departmental loyalties on the part of officers of other departments in the district was much rampant, and that the District Officer had no power to force them to comply with his orders. His position vis-à-vis heads of technical departments in the district had become, says, the Bengal Administration Enquiry Committee, "thoroughly unsatisfactory both from the point of view of efficiency of the Government machine and the welfare of the people in the district".[39]

An important consequence of this situation was "the independent and disconnected activities of Government in the mufassal which had reached a point of confusion".[40] The practice, in fact, was that whether the Government wished to take up any new activity, it created a new department by putting a highly paid and well-qualified man at the Government headquarters as Director or Chief with a few regional officers. They were followed by District Officers, gazetted or non-gazetted, at the district level simultaneously or at a later stage, a few field workers were let loose in unmanageable areas without proper training, equipment and facilities. There was no coordination worth the name between the activities of the field staff of any two departments, and they had no sense of 'common objectives'.[41] The result was that development activities in the district lacked unity of approach and were always hampered for want of sufficient field staff for carrying out extension work."[42]

The District Officer in Development Administration

An outstanding feature of the programme introduced since Independence in villages is the Community Development and National Extension Service. It was only appropriate, therefore, that the two reports[43] which influenced most the structure of administrative organization for implementing these programmes suggested a common extension machinery on behalf of the principal development departments of Government.

The Grow More Food Enquiry Committee underlined the need for "an organization for intensive rural work which would reach every farmer and assist in the co-ordinated development of rural life as a whole..."[44] and proposed that since the district occupied an important place in the administrative organization "the development activities should be unified under the Collector as Extension Officer assisted by the Specialist Officers".[45] The Planning Commission also suggested that the re-organization of district administration should provide for:

> "(1) strengthening and improvement of the machinery of general administration ...
>
> ....
>
> (2) integration of activities of various development departments in the district and the provision of a common extension organization..."[46]

The Planning Commission emphasized that in making the detailed administrative arrangements, the States should keep in view an essential point, that is, "the position of the Collector as the head of the district, with the District Officers of the development departments working with him as a team."[47]

These suggestions were not only logical but also natural because in the past the role of the Collector as "the Government's principal representative".[48] had come to be recognized and accepted. Besides this, his functions were never entirely regulatory, and in course of years a great deal of development functions had come to be grafted on his original regulatory functions. He was, by virtue of his position in the official hierarchy, the natural leader of the official team at the district level. He was also capable of becoming a multi-purpose man and was expected to take the lead in the development of the areas entrusted to him.

It took, however, a few years before the District Officer could actually assume the role intended for him in the development administration. The Community Development Project Administration, which was inaugurated in October 1952, was, initially, not an organic part of the normal administrative machinery and the project areas were "virtual islands in the existing administration".[49] The Project Executive Officer had to work directly under the control and supervision of the Development Commissioner, and the District Officer was completely out of the line of the development administration.

Consequent on the opening of the N.E.S. Blocks, the programme further expanded and the Development Commissioner found it increasingly difficult to exercise proper supervision and control, to provide for supplies like iron, steel, cement, seeds, fertilizers etc., and to ensure the flow of the best technical advice available to the field worker. Speedy execution of the programmes was also being hampered by lack of proper delegation of financial and administrative authority.[50]

The experience of the working of the Community Development Projects (basic type) of 1952 further made it clear that it was not adequate to bring about co-ordination among the various heads of departments at the State headquarters. In order to make this a success, it was necessary to ensure co-ordination among the district and sub-divisional heads of departments. The obvious course, therefore, was to confer on the District Officer the kind of co-ordinational functions which had been conferred on the Development Commissioner at the State level, otherwise "neither unity of quality, nor speed of progress can be maintained."[51]

By 1955, such a suggestion was "universally accepted in principle"[52] and the Collector was "well on the way to becoming the principal development and welfare officer of the district".[53] The progress towards actively associating him with the execution of development programmes went apace in the subsequent years and the entire programme came to be integrated, in course of time, into the administrative system of the country. The U.N. Evaluation Mission Report found in 1959 that "the line of authority and supervision was that if the general administration",[54] and that the Collector functioned "as the co-ordinating officer and the captain of a team consisting of technical officers of the respective Departments".[55]

The pattern of supervisory authority and control of the Collector can be said to have a theoretical basis in what is called "dual hierarchy" which, according to Dimock and Dimock, "is so far the best method of solving the problems of co-ordination."[56] This theory was first brought into prominence by Arthur W. Macmahon, John D. Millet and Gladys Ogden in their book, *The Administration of Federal Work Relief*.[57] This theory is a vital organizational concept and John D. Millet is of opinion that "only in the theory of dual supervision will we find the means of building an integrated field structure for administrative operations".[58] It rests on a dichotomy between the specialist and the generalist and assumes a dual line of supervision and control from the top down and a dual set of loyalties from the bottom up. "The crux of the problem", remark Dimock and Dimock, "is that certain officers must be 'administratively' responsible to one superior and 'technically' responsible to another."[59]

District administrative organization in India, like the Prefect system in Western European countries, is an example of the system of integrated field structure, with an area specialist at the head of it. "Area administration with one officer having over-all charge of a particular area has long been a basic concept in Indian administration."[60] The District Officer embodies the principle of organization by area and the principle of general administration.

The District Officer in the Scheme of Democratic Decentralization

With the publication of the Balwantray Mehta Study Team Report (1957), "the most influential survey of local administration which has appeared since Independence",[61] the question as to what place the District Officer should occupy in the scheme of democratic-decentralization came to agitate the minds of the planners and administrators. The Mehta Team itself recommended that "the

Collector will be the Chairman of the Zilla Parishad and one of his officers will be the Secretary".[62] The first official conference held at Bangalore in November 1960 studied this problem carefully and resolved:

> "The Collector should be kept outside the three-tier system and should be the agent of the Government informed of the happenings and the general trend of events, and, where the Government so decides, to take necessary corrective action. For these purposes, he may be entitled to attend the meetings of the *Zilla Parishad/Panchayati Samiti* or its sub-committees and also call for their records.[63]

A few months later this question, among others, was discussed at the Tenth Development Commissioners' Conference in July 1961, at Hyderabad. The question framed for discussion was as follows:

> "What should be the proper relationship between officials and non-officials? In particular, what place should the Collector occupy in the Zilla Parishad?"[64]

The Conference discussed the question in much detail and resolved that "the Collector should keep in constant touch with the Zilla Parishad with regard to the planning and implementation of the various development programmes",[65] but it left to the States to experiment on one of the four available alternatives, namely:

(*i*) The Collector should be fully associated with the Panchayati Raj institutions and should be a member and chairman of the Zilla Parishad.
(*ii*) The Collector should be a member of the Zilla Parishad and Chairman of all its Standing Committees.
(*iii*) The Collector should be just a member of the Zilla Parishad with or without a right to vote.
(*iv*) He should be completely outside the Zilla Parishad but with a right to take part in the deliberations whenever he considers this necessary.

To these alternatives may be added a fifth one which has been proposed by an important group of public men. Association of Voluntary Agencies for Rural Develoment.[66] The alternative is:

The Collector should be the Chief Executive Officer of the Zila Parishad.

It may be said in favour of the fourth alternative that as an official the District Officer has no place in a purely elective body. He should, therefore, function as an agent and representative of State Government reporting to it periodically about the activities of the Zilla Parishad and other Panchayati Raj institutions much in the same manner as he does for the municipalities today or did for the District Board previously. The merit in this suggestion is that it relieves the Collector of a great deal of work and enables him to function as an umpire removed from the din and bustle of local politics. The Maharashtra Committee on Democratic Decentralization opined that the Collector should be outside the Zilla Parishad so that "the Government will have in him an independent officer who can also evaluate impartially the functioning of the local body and who will also be available for keeping Government informed on any matter which is of sufficient importance".[67]

It seems, however, that complete isolation of the District Officer, as suggested by the Maharashtra Committee, from the work of the Zilla Parishad will amount to his complete separation from the mainstream of development efforts in the district. It is difficult to see in what manner he can watch the work of the Zilla Parishad unless he has a right to participate in its deliberations whenever he deems it necessary. The exhortation in the Third Five Year Plan to the District Officer to "assist democratic institutions...in developing the right conventions in the day-to-day work..."[68] would remain a will-o'-the-wisp. It is felt that his occasional presence in the Zilla Parishad, when an important matter is being discussed, will furnish to the Parishad the advice and guidance of a mature and experienced officer who has considerable prestige in the eyes of the people. But he should not be a voting member of the Zilla Parishad for he should be embroiled in group politics in the district. His presence should be to clear up certain misunderstandings, to provide some important information, or to give a mature and impartial advice to the Zilla Parishad on a controversial or difficult question.

An important section of public men is of opinion that the District Officer should be the Chief Executive Officer of the Zilla Parishad in the same way as the B.D.O. is the Chief Executive Officer of the Panchayat Samiti.[69] In order that the State Government is not weakened in relation to these bodies, the AVARD Study Team suggests that "The State Government...can arm itself with the same powers of cancellation and suspension of resolutions in respect of the Zilla Parishad as it has in respect of the Panchayat Samiti." With regard to the emergency powers of the District Officer, the AVARD Report on Panchayati Raj in Andhra Pradesh has observed that "he could have an independent jurisdiction regarding law and order. In a similar way he should be free to execute such duties as the State Government directs him to do".[70]

But it is difficult to visualize how a Collector subordinate to the Zilla Parishad as its executive officer can exercise responsibility towards law and order independently or perform other duties as prescribed by the State Government without being a suspect to the Zilla Parishad. With the District Officer subordinate to the Zilla Parishad, the State Government will be left without any independent observer on the district scene.[71] The new role of the District Officer, therefore, in relation to the Zilla Parishad should involve periodical and informal discussion of affairs of the Zilla Parishad and senior officers of development departments in the district. It should be the duty of the Chief Executive Officer of the Zilla Parishad to keep the District Officer regularly informed of the intentions and actions of the Zilla Parishad and to avail himself of his advice. It should also be possible for the chairman of the Zilla Parishad and the District Officer to meet at least twice a month and discuss matters relating to the development of the district with special reference to the activities of the Zilla Parishad. It would be from such consultations that the District Officer would be able to know when to offer the general advice to the Zilla Parishad by being present in its meetings.

There is a mist of uncertainty surrounding the future role of the District Officer in Panchayati Raj. There are two schools of thought easily discernible through the mist. One like the AVARD regards the District Officer as a sort of scaffolding which is used when a building is in progress, but which must be removed once the building has been completed. But this school is not able to say precisely when the 'scaffolding' should be removed.[72] The other school consisting of planners and administrators hold that even with the establishment of a full-fledged Panchayati Raj the office of the District Officer should continue, for the State Government must have a trusted agent in the district to act as the ultimate authority for maintaining law and order and as a focal point for common local interests between various authorities.[73]

V

THE TRADITIONAL FUNCTIONS OF THE DISTRICT OFFICER: CHANGES AFTER INDEPENDENCE

District Officer as Collector

For long the revenue administration was the only center of Government in the district and absorbed all the governmental authority that operated in the district.[74] In its early days the administration in the district was connected by a single organization which the Revenue Department and the District Officer represented. It was a multipurpose department and the officers of the department was multipurpose functionaries. After Independence changes have taken place in the nature and contents of his revenue functions. The abolition of zamindaris has placed new responsibilities on him. Instead of dealing with a few intermediaries responsible for the payment of land revenue, he has now to deal with hundreds of thousands of cultivators in connection with land revenue, canal dues, taccavi loans, and many other such things. A huge staff ranging from Karmacharis to Circle Officers has to be engaged and supervised and their service conditions and other things have to be looked into.[75]

Land ceiling laws, levy on land improvement and agricultural income-tax have imposed additional burden on him. Political pressures, in the process of realization of taxes and dues like taccavi, canal, etc., are occasionally brought to bear upon his officers. Complete recovery of dues is an ideal difficult of realization.

Consolidation of land holdings and land acquisition are other problems of very difficult nature subsequent to Independence. Land acquisition used to be nominal before Independence. Now, due to various industrial projects and development schemes, considerable land has to be acquired for public purpose. Though he is assisted in the discharge of his heavy revenue work by an

Additional Collector or a Revenue Officer, as the case may be, the main brunt of responsibility has to be borne by him. He is also called upon to dispose of a specified number of revenue cases, besides inspecting Tahsil and sub-divisional offices. Though in some of the States the task of rent collection is being gradually made over to the village panchayats, the ultimate responsibility still rests with the Collector.

The District Officer as Magistrate

The magisterial functions of the District Officer may be dealt with under: (*i*) maintenance of law and order, and (*ii*) trial of criminal cases and supervision of magisterial courts, that is, functions which are essentially judicial.

(*i*) *The maintenance of law and order*: The first set of magisterial functions has two facets; (1) the detection and prevention of crime in general, and (2) the prevention and quelling of riots and more serious disturbances. The first is performed mainly by the police, but in the performance of the second, the District Magistrate plays an important part. The relation between the District Magistrate and the police is delicate and ill-defined. On the one hand, the police of the district have to work under the District Superintendent of Police and no one else, but on the other the District Magistrate is required to exercise a general control over the criminal administration.

Before Independence, the District Magistrate and the District Superintendent of Police, usually worked together in harmony and co-operation, but instances of clash between them are now often cited. The Uttar Pradesh Police Commission (1960-61) has found that the existing relationship between the District Magistrate and the District Superintendent of Police, based on Section 4 of the Police Act (Act V of 1861), which used to be taken for granted, has assumed the character of a 'controversy'. It is now being argued by the police that "the exercise of supervisory powers by the District Magistrate weakens the authority and reduces the position of the

Superintendent of Police".[76] A similar controversy was raised before the Bihar Police Commission (1961) which examined the relationship that should exist between the District Magistrate and the Superintendent of Police. The Commission was of opinion that "the present conflict wherever existing, is due more to a conflict of personalities than a conflict of the system itself".[77] It did not recommend a radical change in the relationship which has been existing between the two since 1861.

(*ii*) *The trial of criminal cases and supervision of Magisterial Courts*: This particular aspect of the Collector's magisterial functions has been affected in those States or parts of State where the scheme of separation of judicial and executive functions has been introduced. The separation scheme of the State of Bihar might illustrate to what extent the magisterial (judicial) powers of the District Magistrate have been affected. The scheme envisages that all Magistrates and Munsif-Magistrates trying criminal cases will be under the control of the High Court through the Sessions Judges, and that the District Magistrates and Sub-Divisional Magistrates will not have any control over them nor will they have anything further to do with a criminal case after it has been transferred for trial to a Munsif or a Judicial Magistrate. It is only the Sessions Judge who is to record annual confidential remarks on the work and conduct of the Magistrates employed on the judicial side. In the matter of vesting the Judicial Magistrates with higher powers the Sessions Jude is to be consulted. The High Court has been vested with the powers of transfer and posting of, and grant of leave to, Judicial Magistrates.[78]

Now, under the separation of scheme, the District Magistrate does not inspect trial-registers and case records. Inspections are done by the Sessions and Assistant Sessions Judges and the responsibility for proper and speedy disposal of cases is theirs. Functions, however, which are essentially police functions, e.g., the handling of law and order and those of an administrative character, e.g., issue of licenses for firearms continue to be discharged by the District Magistrate and executive magistrates subordinate to him.

VI
CONCLUSION

The institution of the District Officer has a long history behind it. From time-to-time there have been changes, additions and subtractions in the duties of the District Officer. But on the whole his duties have expanded while his powers have diminished. With the outbreak of the Mutiny the paternalist system of district administration came into prominence resulting in the absolute supremacy of the Collector in the district. This trend was, however, soon countered by the growth of governmental functions demanding specialized direction and treatment.

The introduction of diarchy in 1921 which transferred the control of nation-building departments to Ministers further restricted his powers. During the Second World War and the post-war period, his functions came to expand for a short while, but simultaneously a tendency to departmental autonomy and disconnected functioning of technical departments was also discernible. With the separation of judiciary, the District Officer became more and more exclusively an executive magistrate and a collector of revenue.

In the context of Community Development and N.E.S. Programmers, he was recently invested with co-ordinational and supervisory power over the district heads of technical departments. But again, a tendency in the opposite direction is appearing with the introduction of Panchayati Raj. Under this scheme, his extension functions are being transferred to local bodies and he is being entrusted with the task of guiding, educating and advising them. Full implications of the impact of the scheme on his office are not yet in sight. But it is not unlikely that after the successful working of the Panchayati Raj institutions over a reasonable period of time, he may be left with regulatory functions alone.

REFERENCES

1. Erick Stokes, "*The English Utilitarians and India*", The Clarendon Press, Oxford, (1959), pp. 1-3.
2. L.M. Penson, "The Bengal Administrative System (1786-1818)", *The Cambridge History of India*, Vol. V, ed. H.H. Dodwell, S. Chand & Co., New Delhi, p. 133.

3. *Ibid.*, p. 133.
4. A.Aspinall, *Cornwallis in Bengal*, Manchester University Press, (1931), p. 132.
5. Erick Stokes, *Op cit.*, p. 4.
6. H.V. Lovett, "District Administration in Bengal (1818-1858)," *The Cambridge History of India*, Vol. VI, ed. H.H. Dodwell, S. Chand & Co., New Delhi, (1958), p. 29.
7. *Ibid.*, p. 28.
8. E. Thompson and G.T. Garrat, *Rise and Fulfilment of British Rule in India*, Central Book Depot, Allahabad, (1954), p. 424.
9. *Ibid.*, p. 426.
10. Philip Woodruff, *The Men Who Ruled India*: *The Guardians*, London, (1954), p. 14.
11. L.S.S. O'Malley, *The Indian Civil Service*, 1601-1930, John Murray, London, (1931), p. 110.
12. C.E. Buckland, *Bengal Under the Lieutenant-Governors*, Vol.I, Calcutta (second edition, 1902), p. 519.
13. *Ibid.*, p. 519.
14. *Report on the Administration of Bengal*, (1871-72), Calcutta, (1872), p. 65
15. *Ibid.*, p. 66.
16. *Ibid.*, p. 67.
17. H.V. Lovett, *Op. cit.*, p. 252.
18. Report of *The Royal Commission Upon Decentralization in India*, Vol. I, (1909), para 539.
19. *Ibid.*, p. 539.
20. P. Woodruff, *Op. cit.*, p. 218.
21. *Report of the Bengal District Administration Committee* (1913-14), Calcutta, (1914), p. 18.
22. *Report on Indian Constitutional Reforms*, Calcutta, (1918), p. 80.
23. *Ibid.*, p. 81.
24. *Report on the Working of the Reformed Constitution in Bengal*, 1921-27, Government of Bengal, Appointment Department (Reforms), Bengal Secretariat Book Depot, Calcutta, (1929), p. 188.
25. *Ibid.*, p. 189.
26. *Memorandum submitted by the Government of Bihar and Orissa to the Indian Statutory Commission*, Vol.XII, H.M.S.O., London, (1930), p. 293.
27. *Report on the Working of the Reformed Constitution in Bengal*, (1921-27), *Op. cit.*, p. 189.
28. *Memorandum submitted by the Government of Bihar and Orissa to the Indian Statutory Commission*, *Op. cit.*, p. 292.

29. *Report on the Reformed Constitution (1923-26) in Bihar and Orissa. See, Reports on the Working of the Reformed Constitution, (1928)*, p. 424.
30. *Report of the Committee appointed by the United Provinces Legislative Council to Co-operate with the Indian Statutory Commission*, (1929), p. 25.
31. Frederick William Wilson, *The Indian Chaos*, London, (1932), p. 29.
32. *Ibid.*, p. 286.
33. *Memorandum submitted by the Government of United Provinces to the Indian Statutory Commission*, Vol.IX, H.M.S.O., London, (1930), p. 47.
34. *Indian Statutory Commission*, Vol.I, H.M.S.O., London, (1930), p. 291.
35. *Ibid.*, p. 286.
36. Philip Woodruff, *Op. cit.*, p. 273.
37. *Ibid.*, p. 303.
38. *Ibid.*, p. 303.
39. *Report of the Bengal Administration Enquiry Committee,* (1944-45), Superintendent, Government Printing, Bengal Government Press, Alipore, (1945), para 64.
40. *Ibid.*, para 66.
41. *Report of the Grow More Food Enquiry Committee*, Government of India, Ministry of good and Agriculture, (June 1952), p. 53.
42. *The First Five Year Plan*, Planning Commission, New Delhi, p. 129.
43. These two reports are: the *Report of the Grow More Food Enquiry Committee* and the *First Five Year Plan*.
44. *Report of the Grow More Food Enquiry Committee, Op. cit.*, p. 53.
45. *Ibid.*, p. 63.
46. *The First Five Year Plan*, Planning Commission, p. 130.
47. *Ibid.*, p. 130.
48. *Ibid.*, p. 128.
49. *Road to Welfare State*, the Publications Division, Government of India, New Delhi, (second edition, 1957), p. 19.
50. U.L. Goswami, "The Structure of Development Administration", *The Indian Journal of Public Administration*, Vol. I, No. 2, April-June, 1955, p. 110.
51. *Evaluation Report of the First Year's Working of Community Projects*, Planning Commission, P.E.O., (1954), p. 12.
52. *Evaluation Report of the Second Year's Working of Community Projects*, Vol.I, Planning Commission, P.E.O., (1955), p. 5.
53. *Ibid.*, p. 4.
54. M.J. Caldwell, R. Dumont & M. Read, *Report of a Community Development, Evaluation Mission in India*, (Under the U.N. Programme of Technical Assistance) Ministry of Community Development and Co-operation, Government of India, (1959), p. 13.
55. *Ibid.*, p. 13.

56. Marshall E. Dimock and Gladys Ogden Dimock, Public Administration, Rinchart and Co., Inc., New York and Toronto, (1954), p. 331.
57. Arthur W. Macmahon, John D. Millet, and Gladys Ogden, *The Administration of Federal Work Relief*, Chicago, (1941), pp. 264-68.
58. John D. Millet, *New Horizons in Public Administration: A Symposium*, University of Alabama Press, (1945), p. 99.
59. Dimock & Dimock, *Op. cit.*, p. 331.
60. V. Nath, "Area Development", *Kurukshetra*, Anniversary Number, Vol. 6, No. 1, October 2, 1957, p. 45.
61. Hugh Tinker, "Authority and Community in Village India", *EROPA Review*, Vol.I, No. 1, December, 1960, p. 119.
62. *Report of the Team for the Study of Community Projects and National Extension Service I*, p. 19.
63. *Kurukshetra*, Vol. 9, No. 4, January, 1961, p. 12.
64. Hyderabad Conference Special, *Kurukshetra*, Vol. 9, No. 12, September 1961, p. 4.
65. *Ibid.*, p. 19.
66. The Association of Voluntary Agencies for Rural Development is a voluntary organization devoted to the welfare of rural community through development of mutual cooperation and understanding among voluntary agencies. (Vide: *Report of the Study Team of Democratic Decentralization in Rajasthan*, 1961, p. 19). Also see Report of a Study Team on Panchayati Raj in Andhra Pradesh, 1961, p. 37. The Chairman of the Executive Committee of AVARD is Jayaprakash Narayan, the Sarvodaya leader.
67. *Report of the Committee on Democratic Decentralization*, Government of Maharashtra, (1961), p. 101.
68. *Third Five Year Plan*, Government of India, Planning Commission, (1961), p. 340.
69. *Report of a Study Team on Democratic Decentralization in Rajasthan*, AVARD, (1961), p. 19.
70. *Report of a Study Team on Panchayati Raj in Andhra Pradesh* (1961), p. 37.
71. *The Maharashtra Committee on Democratic Decentralization* has objected to the Collector becoming the Executive Officer of the Zilla Parishad. It says, "The Collector's appointment as Chief Executive Officer is also likely to place him in an embarrassing position as he will have to divide his loyalty between the Government and the Council...His position will become particularly difficult in matters where there is difference of opinion between the Government and the Council. It will be extremely difficult for him to divide his loyalties in compartments and show different personalities at different times according to the authority under which he is operating." (*Vide* Report, p. 102).

72. *Report of a Study Team on Panchayati Raj in Andhra Pradesh*, p. 37. It says, "The Collector should work as the Secretary of the Zilla Parishad, so far as the development departments are concerned. He could have an independent jurisdiction regarding law and order...This, of course, will be a necessary preliminary step to *the complete transfer of all the present functions of Government to the Zilla Parishad.*"
73. *The First and Second Five Year Plans* suggested various measures for strengthening the position of the District Officer. *The Third Five Year Plan* also assigned an important role to the District Officer in facilitating the success of Panchayati Raj and implementing development programmes. It says: "He has the duty of ensuring co-ordination at the district level between the Zilla Parishad and the technical officers in different fields...and a continuing flow of technical advice and guidance from departments at the state level." (Vide: p. 340). *The Maharashtra Committee on Democratic Decentralization*, which is said to be more radical in its approach to democratic decentralization than the *Mehta Study Team*, favoured the retention of "the state sector" in the hands of the District Officer. It did not foresee a complete transfer of the whole gamut of district administration to the Panchayati Raj institutions.
74. M. Ruthnaswamy, *Some Influences That Made the British Administrative System in India*, Lucaz & Co., London, (1939), p. 321. Ruthnaswamy observes: "Not tribal settlements, nor historical influences, nor political considerations—such as created the English county or the French province of the ancient regime—created the Indian district. It was the offspring like the French department of the Revolution of administrative convenience."
75. This is especially true of Bihar whose land revenue administration was governed by the Permanent Settlement of 1793, and which, before independence, did not have revenue agencies below the Sub-Divisional Officer.
76. *Report of the Uttar Pradesh Police Commission* (1960-61), Superintendent, Printing and Stationery, Allahabad, (1961), p. 15.
77. *Report of the Bihar Police Commission* (1961), Superintendent, Secretariat Press, Patna, (1961), p. 150.
78. See Bihar Government's Additional Secretary's Letter No. II-HI-301/50-A-11860 dated December 20, 1950, *Compendium of Circulars and Orders of Appointment Department, Cabinet Secretariat, Government of Bihar*, 1961, pp. 696-701.

8

The Collector in the Nineteen-Sixties in Uttar Pradesh

J.D. SHUKLA

The title of this article implies that the role and the functions of a District Collector have been changing from time-to-time. This is true but in the centre of the change there is a fixity, and in order to evaluate the position and functions of the Collector of a district in Uttar Pradesh in the Nineteen-Sixties it is necessary to examine both aspects of the matter, that is to what extent his functions and position have undergone a change and to what extent they remain as they were. This exercise invites a comparison with his forbears in previous decades.

If John Simple, who was Collector of a U.P. district in the Thirties, came and visited a Collector of U.P. district in the Sixties and spent some time with him, the first impression he would get would be of a vast change which will intrigue an even confuse him. He will notice a large number of visitors and of different types than he was used to. He will also notice that visitors keep no time. It is the Collector who has to adjust his daily routine to suit the convenience of his visitors. And if John Simple sat with the Collector during interviews, he might get the impression that the Collector of these days has wider and larger individual contacts, while in John Simple's days general contact with the public, and particularly with the public in rural areas, was preferred and individual contacts were kept to the minimum. And listening to the conversation at the interviews John Simple may find that the Collector has a large number of individual visitors who were seeking their own interest and that the points raised were very limited and personal and at times John Simple may even think that the Collector was busy appeasing a few influential individuals rather than discussing general policy matters. He will also be struck by the way visitors put up their cases. In John Simple's days the visitors put their cases in a polite, almost submissive and apologetic way and left the decision to the Collector. These days points are put forward aggressively and hints may be dropped that if the decision is not given in favour of the person making the point, he would consider that justice had not been done.

The second point John Simple would notice would be the attendance of the Collector at a very large number of meetings of numerous committees. The number and functions of these committees would bring vividly to the notice of John Simple the great extension of the field in which the District Officer now operates. These committees would reveal the widening and deepening of the area of district administration today. Some of these meetings are concerned with the regulatory matters like price control, rationing of foodgrains, licensing, issue of permits and the exercise of various controls and regulations which cover quite a large field of ordinary citizen's life. John Simple was used in his time to leave these things to the natural play of economic forces and to the resources of the individuals. Today the Collector is the regulator of the life of the citizens over a vast field. If a citizen wants to celebrate a simple ceremony connected with a child's *sanskar*, he must get a permit for sugar from the District Collector; if he wants to repair his house, not to speak of building a new one, he must take Collector's permission to buy cement; even if he wants to give a feast at his own expense, he must ask the Collector before inviting a number of guests larger than that prescribed. These regulatory functions were almost unknown in the Thirties. They became a feature of administration in the Nineteen-Forties owing to the War but have since then continued owing to shortages.

The Collector today rations big populations in towns, provisions them in several ways and regulates their life in a dozen ways.

But some other committees, John Simple would notice, are concerned with what is called development. John Simple had seen the seed of this when late in the Thirties the Rural Development Department was established. But it has now expanded and grown in complexities and scope and has been re-organized. If asked what were the main functions of the District Collector, John Simple would have replied in his days without hesitation: Maintenance of law and order so as to enable the citizens to go about their daily routine in peace and freedom; to look after the revenue administration and to collect taxes promptly in order to provide revenue to the State and also to maintain correctly and up-to-date the land records in which are contained the rights of the millions in rural areas to their land and to look after the rural people when natural calamities visited them; and to dispose of justly, impartially and expeditiously revenue and criminal cases. Today, while these functions remain, the place of pride is taken by development work. John Simple would find the Collector in the Sixties a less relaxed man than John Simple himself used to be, but if he had an opportunity of an evening chat with the Collector, he could easily get a picture of the developmental set-up and the place therein of the Collector. The Collector today is responsible for achieving economic and social goals and, therefore, his functions have become as large as life itself. It is not as if John Simple was not interested in these aspects but that was in a pioneering way. John Simple himself organized a flower show, was president of the district club which he visited pretty often, helped in setting up rifle clubs, organized various kinds of exhibitions, helped in organizing local charities, promoted education and public health and hygiene, organized sports and took part in them. He also promoted better agriculture, advanced loans for digging of wells, for buying of bulls and agricultural implements inspected Village Panchayats and schools and in a number of ways promoted social welfare of the people in his charge. His wife organized maternity shows and sometimes Purdah clubs. She also distributed medicines when camping with her husband in the rural areas and indeed sometimes performed other health services as she was closely associated with the local Red Cross. Some rural dispensaries were opened in her name and she ran the Dufferin Hospital at the district headquarters. Nevertheless John Simple could not have the idea of the present-day Collector's developmental activities until he sat at various committees and toured with the Collector in rural areas.

While the Collector is responsible for increase in agricultural production, for setting up rural industries, for reclaiming *Usar* land and conserving soil, for promoting fishery and poultry and while he is specially charged with the welfare of the backward castes and tribes and women and is generally expected to promote all developmental activities of various departments, the developmental organizational set-up is, more or less, entirely non-official, consisting of the representatives of the people. The Collector is neither Chairman of the Zilla Parishad nor is its member, nor he has any worthwhile powers over the Zilla Parishad or the Kshetra Samitis (Panchayat Samitis or Panchayat Unions). The Zilla Parishad consists of the Pramukhs of the Kshetra Samitis and some other persons with an elected Chairman. District level officials of the development departments of the Government have been deputed to the Zilla Parishad to carry out in an integrated and co-ordinated manner development work under the aegis of the Zilla Parishad; they are headed by an official called the Distict Planning Officer. Similarly, at the block level the Block Development Officer with his assistants has been placed on the staff of the Kshetra Samiti which consists of elected members with an elected Chairman. The organization at Gaon Sabha level is simpler; it is also an elected body with an elected Pradhan. The Panchayati Raj consisting of elected representatives of the people and organized at three levels and assisted by Government officials deputed to them is charged with the task of development and making the country prosperous through increased production in various fields. The philosophy was and is that such a tremendous task of raising the country from poverty to prosperity can be performed only by the people themselves and not by a few officials. People are aware of their felt needs; they are in the best position to frame their plans and to implement them and to know their results and to correct irregularities and remove irrelevancies, rectify mistakes and progress developmental activities along right lines.

On such a theory and such an organization, it seems inexplicable, on the face of it, as to why the Collector's functions and importance should increase. Many people held the view that an all-purposes officer like the Collector was suitable only for a bureaucratic type of administration but would not fit in with a democratic organization where the people's representatives at various levels would be sitting and debating and deciding, where the problems to be dealt with will be economic and social and where even various Government departments would be functioning under their own political heads. What is the explanation that this opinion has not turned out to be true and the Collector's functions have expanded rather than contracted and his role in the developmental field overshadows his role even in the basic functions of Government. This development also contradicts the obvious view that as the people's representatives take on more work to themselves, assume more functions and responsibilities, to that extent the Collector's position will become less prominent and indeed he would, in due course, fade away. The fact of the matter is that whatever may be the set-up, function and power belong to those who can wield power and discharge functions. While there are some excellent people in the people's organization, well-intentioned and able to achieve, yet no organization, whether at the district or the block or the village level, can rival the effectiveness of the District Collector. He is the pivot and pillar of administration and to the administration still attaches in this country considerable prestige. The Collector also stands out above parties and away from them and the general people still look up to him for an impartial and just decision. He has also a faithful band of officials trained in the art of administration and, what is more, subject to strict official discipline. He is their chief and when he commands them into action it makes a stir. The Collector still represents the unified administration in a district, is directly in touch with Government departments in the Secretariat, is consulted by Government in all controversial matters; he has the resources of the Revenue staff and the district police at his disposal. He, therefore, has the sources of power which he can effectively use. This is the explanation of his position today; a job has to be done. The job is pressing and it has to be done urgently; the man, therefore, who can do it will do it. Indeed the representatives of the people themselves look up to him for guidance and support. Today the test of a District Officer is whether he can draw out the co-operation of the people. To guide the representatives of the people in the art of the administration, to hold balance between the various parties wherever necessary, to adjudicate and to activise the implementation machinery have become the main functions of the Collector today. The people in rural areas still look up to him for receiving justice and sympathy, detached and impartial decisions, and even though sometimes voices are raised that the district official was suborned or weak, by and large the picture of a District Officer as an impartial adjudicator at the district level for redress of grievances remain untarnished.

The Collector of a district in Uttar Pradesh in Nineteen-Sixties is well-supported by the Government and his seniors. Doubtless he is no longer the only ear and eye of the Government. There are other eyes and ears. But there are differences between eyes and eyes and ears and ears and the Government often consults the Collector to find out the correct position or the correct decision when rival and partisan forces are at work whether at the district level or at the State Headquarters. In any case, there may be other eyes and ears but the hands of the Government are still the district executive machinery and the Government is interested in keeping its hands strong and effective. The Government relies on the District Officer for presenting them an unbiased picture of a district and the Government is also aware that the district administration has to carry out many unpleasant but necessary duties in the process of which it is apt to annoy powerful influences against which the district administration should be protected. Sometimes rival and partisan forces negative each other and by this simple process the Collector emerges supreme. John Simple would, therefore, feel re-assured to see this even though he may take some time to find this out.

II

John Simple would also notice that the Collector deals with a bigger dak and if he were permitted by the Collector of the Sixties to read the papers, John Simple would be struck by a large number of enquiries which the Collector scrutinizes. After John Simple left the service, a significant development happened in the matter of public complaints. The public were invited to lodge complaints against officials in the belief that there was much to be complained against–but the public was too frightened to do so–and in the hope that honest and genuine complaints will pour in, providing a basis for action which will cleanse the administration. Every mode of human activity is diverted to ends and purposes other than those for which it is devised and it is not only the genuine complainants who came forward but blackmailers who wanted to suborn the district executive officers to their will by harassing them by false complaints. The filing of these complaints and enquiries that followed considerably shook and demoralized the officials. The honest and the good were more demoralized, for they could hardly relish the loss of dignity involved in an enquiry even though ultimately the accused may be acquitted. The number of anonymous and pseudonymous applications multiplied. The techniques of weaving true facts into false stories developed into a fine art and the Government got concerned. First, the Department of Complaints was abolished, then orders were issued that anonymous and pseudonymous complaints should not be entertained. The threat of the blackmailers and suborners was during the later Forties and early Fifties but the Collector of the Sixties is comparatively better off in this respect. The blackmailers and suborners have been fully exposed for they over-reached themselves. The emphasis now is on the principle that an honest, effective officer is not mutilated in search of a dishonest officer. The District Collector has survived a difficult period in this respect and is now comparatively in a comfortable position, even though he is subjected at local levels sometimes to undue influences. But this is an exception rather than the rule. To John Simple the present position would not seem very satisfactory but doubtless on further refection he would understand that in a democratic set-up you cannot stop complaints and assertions by people. All that you can do is to ensure at Government level protection of the honest, upright and effective officer. District officials' protection is in their own hands, namely in straight-forward and honest work.

Looking at other papers John Simple would still recognize the territories known to him then, though they have expanded and thrown up new features, some hills and other valleys. He would miss his beloved Court of Wards. But he will find that the range and complexities of district administration have tremendously increased. This tremendous increase is merely a reflection of the increase in the functions of the Government itself. All Government policies are executed at the district level by the District Officer and as the functions of Government have increased by taking on more regulatory and developmental functions so has the field of district administration at the district level increased. In John Simple's times the function of the State was an enabling one, holding the ring, promoting basic activities in various fields and enabling the ordinary citizen to promote his interests, to engage in business, to make profit and loss, to increase his produce and to improve his well-being etc. In the Sixties the functions of the State have become positive. The State run industries, actively intervenes in labour affairs; the programmes of *Usar* reclamation and soil conservation and promotion of fishery and poultry have been planned on a very big scale. Even welfare activities are being promoted by the State. The State is actively involved in the promotion of sports and even cultural activities. The State has become as large as life. The responsibilities of the Collector as the Government's representative at the district level, have therefore, expanded accordingly. But apart from increase in his own work, he has also to overser, promote and coordinate the work of other departments in a way in which this was not done in John Simple's time. District level officials of various departments are subordinate to him today in a way that was not in the Thirties. He writes the character rolls of all these officials, encourages and guides them and also, when occasion arises, reprimands them. The Collector today is primarily charged with the task of increasing agricultural production. In this field he works with the representatives of the people and people's institutions on the one hand and officials of the various departments on the other. He has also to see that the various schemes of Government are well-planned, well-executed and there is no wastage of money. He inspects the work of all and when occasion demands enquires into the conduct of the officials and the non-officials and reports to Government. The statutory portion of the Collector in this respect is neither well-defined nor well-established, but he works more through influence than through statutory powers. His strength is that he is consulted and trusted by the Government and is trusted and respected by the general public. He is in constant touch with the people and with facts. Even the development department in its executive sphere works through officials of whom the Collector is the chief and the officials look up to the Collector not only for guidance and encouragement in executing their duties but also for protection. Besides, the Collector is the Chairman of a number of advisory committees.

All this has made the Collector somewhat of a public leader also. Indeed this aspect has been recognized by Government by providing the services of one or two District Information Officers. They are constantly putting out to the public through the press and the pamphlets and through various visual and auditory channels the welfare and development work done in the district and also other aspects of district administration. Today the

Collector works not so much by merely giving decisions as by explaining them all the time. There is need to explain all the time and this development would make John Simple somewhat impatient for he was taught to do the right thing and not to explain or apologize. The picture of the district administration, as it has emerged now, is one where official and public aspects of administration merge, where not only decisions are given but also explained, where not only general contact with the public is maintained but also individual contacts are cultivated or are forced upon, where more and more problems are referred to the Collector and solutions expected of him. John Simple would, however, see that the seed of this was always there because even in the Thirties it was a common saying "When in doubt go to the Collector. When you have no place to stay, stay with him." But John Simple, would definitely carry the impression that district today was over-administered.

John Simple will notice that elections now are more frequent, and a bigger affair. The Collector of the Sixties is all the time either planning or preparing or carrying out elections for one body or the other. This not only means tremendous work but confronts the Collector with one of the most difficult and delegate jobs giving rise to all kinds of complaints and the Collector all the time explaining and defending.

John Simple would very much like to know something about tours of the District Officer for he would get an impression that the District Officer of today is more tied to his desk than John Simple was. This is true in a way but those District Officers who are keen on touring still do it. It is not as if touring has gone into disuse even though tentage and horse have. District Officers in Uttar Pradesh tour fairly well and do a good job on tour for they look to the basic revenue and police administration, and also to the impact of development plans on the people in rural areas. Therefore, they come to know the general reputation for honesty and efficiency of officials of the various departments; they come to know what people think of governmental activities, particularly in the development field; they have an opportunity to verify where the resources mobilised for agricultural production have gone and to what use they have been put; on tour they can find out from the man himself what his views are about Government policies, what are his priorities and what is important to him. They can see progress of various departmental schemes, like reclamation of *Usar* and soil conservation. Most important, they can find out whether the schemes are being so run as to make the expenditure thereon worthwhile or they are merely white elephants damaging general economy. Practical difficulties on the spot can be found and resolved or brought to the notice of the Government. On tour the Collectors inspect the Tahsils and Thanas and a number of Government institutions, organizations, works and projects, John Simple will notice some changes. He would first see that the *abadi* (residence) of the Patwaris in their charges, on which he was so keen, is not strictly enforced now and quite a number of Patwaris are *ghair-abad.* He would also notice that there is not paid that detailed attention to the Patwaris' records as was in the past and that there is increase in the collection of statistics and figures even though they are not very reliable. But John Simple would recollect that in his time also he held the view that statistics and figures were not very reliable and that the best thing was to trust one's ears and eyes.

John Simple would also notice the absence of the landed gentry and the courtesy calls of the Zamindars, dressed in colourful clothes and sometimes carrying a sword. In their place he will find a number of visitors drawn from the masses of the people, Pradhans, members of the Block Committees and Zilla Parishad, representatives of the people, new local leaders, etc. He will observe that the Collector holds a larger and bigger number of meetings of villagers than in the Thirties and the women participate in large numbers. The Collector still holds successful meetings and is listened to respectfully. People of various political parties like to speak from his platform. The District Officer is still looked upon by the common village-folk as the embodiment or governmental authority and the head of the officialdom at the district level. They still put to the Collector on tour their difficulties in an honest and sincere way in the faith that they will get redress. John Simple, however, would also notice a number of individuals who meet the Collector seeking their own interest and sometimes not averse to trying to suborn the Collector to their way. As a matter of fact, the points of contact of the Collector with the villagers have increased in the Sixties owing to the implementation of the Community Development Programme in the villages. The villager now speaks to the Collector not only about revenue and police matters and general administration as in the past but also concerning the whole range of Community Development schemes. Here he has much to say and the Collector has much to listen to and much to do. It is satisfying that the relationship between the Collector and the villagers has deepened and widened. John Simple would be quick to notice that the villager now stands more erect than before and there is an element of demand in what he says rather than entreaty. He has become more assertive and the District Officer no longer works at and for a passive population but rather explains and satisfies the demands of an awakened peasantry no longer under the restrictive discipline of the local zamindars. The villager, however, still needs the protection of the district officials for the trouble now comes from a less responsible element, namely the village bullies.

John Simple would, however, miss the *Shikar* and notice that the Collector does not relax so much as in his days nor engages into physical exercises like the *Shikar* or horse-riding. In John Simple's time it was both "On Parade" and "Off Parade", but now it is only "On Parade".

III

John Simple would hear much about the establishment of the Welfare State in Uttar Pradesh, indeed in India, and will be a bit intrigued about it, as he will neither find a system of universal old-age pension nor free and compulsory education up to the age of 16, nor unemployment allowances nor full employment; he will also not find free medical services of a high order nor free dentistry, free provision of spectacles, nor free provision of vitamins. In 1947, it was often said that the Police State was ended and the Welfare State had come. In this was involved a double misconception. The Police State cannot be abolished, it must always remain; indeed the Welfare State is a super-structure built on the Police State; the super-structure would collapse if the foundation disappeared. Also a Welfare State is not established by a declaration. What happened in 1947 was that the objective was defined as a Welfare State and developmental activities were started in order to find the wherewithals with which to establish the Welfare State. If intentions were horses, everyone would ride. We are still in the process of producing and assembling the wherewithals through increased production of every commodity including food and consumer goods in order to bring about the Welfare State. At present we are in the midst of a developmental state in which the State machinery is actively sponsoring and promoting economic activities through the public sector. The Government has assumed many responsibilities in the economic and industrial field and these duties and functions are reflected in some way or the other at the district level and the District Officer is involved in them.

These developmental functions loom large in public view but they have not taken away from the Collector his basic responsibilities nor divested him of basic administrative duties. The basic structure of district administration remains unaltered; and even when it has undergone some changes, there has been no break from the past; the changes have a continuity about them. Indeed there has been a renewed emphasis on maintaining law and order and public peace and on collection of taxes. The Board of Revenue has re-emphasized the need of keeping the accounts in good order and improving the quality of land records. For some time law and other, collection of taxes, maintenance or records and disposal of cases were taken for granted. This attitude resulted in neglect of these subjects with the result that conditions deteriorated in these fields of administration. The role of the District Magistrate of late has again emerged prominent and he is today armed with more legal powers than his predecessor. John Simple will be quick to notice this. Collectors are busy improving land revenue and taccavi accounts; arrears of taxes have mounted up and from time to time Collectors are reminded to justify their designation of Collector by quickly collecting the arrears. Government and Commissioners of Divisions have reminded the Collector of the importance of looking to routine Revenue administration. The old values have been re-emphasized and in this field of basic administrative duties, the work of the Collector is now heavier and more difficult owing to democratic pressures.

John Simple would notice that the District Magistrate is armed with more legal powers and is, therefore, more powerful and that the Collector has become bigger than he was in his times. He has become a direct Collector of taxes employing an army of petty revenue Collectors and collecting taxes directly from the cultivators, without the intervention of Lambardars as in the days of John Simple. As a representative of the Government in the district also the Collector's personality has expanded. These days he writes to Government more often and hears from them from often. He comes in touch with more V.I.Ps. and more frequently than John Simple did; and he is consulted on a larger number of subjects, over a wider field than Government consulted John Simple. Thus as a District Magistrate, as a Collector and as a representative of the Government, the District Officer of the Sixties is bigger than he was in the Thirties.

IV

Seeing all this, the question that would arise in the mind of John Simple would be how does the Collector of a district in the Nineteen-Sixties manage to discharge all these duties and responsibilities. There are two answers: First, the Collector has been either relieve of some of his former duties or has ceased to take interest in some of them under the influence of changed conditions. Secondly, he is now assisted by a much bigger staff than in the Thirties. To take the first point first. The District Officer these days practically does no case work, neither original nor appellate, neither revenue nor criminal. He remains the head of the criminal administration of the district with control over the police and the Sub-Divisional Magistrates and exercises powers under the Cr.P.C. and other extraordinary criminal laws, but as regards the Criminal and Revenue case work this has been transferred to an Additional District Magistrate called A.D.M. (Judicial) who has under him a number of Judicial Officers with revenue and magisterial powers. All the cases under the I.P.C. and all the cases under Rent and Revenue Laws are now disposed of by this body of Judicial Officers. This body functions directly under the administrative control of the Commissioner of the Division. These officers are still available to the Collector for ordinary magisterial duties in times of emergency or on festivals, etc. The Sub-Divisional Magistrates and Sub-Divisional Officers function under the District Magistrate and the Collector but they mostly deal with cases under the Cr.P.C. and under some miscellaneous Criminal Acts and with Revenue cases under the Land Revenue Act and some other miscellaneous Revenue Acts.

The taking away of the case work from the District Officer has been a great blow to his position in the sense that now he does not know what is happening in a most important field of administration. He does not come to know how the Courts administering justice between parties are functioning, whether records are being promptly sent to courts, whether witnesses are produced and examined on days fixed and whether effect to decisions is given in records quickly. Administration of justice has a great impact on public life and by doing cases the Collector came to know many things concerning the life of the people and also the work and worth of the subordinate judicial officials. He is now deprived of this experience. The junior magistrate of the I.A.S. and P.C.S. have greatly suffered from this development. Particularly in the old days the junior officers of the All-India Service during their first five years did a lot of revenue and criminal case work, which gave them a very good training in the matter of weighing evidence and giving decisions; it gave them a good insight into the life of the people; it improved their personality, made their minds sharp and alert, engendered a spirit of listening to and following arguments; their minds were sharpened by the impact of facts and laws and they acquired a habit of hard work. All this training is gone. Dealing with cases and applications under the Land Revenue Act and miscellaneous criminal cases is no substitute for the old training.

In the changed circumstances the Collectors occupy themselves less with Municipal Boards and Notified Areas, etc. than they did in the past.

To come to the second point of staffing. Here John Simple would see a tremendous change. Let us take two districts, Kanpur and Fatehpur. The position regarding the strength of officers (including Judicial Officers) on the staff of the Collector at Kanpur and at Fatehpur is as follows:

	Kanpur		*Fatehpur*	
	Joint Magistrates & Deputy Collectors	*Judicial Officers*	*Deputy Collectors*	*Judicial Officers*
1965	19	11	7	3
1935	12	x	7	x
1925	11	x	7	x
1915	11	x	4	x
1905	6	x	3	x

The data will show the tremendous increase in the district staff that has taken place recently. "This has necessarily the effect of changing methods of work on the part of the Collector. He does less original work now than before. He more and more concentrates on making others work and on guiding and supervising them. The clerical staff of his office has also increased and the number of officials in the Tahsils has increased greatly, partly because of the method of direct collection of land revenue. The Collector in the Sixties cannot, therefore, minutely go into the inspection notes of the Supervision Kanungos or examine the Patwari records and Jinswars as meticulously as his forebears did thirty years ago; nor does he find time to devote enough attention to the scrutiny of statements showing disposal of cases by various courts. This used to be one of the big pre-occupations of his forbears thirty years ago. He also cannot find time to scrutinize in detail the various annual reports and other statements. He cannot go through many items of work as thoroughly as he would like and has necessarily to leave the administration of many matters to his subordinates. He cannot even find time to follow up the progress of various matters entrusted to the case of his subordinates.

It might be true in a sense to say that the District Officer in the Sixties tends to do less of original work and pays less attention to details of administration and to inspections but spends more of his time on making a large number of subordinates work, supervising their work in a general way, co-ordinating and integrating it, building up personnel at various levels, deciding plans and policies, smoothing up difficulties, seeking co-operation and participation of the people in various schemes in which this is very necessary, keeping up constant relationship with the public and looking to those aspects of the administration which brook no delay and which for some reason or the other must be dealt with at his level. Owing to force of changed circumstances sometimes he has to deal with certain matters of comparative unimportance at his level and leave other matters of basic importance to his subordinates. Today if he has to succeed, he must be a hard task master and must be a good leader of a large number of officials on his staff and a large number of officials indirectly associated with him. He has also to be a leader, to some extent, of the non-officials, particularly public workers and public representatives. He has to draw upon their energies, interest and resources not only to make developmental schemes successful but also to make administrative decisions acceptable to the people at large. The increase in the work of the District Officer is partly due to the fact that he has now to function under parliamentary system of Government where there is rigorous public accountability for everything done. But apart from this, administrative decisions have to be explained at various levels not only to the representatives of the people and their organizations but also to the individuals. Thus the face of the District Magistrate is not the same as in the Thirties though the face is of the same man.

The size of a district makes no difference to the functions, duties and role of the Collector. Mirzapur district has the biggest area of 4,263.4 sq. miles with a population of 12,49,653 (1961 census) and Meerut district has the largest population of 27,12,960 with an area of 2,322.9 sq. miles. Rampur district has the smallest area of 916.7 sq. miles with a population of 7,01,537 and Uttar Kashi has the smallest population of 1,22,836 (1961 census). But these figures do not indicate much because a large area of a district may be uncultivated or under forest and mere population need not indicate the complexities or difficulties of administration. Some districts are difficult because of problems connected with natural calamities, floods, draught, and famine which are their regular features; other districts are difficult because of political reasons; some other districts have special problems of labour or ordinary crime and yet other districts have special schemes which require special attention. The nature of the work in a district remains basically the same and bigger the district bigger the staff. The Collector's position, however, is the same in every district. Thus a picture of the District Collector of a U.P. district in the Nineteen-Sixties emerges somewhat as follows: His basic functions remain all the same, indeed in some ways they have become bigger and more complex. Thus John Simple would see that it is not only the label on the bottle which remains the same but much of the wine inside remains the same as in his days. The quality and the flavour have changed only slightly with the passage of time. But on these basic duties are super-imposed several other duties which result from the assumption by Government of many new functions, secondly, from a parliamentary system of Government, thirdly, from a greater association of the public with administration at the district level and, fourthly, from the adoption of the scheme of planned development. The Collector still remains in the centre of things at the district level, wielding considerable powers and influence. Generalizations are misleading but it might be stated that as compared to a Collector in the Thirties the Collector in the Sixties has more powers, though less prestige. The Collector in the Thirties had less legal powers but more prestige. The Collector in the Sixties does not possess "iqbal" as he is not an agent of an Imperial Ruling Power but he possesses something else which can be more potent weapon in his hand. He has power to influence people in his district and, therefore, he gathers considerable authority to carry through various schemes. The Collector remains the kingpin of district administration today as in the past and indeed as in the past so at present no civil servant has so many opportunities over such a wide field as the Collector of a district has to serve the people in his charge. And John Simple would find another thing in common, but is the Collector neither gets nor expects any reward or decoration. As in the days of John Simple so today, the greatest reward of the Collector is when people in his district identify themselves and their interests with him and call him "Hamara Collector".

V

The Collector of a district was firmly established for a long time as the chief administrator of a district but immediately after 1947 his position became somewhat difficult. There was a feeling that in the past the Collector had been unresponsive to public feelings and views, that he did not maintain contacts with people and that all that he was doing was sitting away and giving decisions in a detached and impartial manner. He was not emotionally involved with the hopes of the people and that the Collector should be associated with a number of bodies set up at the district level and consisting of the representatives of the people. These bodies should advise the Collector how to exercise his functions in certain fields. While much valuable advice and assistance came, at times the Collector was torn between factions. His functions increased and impinged on public life more and more including trade and commerce. With this, complaints of corruption grew and this made the administration more vulnerable to public criticism and a demand that there should be even more association with public bodies. At this very time the Divisional Commissioners, who had been friends, philosophers and guides of their Collectors and to whom the Collector had turned in difficulties and who had eased out pressures both at the public and governmental levels and re-inforced the views of the Collector with the Government, were reduced in number and divested of administrative powers. The small number of Divisional Commissioners that remained were virtually judicial officers and no more. This period did not last very long and while advisory committees remained and the emphasis on the Collector and the district administration being responsive to public opinion was maintained, the Collector was given more and more effective powers and many of the local bodies became merely advisory. In the Nineteen-Sixties the Collector's position in his district is pretty strong and while he consults the people and various committees, the prevailing picture is that responsibility for taking action rests on him. The Divisional Commissioners have also come back into their old form and from them he seeks guidance and with them he discusses his difficulties. As a matter of fact, the relations of the District Collector with his Divisional Commissioner are today closer than at any time in the past. The Commissioner of the Division co-ordiantes and pushes forward all developmental work at the divisional level, and all his authority and powers in this connection are available to his Collectors. He also visits the districts more frequently than he did thirty years ago and the opportunities which offer to the Collector to seek his advice and assistance are many more now than in the past.

The interesting question that arises in this connection is whether the District Collector is to be a permanent feature of the Indian administration or he should fade out in due course, yielding place to a network of representative bodies of the people who would effectively and impartially discharge carious administrative functions and public business which today are the concern of the District Collector. Everyone would wish that some time or the other the people should manage their own affairs and these be not left to a single officer of the type of the District Officer. If the Panchayati Raj becomes a success, it should logically lead to the gradual fading away of the District Officer. As people's representatives gather experience in the art of administration, they would displace the District Collector, who however efficient and impartial is not an elected person, even though he may be responsible to a higher elected body, namely, the State Government. If the democratic set-up is to enlarge itself in order to comprehend the various levels of administration, then the Collector must go. On the other hand, if the Panchayati Raj fails and the people responsible for running it prove inadequate to discharge the duties and responsibilities entrusted to them, then it is likely that the District Collector will remain firm in his position, for stability and effectiveness are the indispensable needs of any administration. Let us hope then that the Collector of a U.P. district in the Sixties is functioning only to efface himself in due course, yielding place to an elected council. But in the meantime let him function well. He is an instrument which has been found suitable for administration whether the instrument is wielded by an Empire or a Republic. In fact, he is something more. The Collector is not an individual officer. He is an institution.

> "A Collector should be to his district what a captain is to a ship: he should possess qualifications of command, control, personal influence, and acquirements of science. If one is fully acquainted with the duties of the ship, from the sweeper to the astronomical calculations of the pilot who directs the course, the other should be equally intimate with the dealings of the lowest ryot and the whole internal management of the village, of the effects likely to be produced upon it by any measure of political economy directed by government. If the ship is safely conducted or the district scientifically ruled, the means or application of labour is scarcely a subject of legislative enactment."
>
> — *Board of Commissioners for Bihar and Benares, 1822.*

9

The Evolution of the Office of Collector (1770-1947)

B.B. MISRA

"In India whoever regulates the assessment of the land, really holds in his hand the mainspring of the country."[1] Sir Thomas Munro, a distinguished Madras Civilian, who made this observation on the basis of his own experience as a settlement officer, finally showed the way, and the business of the office of Collector which had under the Cornwallis Code been limited to mere revenue matters, extended to everything affecting the welfare of the people. He became the chief executive officer, the ruler and governor of his district, representing within his jurisdiction the might of Government, and responsible not merely for the collection of revenue, but the interpretation and execution of Government policy as a whole. The object of this article is briefly to narrate the story and to analyse the causes of this change.

THE MUGHAL HERITAGE

According to the constitution of the Mughal Government the collection of revenue was vested in an officer called Amalguzar or Amil. He was the chief revenue officer of a district called Sarkar. In the collection and management of Government revenue his duty was to encourage the raiyats to bring waste lands into cultivation and to take all such measures as he deemed necessary for the promotion of agriculture and the protection of peasants either against natural calamities or the oppressive conduct of groups and individuals. In the discharge of his duty the Amalguzar exercised a certain degree of judicial authority in the settlement of disputed claims and actions arising in the course of assessment and, under certain circumstances, performed a limited executive function, especially on the breakdown of law and order. He was, however, neither a judicial officer nor the Chief Executive Officer of the Sarkar. While the civil judicial function of Government in the district vested in the *Qazi* and the *Mir Adl*, its main executive function remained with the Faujdar, a police magistrate, who maintained a contingent of armed force (*fauj*) and assisted other departments of his district in the execution of their respective duties. The author of the *Seir Mutaqherin* says that "in cases of emergency the Nazim (Provincial Governor) or ultimately the Emperor himself sent troops under his general or royal princes who came to the help of the Faujdar on information being sent for the same and law and order maintained."[2] The Faujdar could thus report directly to the Central Government in times of emergency and seek its assistance in the restoration of peace.

This, however, constituted the official organ of district administration under the Mughals. There was in addition a non-official organ consisting either of village communities of joint proprietors, or government "assignees" and zamindars whose local influence had either obscured or altogether obliterated the rights of such communities. During the vigour of the Mughal Government both the organs worked together in harmony, the latter being subordinated to the former. Like the Faujdar the Zamindars maintained their own zamindari force which secured the peace of the zamindari areas of the Empire and occasionally helped the Emperor in his wars.[3] The land servants of the ancient militia operating either under a village community or a zamindar constituted an agency of both collection and policing. In the exercise of his faujdari jurisdiction a zamindar, for instance, was "subject to a Faujdar who had the superintendence of a district comprehending many zamindaris and had the thanas or inferior stations under the charge of officers and armed men dependent on him, besides a part of the land servants of each zamindari, the rest being employed to guard the villages and enforce the collections. It was the zamindar's duty to give constant intelligence to the nawab (governor) and to assist the Faujdar in the apprehension of robbers and in executing the measures which were required of him for preserving the peace of the country; but this duty first and immediately belonged to the Faujdar, who was the representative of the nazim, and to him the people looked up for justice and protection against their chiefs."[4]

In the Mughal system of district administration, therefore, the District Revenue Officer did not hold a dominant position. The reason was that the local community or the zamindar who was rooted in it was associated with the discharge of two of the most important functions of the state, the collection of revenue and the maintenance of law and order. Together they did most of the collections and in addition kept the peace of the country as a subordinate instrument of the Faujdar who had the superintendence of district administration as a whole without any immediate responsibility for the collections. The whole system was based on custom and consensus, not on any legal definition of rights and obligations. But it worked well so long as the Central Government of the Mughals remained intact.

The political instability which followed the disintegration of the Mughal rule had its first impact on the administration of the districts where the non-official organ, because of its local knowledge and influence, became more powerful and superseded the regular machinery of administration. Even Amils or regular revenue officers of Government whose posts had under the later Mughals become hereditary, followed the examples of zamindars and farmers of revenue. Like them, they stipulated to pay a definite amount to Government and made no scruple to rack-rent the tenants whenever they found that they could not otherwise pay the stipulated sum. Faujdars were likewise invested with revenue function. The collection of revenue had in fact come to be the only concern of Government, and those who engaged to pay the revenues, were left in the exercise of judicial function also, the policing of the rural areas being already in the hands of those who did the collections.

It was in this state that the East India Company obtained in 1765 the diwani (civil administration) of Bengal, Bihar and Orissa. In practice, however, the Company did not take over the whole of civil administration. Its interest was limited to the superintendence of the collections and disposal of the revenue. "We were", wrote Clive, "under the necessity of drawing the earliest advantages from our acquisition of the Duannee. Our army was to be paid, our investment to be made, and the China market to be supplied. To trust these collections, therefore, upon which our credit and security depended, to the management of the Company's servants, totally unacquainted with the business, would have been a dangerous, and at this time would have been termed a criminal, experiment."[5] Clive, therefore, confided in the old officers of the nawab's government and endeavoured to attract them and others to his government "by ties of interest, until experience should render their assistance less necessary".[6]

By far the most serious of the administrative problems which confronted the early English Government, was to reconstitute into sizeable units of administration the districts which had disintegrated into what became known as *chaklas* and *tahsils*, each consisting of a number of the old revenue units of parganas, the size of which was determined by the extent of the influence of the "assignee" who held it. A no less difficult problem was to find able, honest and experienced men of the covenanted service precisely to ascertain the revenue resources of the districts and to superintend their administration in its totality. This was a task which, in spite of competent men being available, could not be accomplished so long as private individuals like zamindars and farmers of revenue as well as public officers continued arrogating to themselves functions which in law did not belong to them. The task was both political and administrative in nature. It involved change in the political constitution of the English Company as well as a re-organization of administration in the districts on a uniform principle. On account of its lead in territorial acquisition Bengal set the norm in the re-organization of the district administration, and the other parts of India adopted it with such modifications as their local conditions required.

ORIGIN AND DEVELOPMENT UNDER THE EAST INDIA COMPANY

Appointment of Supervisors

Administratively speaking, the Company's first experiment in Bengal was the appointment of covenanted servants as Supervisors. In 1769-70 they were appointed to the several existing districts of the diwani provinces. In addition to the general history of the landholders and ancient rulers of the district under their charge, they were required under their instrument of instructions to report on "the state, produce and capacity of the lands"; on "the amount of revenues, the cesses, or arbitrary taxes, and of all demands whatsoever which are made on the rayots either by government, zamindars or collectors (*amils*), with the manner of collecting them, and the gradual rise of every new impost". They were likewise asked to look into the state of justice and to summon Qazis and Brahmans to ascertain whether they possessed any *sanad* from Government authorizing them to administer it. They were also to see that native judges maintained proper registers of cases tried and settled by them. Their instrument of instructions made it clear that within the limits of their charge they were not only to be concerned with the collections, but to have a general knowledge of all that affected the districts.[7] The plan of supervision, however, failed. The Supervisors were for the most part untrained and inexperienced. And although some of them interposed their authority to ensure justice, their interposition remained ineffective because their powers were limited to reporting and their functions were in the main exploratory. Besides, their appointment excited the suspicion of the zamindars, farmers and native officers of revenue and justice who would not readily lend their co-operation except on their own terms.

Creation of the Office of the Collector

It was in these circumstances that in a letter of August 28, 1771, the Court of Directors expressed its determination to "stand forth as diwan" and to take over through the agency of the Company's covenanted servants the entire executive management of the public revenues. Accordingly, Warren Hastings and his Council at Fort William issued on May 11,1772, a general proclamation, and three days later nominated the Supervisors as Collectors, vesting them with the executive powers of management and collection of revenue in addition to the previous duties of enquiry and investigation. The office of the Collector of today was thus for the first time created by the Government of Warren Hastings on May 14, 1772.

The functions attached to the office of Collector, however, exceeded those of his Mughal counterpart, the Amalguzar. The jurisdiction of the former extended not only to cases arising from revenue or rent, but also to the title suits which under the Mughal system fell to the competence of separate judicial officers. The European Collector actually presided in each of the Company's civil courts established in the districts reconstituted in 1772. A criminal court was likewise established in every reconstituted district, and although criminal matters still formed no part of the Company's government, the administration of criminal justice became subject to Collector's supervision and control. He was to see that justice was impartially administered according to the evidence examined and the proofs exhibited in the course of trial.

Recall of Collectors

A reaction soon set in against the appointment of Collectors authorized as representatives of Government to make the settlement with any body on such terms as the Government itself dictated. It affected the interest specially of such of the zamindars as were real proprietors; for any rejection of the terms given to them by a Collector resulted in the loss of their zamindari settled with the highest bidder. The zamindars as a class became disaffected. The Court of Directors, on the other hand, was guided by motives of commercial gains which they found impaired by a sudden increase in civil expenditure without a corresponding increase in the collections.[8] In 1773, it, therefore, ordered the recall of Collectors from the districts,[9] although instead of being removed to Calcutta, they were allowed to remain at the headquarters of six of the divisions into which the districts of the diwani provinces were grouped, with a provincial council established at each of these headquarters. Administrative considerations, however, dictated the expediency of gradually removing one district after another from the control of the provincial councils and placing them under the control of separate Collectors exercising both revenue and judicial powers, especially in the frontier districts. In 1781 the provincial councils themselves were abolished and the collections centralized at Calcutta in a Committee of Revenue which in 1786 was re-organized as the Board of Revenue. The districts had by 1781 thus come to be administered by the Company's Collectors. But the confusion of policy created by their recall in 1773 remained. In March, 1780, Warren Hastings had, in the meantime, drawn a line of distinction between the two types of civil suits arising from two distinct sources of revenue as well as real and personal property, the former being left to Collector while the latter entrusted to separate Civil Judges of the covenanted service. The Faujdars were finally abolished in 1781 and their duties and powers transferred to the covenanted English Magistrates acting primarily as Judges of Civil Courts first established in 1780. But the question as to who should preside over the administration of the districts and what should be his powers remained unsettled.

In his administrative reforms Warren Hastings had ruled out innovations. He believed that the established forms of the diwani provinces were not only best calculated to expedite the despatch of business, but also best adapted to the understandings of the people. His aim was generally to maintain the prevailing and known forms of administration and to deviate from them only where they had been deprived of effectiveness.[10] It was the prevailing forms as well as his desire to impart effectiveness that led him to combine powers in the office of Collector, a principle of district administration which the Bengal Government adopted in 1786-87 after a considerable period of trial and error. An important cause of this deviation from the Mughal constitution was the commercial character of the company with its emphasis on the civil authority being invested with control over the military. It also proceeded from the policy of the state increasingly to interpose through its official agency and to reduce the extent of private participation in the collection and management of the public revenues as well in the administration of justice. The encroachment of law upon custom had thus begun and with it the need for centralization.

The person who came out openly in support of combining powers in the office of Collector was John Shore, a hard working, honest and able Bengal civilian who later became the first President of the Board of Revenue and then rose to the position of Governor-General in 1793. In a note of January 13, 1782, Shore recommended that the system of 1772 should be restored and that a Company's covenanted servant should be appointed to each district as Collector exercising both revenue and judicial functions. He was guided in his recommendations by two main considerations, administrative and political. Administratively speaking, Shore had no confidence in the ability and honesty of the indigenous agency through which revenue accounts passed in the several districts. "The simplest matters of fact", he complained "are designedly covered with a veil through which no human understanding can penetrate."[11] Politically, the integration of the Company's territories, especially in the outlying parts of the country, was of paramount importance. "It is the part of a wise government", Shore pointed out, "to provide against all contingencies, we ought not therefore to rely upon the peaceable nature of the natives or on a supposed attachment to us, but establish such a control in all parts of the country that in case of a foreign invasion...or of the inroads of an eastern enemy or in the event of a rebellion in any of our provinces the payment of the revenues may not be suspended, illicit correspondence or dangerous confederacies may be checked and the contagion of rebellion stifled."[12] Shore thus thought in terms of Collector being invested with such duties and powers as were under the Mughals exercised by the Amalguzar, the Faujdar and the officers of justice taken together. He was to be the sole governor of the district, locally responsible for the execution of Government policy in all its details.

The continuance of war with the country powers, the confusion caused by the earlier orders of the Court of Directors, and the uncertainty of Hastings' own tenure of office, however, delayed the whole thing, and Shore's plan remained in a state of proposal until 1786-87 when both the magistracy and the duties of Civil Judge were united in the office of Collector. The Court of Directors now justified this combination of powers on the ground of simplicity, efficiency and speed. Here again the prevailing practice of the provinces supplied the cue, not the original constitution of the Mughal Government where as said before, the interference of law was minimal and the chief executive officer of the district had no revenue or judicial function.

Reduction in the Collector's Powers

The immediate cause which had led Shore to recommend a concentration of powers in the office of Collector was, basically speaking, the unsettled state of land revenue. It was realized that the revenue resources of the districts could not be ascertained except by investing Collector with sufficient powers to carry on investigation even against any combination of zamindars. But the position changed under Cornwallis in 1793, when from poilitical and other motives, he settled the land revenue in perpetuity with them or persons of their description without ascertaining the rights of the several classes engaged in agriculture. The case for a union of functions lost much of its force; for the exigencies of adjusting disputed claims which might otherwise have necessitated such union during the progress of settlement operations, ceased to exist where the entire responsibility of determining rights to property was on the principle of separation of powers entrusted to regular civil courts, Collector being considered directly or indirectly involved as a party representing Government in revenue matters. The reforms of 1793 in fact divested Collector of even that part of the judicial authority which proceeded from his connection with the control and management of the revenue. The determination of both revenue and title suits was transferred to the Civil Judge of the district who was also to act as magistrate. Instead of Collector, the Judge-Magistrate thus became the chief executive officer of the district.

Revision of the Cornwallis System

Though consistent with the strict principles of equity and justice, the system established in 1793 was a failure in practice. The permanent settlement resulted in a considerable increase of litigation; for it necessitated resort to judicial action as the only means to have the respective rights of zamindars and tenants duly ascertained. The transfer of revenue suits to judges added to their burden still more. Then came the difficulties arising from the incompatible union of the magistracy in their own office. "The duties of judge", wrote the Marquis of Hastings, "necessarily confine him to his court house. The duties of a magistrate can perhaps never be so properly executed as while he is engaged in a personal visit to every part of the district. The administration of civil justice requires the patient and cool deliberation of mature age. The preservation of the peace of a district calls for all the active energy of early youth. A judge should perhaps be abstracted from all private converse with the natives. A magistrate must maintain a most intimate communication with them and carry his researches into the most in most recesses of their privacy. Justice should be blind, but police requires the eyes of Argus."[13] The combination of these two diverse functions in the same person thus prejudiced the administration of both. It, therefore, necessitated by 1812 the restoration of certain old powers of Collector and the appointment of separate magistrates and joint magistrates, vested with judicial authority to punish crimes within certain limits, a function which did not belong to their Mughal predecessor, the Faujdar.

The urgency of revising Cornwallis' system by uniting the magistracy with the office of Collector and investing the latter with a measure of judicial authority in revenue matters, however, arose in the ceded and conquered districts of the North-Western Provinces, where in the very first decade of their acquisition the lands of a numerous class of joint village proprietors had been alienated by the collusive conduct of revenue farmers and court officials. They did it by illegal manipulations of fictitious balances and public sales to meet fraudulent claims of revenue. All these happened because the Collector had been deprived of his opportunity of mass contact previously maintained through the exercise of judicial authority in the determination of revenue suits. Several of the cases of fraudulent transfers and the consequent ruin of a large number of joint proprietors come to light in the course of a local enquiry made by Holt Mackenize, a leading Bengal Civilian. On the basis of his recommendations the idea of a permanent settlement of the Bengal type was finally rejected and a Special Commission was constituted under Regulation I of 1821, to investigate all cases of abusive alienations as well as to determine suits for the recovery of the lands so alienated during 1801-10. This was an open challenge to the principle on which the Code of 1793 had been founded. The Judges of the Sadar Court naturally opposed the measure, for they took a purely legal view of the whole thing, and the social injustice arising from a large-scale alienation of landed property formed no part of their consideration. The Government, however, enacted the measure in spite of that opposition, and finally decided to form the settlement only for a period, and that too after determining the respective rights of all such classes as engaged in agriculture. Consistently with this change in land policy, the Government passed at the instance of Holt Mackenzie himself a resolution on August 1, 1822. It was designed to enable Collector to conduct his enquiries on the spot, "village by village, proceeding upwards from the persons who till the ground to the Government itself, noticing distinctly all the classes who share in the produce or rent of the land, the extent of the interest of each, and the nature of the title by which it is held."[14]

To secure the execution of this policy the Governor-General in

Council enacted Regulation VII of 1822 which restored on a wide scale the judicial authority of Collector and other revenue officers to hear and determine suits, claims and actions arising in the course of settlement proceedings.[15] Their decision in such cases was to remain in force so long as it was not proved to be wrong on a regular suit brought to determine the question of title in a civil court. Lord William Bentinck created under Regulation IX of 1833 a cadre of Deputy Collectors to assist the Collector in the execution of this new policy.

As for the magistracy, it remained tagged on to the office of Civil Judge, for the influence of Cornwallis had become so deep-rooted that any radical deviation from the basic principle of his system was more or less regarded as an act of heresy. The person who effectually acted against that tradition was again Holt Mackenzie himself. As a member of the Civil Finance Committee appointed by Lord Bentinck in 1828 to suggest administrative reforms Mackenzie recorded a minute on October 1, 1830, where he asked the Government to provide in the administration of the districts "the completest possible unity of purpose throughout all the departments, and in all their grades", by making the office of Collector "a sufficiently strong connecting link", an object which he wished to accomplish by uniting in that office magisterial, revenue and certain limited judicial functions. "In a word", he said, "to disjoin the several parts of government in a country, which is not self-governed, is like placing the different members of the body in charge of different physicians, severally acting with their respective limbs according to individual theory, without reference to the treatment of other parts, and each holding in his hand the power of destroying life, but helpless to save, from the blunders of his brethren."[16]

Mackenzie thus looked upon district administration as a unified whole and Collector as its chief controller, especially in the unsettled districts where any act of indiscretion on the part of Government servants had the tendency most seriously to affect the interest of society, touching at every point the properties and institutions of the people. What he wanted, therefore, was that responsibility for the administration of the district as a whole must vest with one officer, the Collector whose business it should be to ensure "unity of action in the different branches", not the execution of details in any one of them; for, as he clearly pointed out, "real control is not exercised through a busy intermeddling with the details of individual cases, and the efficiency of a ruler is to be measured not by what he does, but by what he causes to be done".[17]

From a close perusal of the whole of his minute it appears that although there were financial reasons also to justify his proposed union of the magistracy with the office of Collector, Mackenzie's main emphasis was to secure by a combination of powers unity of purpose and action which he considered necessary to secure the execution of the State's extended function of defining and recording the rights and obligations of agricultural classes. It is true that his proposed combination of powers was based on the assumption that "all the civil servants of the Company are or will be men of fair capacity and character, fully qualified to discharge, after a sufficient course of service, the duties which attach to the Collectors and Magistrates of districts."[18] But that was altogether a different question. It involved problems of education and training of civil servants for which adequate provision was soon to be made by a Parliamentary Act. His emphasis on increasing the powers of Collector remained; for he clearly pointed out that if a district happened to be too large or populous for the Collector-Magistrate to manage, it was necessary that the district should be divided, not that his functions should be separated. Bentinck's reforms of 1831 proceeded on this principle. The magistracy was united with the office of Collector who once again became the chief administrator of the district.[19]

The whole trend of administrative reforms in the course of about twenty-five years prior to 1833 was in fact to strengthen the office of Collector on one hand and to provide for the inspection of that office in the exercise of its extended powers on the other. It was precisely for a proper discharge of the latter function of inspection that the Governor-General in Council appointed under Regulation I of 1929. Divisional Commissioners, so that they might watch the conduct of Collectors locally within a limited jurisdiction of four to five districts. In fact, the extension of the Collector's responsibility and the provision for the local inspection of the district offices both proceeded from the increasing activity of the state to secure private property on one hand and to promote the revenue resources of Government on the other.

Madras made no provision for Divisional Commissioners. The Presidency was divided into districts, each under a Collector who was responsible immediately to a Board of Revenue constituted in 1786. As the average size of the districts in Madras was larger than elsewhere, the Collectors there were in 1792 assigned Covenanted Assistants, with fixed territorial jurisdiction being attached to them under the designation of Head Assistant or Sub-Collector. These jurisdictions consisted of taluks, each taluk being under an Indian revenue officer called tahsildar.

The duties, powers and codes of conduct of Collector were laid down by the Madras Regulation I of 1803, modelled more or less on the same lines as the Bengal Regulation II of 1793, divesting the Collector of his judicial powers and uniting the magistracy with the office of Civil Judge. But as the main system of land revenue in Madras was raiyatwari, the Collector there exercised a degree of executive authority and the Board of Revenue a degree of supervision and control which their counterparts in the Lower Provinces of Bengal hardly ever did. Under the influence of Sir Thomas Munro, a great supporter of the raiyatwari system, the Governor-in-Council re-invested village officials with civil criminal jurisdiction and restored to Collectors their magisterial powers and supervision over the police. The separation of the magistracy and police from the office of Civil Judge and their reunion with the office of Collector was by far the most important of the reforms effected in 1816, and although Bengal had under Hastings led the way, it was Munro who first shook the foundation of the Cornwallis system and influenced the course of administrative reforms in the districts of the North Western Provinces.

In Bombay, the British system of district administration was organized on the final defeat of the Marathas in 1818. Under the Marathas a district constituted the charge of an officer called mamlatdar. What the English did in 1818 was to reconstitute the jurisdictions of a number of mamlatdars into what they called a zillah and placed each such zillah under the charge of a European Collector who was to be a covenanted civil servant. This was the arrangement introduced in Bombay by Mountstuart Elphinstone who was the first to form the settlement of the Deccan and Khandesh. By placing a European Collector over a number of mamlatdars Elphinstone preserved, from political motives, the practice of the Maratha government without impairing the authority of the British. The mamlatdar became reduced to the position of a tahsildar and his jurisdiction to that of a taluk of

Madras. The system so introduced in Bombay differed but little from that of Bengal except that the former created no Board of Revenue and that its Collector exercised in the course of his raiyatwari settlement a measure of executive and judicial authority which his counterpart in the Lower Provinces of Bengal never possessed. In 1827, the Bombay Code defined the duties and powers of Collector in respect of assessment and collection; invested him with the powers of magistrate, and in addition authorized him to decide certain civil suits and to try claims of exemption from the payment of land revenue.

By 1833, therefore, the Collector had in most cases become magistrate also. In the exercise of his magisterial and criminal judicial function his determinations were, however, subject to review by the Sessions Court established in 1831-32. Lord Auckland obtained in 1837 the sanction of the Court of Directors gradually to separate the magistracy from the office of Collector, the object being to enable the Collectors in the unsettled districts to concentrate on the completion of the survey and settlement operations. Its result, however, was that on account of a Magistrate's salary being lower than that of a Collector the magistracy fell into the hands of junior civil servants. This affected law and order and impaired the quality of criminal justice. Legislative provisions were made in 1843 for the appointment of uncovenanted Deputy Magistrates. But that did not improve the situation. In the light of the experiences of the Mutiny the offices of Magistrate and Collector were reunited on a general plan throughout the country in 1859. The mass contact acquired by the Collector in the management of revenue and the promotion of agriculture was considered conducive to the maintenance of law and order also. The union of the two offices so effected in Collector has, therefore, remained unchanged ever since. As District Magistrate the Collector was authorized under the Criminal Procedure Code to have control over the District Superintendent of Police. He could administer criminal justice and punish to a maximum limit of two years and a fine amounting to one thousand rupees. He could commit prisoners for trial to the Sessions Court and call for any of the criminal files from the court of another Magistrate. In short, he became the guardian of law and order in the district.

In the non-regulation province like the Punjab, for instance, the position of Collector was even much stronger. Each of its districts was placed under an executive officer called Deputy

Commissioner, the counterpart of Collector in the regulation provinces. He combined in his office not only revenue and magisterial functions, but the duties of civil as well as criminal judge also. He exercised these powers without his action being subject to any appeal to a separate judiciary the district.

THE COLLECTOR UNDER THE BRITISH CROWN (1) PERIOD: 1858-1919

New Tasks

The period of fifty years that followed the Indian Mutiny was one of peace, and the problems of Collector arose not from internal disquiet or external invasion, but from the expansion of the State activity, such as municipal and local bodies, roads and railways, commerce and industry, education and statistics, agriculture and co-operation, cadastral surveys and census operations, epidemics and famine reliefs. Of these, the exigencies of recurrent famine specially threw up a serious challenge. It called for a review of the executive administration, more especially of the districts, to see if the office of Collector could deliver the goods without any radical modification of structure and statutory function.

Of the provinces of India, Bengal alone was found wanting in reliable means of. contact with the rural population. In between the districts and villages there were in Madras and Bombay smaller units of executive administration called taluks, administered respectively by a tahsildar and mamlatdar. There were corresponding units of revenue jurisdiction called tahsils in the North-Western Provinces and the Punjab, each placed under a tahsildar who, like his counter-part in Madras and Bombay, had grown within the framework of indigenous institutions, performing revenue, magisterial and police duties and acting as a local executive agency of Collector at the district headquarters. There was no such subordinate revenue jurisdiction in Bengal. There were police darogas created by Cornwallis in 1792 in place of zamindars. But they were mere police officers. They had no revenue duties to perform, nor could they act as Magistrate exercising a certain degree of executive and judicial function. Above all, police darogas were a British creation. They had not grown indigenously.

The Police Committee appointed by the Governor of Bengal, under W.W. Bird, had in its report of 1838, suggested the creation of subordinate magisterial jurisdictions to bring the protective machinery of Government nearer to the people.[20] The proposed sub-divisional magistrates were to be placed under junior covenanted servants as Assistant Magistrates, or under uncovenanted Deputy Magistrates specially created, for the purpose, or, according to a suggestion of the Finance Committee (1842), under Deputy Collectors vested with magisterial powers. The Government finally decided under Act XV of 1843, to create Deputy Magistrates, and on the receipt of the orders of the Court of Directors in 1844[21] actually sanctioned on an experimental basis the creation of sixteen sub-divisional officers in Bengal, each consisting of four to five thanas.[22] By 1856, the number increased to thirty-three. But as this was still too small a number to secure any effective rural administration, F. J. Halliday, then Lieutenant Governor of Bengal, proposed to raise that number to a hundred. But his proposal remained shelved for a time; for it was feared that the extension of the sub-divisional system might be a potential danger to the authority of the District Officer—the keynote of the district system. Then came the Police Act of 1861 which actually reduced his authority by constituting the police into a separate department, distinct from the magistracy. The net result was that by 1866, the year of the Orissa famine, the Bengal sub-divisions remained in size twice as big as the tahsils or taluks. And above all, their function was purely magisterial. It did not extend to revenue, the real means of contact with the people.

Another serious drawback in the administration of Bengal was that in spite of the suggestions made by Holt Mackenzie in 1830 the Collector-Magistrate had continued to be immediately responsible for the administration of other departments operating in the district under the control of their departmental chiefs at the provincial headquarters. All these departmental chiefs, such as the Inspectors-General of several departments and the Director of Public Instruction, acted as so many masters of Collector, with the Divisional Commissioner functioning as their local superintending authority. The District Officers were in fact acting as "drudges of so many departments and masters of none." Even so, they would not like to part with any of these.

Then there used to be frequent transfers arising from the promotion of an executive officer from Collector to Judge, from Judge to Commissioner, and so backwards and forwards between executive and judicial departments, in a way which seriously affected efficiency and rendered long experience in any department almost impossible.[23] *The Bengal Administration Report* (1871-72) thus pointed out that only six Collectors in the whole of the regulation province of Bengal had been in-charge of their respective districts for full two years, and two out of these six for four years.

Campbell's Reforms

These defects were brought to light by the Orissa Famine Commission (1866-68), with Sir George Campbell, an eminent civil servant, as its Chairman. As the Chairman of the Commission Campbell made a number of recommendations which he himself implemented as the Lieutenant Governor of Bengal in 1872-73. He increased the number of sub-divisions, placed each of them under a covenanted servant or Deputy Magistrate, with extended authority and function, and created a new subordinate cadre of Sub-Deputy Collector who like a tahsildar might be deputed to rural areas for a variety of executive purposes. To enable civil servants to acquire experience of specialized departments, Campbell introduced what he called the system of Parallel Lines of Promotion under which a civil servant instead of being almost of necessity changed from the executive to the judicial line and *vice versa* at every frequently recurring step of promotion was to be invited after some years' service to choose one line or the other, and having once chosen was ordinarily to be kept to that line. This was a principle of administrative organization which applied to the separation of the judicial branch of the civil service; but it was so flexible that its operation might, if necessary, be extended to other branches where with appropriate education and training a civil servant could acquire equal proficiency required in the conduct of his business. So far as Collector's relations with "special departments" were concerned, Campbell made the chiefs of those departments the "agents and inspectors on the part of the Government, bound to aid, consul and guide local officers, each in his own department, without exercising absolute authority over them, and to criticize, collate and compare local facts for the information and guidance of the Government". The Collector, on the other hand, was to exercise as the head of the district "the general controlling authority over all departments in each district".[24] The object of this arrangement was to free the District Officer from the departmental responsibilities vested now in their separate local officers, and to limit his function to general administration and control over the various departments. Campbell's aim was in fact to separate the technical functions of the Government from the general and yet to vest in the generalist a degree of controlling authority necessary for co-ordination and unity of action. The Collector continued to report on local departments. But his report was to be of general nature indicating whether or not local departments functioned according to Government policy.

A question arose whether in view of the urgency of relief operations the magistracy could be divested of its criminal judicial duties. Sir J.F. Stephen, the Law Member of the Government of India, tried to answer the question in a minute he recorded on the administration of justice at the time Sir George Campbell was introducing his reforms to impart speed and efficiency in the execution of the extended and positive functions of the State. Though inclined to consider the expediency of relieving such Magistrates of judicial duties as engaged in relief operations, Stephen; like Campbell, strongly held that so far as the Collector was concerned, he must under all circumstances remain vested with all the powers of Magistrate, for he was for all practical purposes "the Government" within the limits of his charge, and he must continue to be so through the exercise of his criminal jurisdiction, "the most distinctive and most easily and generally recognized mark of sovereign power".[25]

Famine Commission's Views

The Indian Famine Commission (1880) which looked into: the state of rural administration, held a similar view about the office of Collector. It pointed out that a system which was best suited to the requirements of the country in ordinary times might as well "conduce to efficiency in times of distress". What was needed was to supplement it "by such special aid as the temporary urgency of each case may demand", *e.g.*, the extension of the sub-divisional system, tours in rural areas for at least four months a year, and promotion on the basis of pure merit and achievement. But the sub-division of work arising from increase in the load of public business should on no account be allowed to withdraw from Collector that general control which "invests him in the eyes of the people with the position of the local head of the civil government. His time should not be occupied with the details of magisterial, police, revenue, fiscal, or any other business to a degree which will deter him from watching the effect produced on the people by the operations of all the departments of Government. The Collector...should administer details chiefly through his assistants".[26]

Historically, therefore, the Collector, with the exception of certain breaks in the earlier period, did continue to be in the sole executive charge of the district. From the 1880 onwards there gradually developed a socio-political force which acted in two main directions administrative and political, expressing itself in the form of a growing Indian demand for the separation of the executive and criminal judicial functions on one hand and for the extension of self-governing institutions on the other. This tended to weaken the powers of Collector, or in fact, of the bureaucracy as a whole who believed that while the union of functions was necessary for a society susceptible to sudden violence from-caste and religious motivations, the extent of political progress must be in keeping with the degree of educational advancement. Such eminent Home Secretaries as Hewitt, Ibbetson and Risley, who served under Lord Curzon, followed the arguments of Sir James Stephen and rejected after a thorough examination the demand for the separation of executive and judicial functions. The private collections of the Viceroys and the Secretaries of State, on the other hand, contain several letters indicating that although able, honest and hard working, the bureaucracy as a class failed signally to lookout of the window and to scan the political weather which changed from time to time according to the emergence of new forces in society. There was in fact imbalance noticeable on both sides. While the bureaucracy emphasized administrative efficiency, the Indian leadership concentrated on political demand. Dyarchy was in these circumstances of mutual suspicion introduced in 1921, with the centre of political gravity being slowly shifted in favour of the latter.

(2) PERIOD : 1919-47

Problems of Democratic Confrontation

The Collector who came to preside over district administration during the period had new problems to face. With the growth of revolutionary and revivalist nationalism political acts of violence became more and more broad-based, and in spite of the efforts of Mahatma Gandhi to bridge the traditional gap between Hindus and Muhammadans there began in the wake of the khilafat and the non-cooperation movements a period of communal disturbances that broke all previous records. There appeared at the same time a new economic force arising from the growth of industrial workers and landless peasants. It was a secular force, based on the Marxist concept of class war and led in the beginning by the Communists who emerged as a threat to the political authority established by law in the country. Then there was the prospect of a responsible self-government in India held out for the first time by the famous policy statement of August 20, 1917 and the subsequent constitutional progress made in keeping with that statement. This acted in two ways. In the first place, it caused awakening among the socially, depressed and backward classes, which expressed itself in caste rivalry and occasional caste riots. Secondly, the ruling bureaucracy tended to become racially oriented; for the policy of progressive Indianization of the Civil Service produced a sense of insecurity among European members who formed a separate. Association of their, own, and vied with the Association of the Indian members of the superior services. Professionalism was thus being recast into racism. A cumulative effect of all these was to weaken the legal foundations, of authority. For the popular forces were emerging as an alternative to British Government and dislocating loyalties without themselves being in law yet recognized as entitle exercise of sovereign power.

The most serious of the pre-occupations of the Collector-Magistrate during this period was the question of law and order. He was naturally armed with new powers either in the form of legislative amendments of the Cr. P. C., or of the Ordinances and the Defence of India Rules.

Pre-occupations with the problems of political crimes and communal disturbances operated as a serious check to the progress of the "nation building" departments transferred for the first time to the control of Indian Ministers under the Government of India Act (1919). But there were other factors which explained why the I.C.S: men who had the charge of the districts and were for the most part Europeans in the earlier part of this period, remained by and large indifferent to the administration of such "transferred" subjects as education and agriculture, medical and public health, industry and local self-government. It is not that they were under the Act not responsible for the administration of these departments. They were to look after both the "reserved" and the "transferred" subjects. What happened was that in the administration of the latter, the knowledge of experienced European officers went unutilized. The Reports of the Local Governments on the working of the Reformed Constitution (1924) pointed out that hitherto the motive power which made progress possible came from above, especially from the European officers. But the Reforms Scheme meant definitely that this was to cease and that the impulse to improvement, if it came at all, must come from the educated Indian, particularly his elected representative and the Minister who, however, did not have the knowledge or experience to enable him to use his opportunities to the fullest extent. In view of the constant political agitation on a racial basis the European member of Civil Service lost much of his incentive to constructive effort, more especially when he had no assurance that what he did for the improvement of development departments would not be reversed. Moreover, he had no longer the same powers to carry through improvements. Before any of his schemes could be accepted he was now required to convince different sets of critics in the Legislative Council, guided not by the quality of the schemes submitted for approval, but by considerations of caste and group interests in the Council. The Chief Secretary to the Government of Bihar, for instance, complained that this tendency was specially marked in the Settlement Department, and that so far as the Local Self-Government was concerned, the District Officer was practically excluded after the introduction of the Reforms.[27]

Moreover, in making appointments, a popular Ministry was for the most part guided by considerations of caste and individual interest, not of merit and efficiency. This generally led to caste and religious rivalry. While this developed between Bhumihars and Kayasthas in Bihar, it went on between Brahmans and non-

Brahmans in Madras and Bombay, and between Hindus and Muhammadans in Bengal and the Punjab. The exercise of patronage was naturally vitiated. These factors contributed to corruption, delay and inefficiency in the administration of the self-governing institutions.[28] The Collector could not help it. He remained a passive onlooker.

After the passing of the Government of India Act (1935), the position of Collector perhaps became worse; for the *Report of the Bengal Administration Enquiry Committee* (1944-45) said, "the present position is, in our judgement, thoroughly unsatisfactory, both from the point of view of the District Officer himself as well as from the point of view of efficiency of the Government machine and the welfare of the people in the District. ... He is expected to see that nothing goes wrong in his District, but he has little power outside the Magistrate and Collector field to see that things go right.... He can cajole and persuade: he cannot compel. He is regarded as responsible for stimulating the activities of the officers of other Departments, but he has no real control over them, and, though they are under an obligation to keep him informed of their activities, the extent to which this obligation is discharged depends in most cases on the personal factor."[29]

There was another handicap, especially in Bengal where for a century and a half there had been no revenue staff providing "representatives of Government right down into the villages with a hierarchy of superior staff through kanungos, naib tahsildars and tahsildars right up to the district headquarters." Circle officers, it is true, were appointed under the recommendations of the Bengal Administrative Committee (1913-1914). But their jurisdiction was large and their number small. The assistance they afforded to Collector remained, therefore, inadequate. So far as Bihar was concerned, nothing of the kind had been done before 1956 when circle officers were, for the first time, appointed on the basis of a scheme formulated by Shri L.P. Singh, then Chief Secretary to the Government of Bihar. They united in their office both revenue and development functions.

The weakness of Collector arose yet in another way. After the abolition of most of the All-India Services under the recommendations of the Lee Commission (1924), there rapidly grew a tendency on the part of every department to think in terms of a "Provincialized Service". This tendency bred a spirit of departmental independence prejudicial to the work of co-ordination in the district under a single administrative head. Then, with the advancement of science and technology, there arose a problem of how best to work out mechanisms and techniques of technological and administrative co-ordination. Here too the tendency was to assert an independence arising from the growth of specialization and expertness. The Rowlands Committee examined these problems in some detail and emphasized the need to restore the powers of Collector for the purposes of co-ordination. Some of the departments actually regarded this proposal as "revolutionary". In reply, the Committee quoted Campbell and pointed out that its emphasis on strengthening the hands of Collector was "merely a restoration of the position established by Sir George Campbell in 1872", a position which recognized the Collector as "the real executive chief and administrator... supreme over everyone and everything except the proceedings of the Courts of Justice".[30] The expediency of "restoration" and greater "delegation of authority" to the District Officer in fact arose from a policy of planned development introduced in 1944. The Committee realized that the local status and prestige of the Collector-Magistrate was by far the highest in the eyes of the people and that it was desirable to utilize this position and harness it to the work of development.[31]

According to the proposals of the Rowlands Committee, 'therefore, the functional plans of a province were to be turned into district plans by the District Officer as the undisputed head of all other Government agencies operating in the district. He was to decide *what* was to be done, *where* it was to be done, and *when* it was to be done. The technical officer, on the other hand, was to suggest *how* a particular project was to be carried out. Here too the District Officer could modify the methods of execution suggested by a technical officer, so that the development of the entire district might proceed as a combined operation. The technical officer was in fact to be the direct subordinate of the District Officer; but while the former was to correspond direct with the head of his own technical department, the latter was to report to the Chief Secretary on the progress of each part of a plan. Under this arrangement the administration of the beneficent welfare activities of the state was thus to remain united with the coercive functions of a police and a tax gatherer. The Committee realized that it might in future be necessary "to hive off development activities from those of law and order" and "to transfer to the separate Development Officer powers now vested in the District Officer as Magistrate and Collector".[32] But this did by no means signify that the Collector would then cease to be the sole representative of Government in the district.

Though historically consistent, these proposals took little or no account of people's participation in the activities of their own direct interest. The Committee suggested administrative improvements at the provincial and district levels. It dealt with the problems of personnel: management of bribery and corruption, of training and recruitment, of financial control and service conditions. But, so far as the problem of securing popular participation in development activities was concerned, the Committee did not go beyond making a few suggestions; about the existing municipalities, district and union boards. Of the total number of 140 pages covered by the Report the "Local Self-Governing Bodies", for instance, could claim not more than 2½ pages.

CONCLUSION

Democracy and specialization were in fact two of the important factors which in the; post-Independence period tended to affect the power and prestige of the District Officer. The disruptive force of specialization has not yet been formally recognized. But the general pattern of reforms that proceeded in the various states, followed, by and large, the principle of the recommendations made by the Rowlands Committee in regard to the office of Collector,"and in addition supplied its inadequacy by enacting measures to create the Panchayati Raj institutions as an instrument to secure popular participation in development activities. The object was to provide for political security on one hand and extended field for education and training in democracy on the other. But since a spirit of mutual understanding and psychological re-adjustment is still lacking on the part of both the District Officer and the elected representatives of society, the dichotomy between the two continues. While history favours the former politics lends support to the latter. If democracy is to survive, both must learn to live together in peace and harmony. The elected leaders of the community must show respect for law, while the Collector for the electorate as the ultimate source of sovereign power. If the country is to remain politically integrated, it is the Collector, not the elected head of a representative council, who is to be ultimately responsible for the administration of the district. That is a lesson which we must not omit to learn from history.

> "The District Officer has many executive duties, of which it is impossible to give a complete list, for they vary from place to place and from season to season".... "And when government has evolved some scheme for benefiting the people, he will be requested first to advise upon it, and in due course, to put it in operation. In times of stress, the burden of his responsibilities becomes well-nigh intolerable."...Whatever, the trouble may be, the District Officer must see to it. In the old Roman formula, he must take care that the state suffer no harm. He must prevent the trouble, if he can if he cannot, then he must alleviate it, or quell it, or pacify it. He may divide the work, but he cannot divide the responsibility. That is his."

REFERENCES

1. *Selections from Revenue Records of the N.W. Provinces,* Allahabad, 1873, iii, p. 65.
2. Saiyid Ghulam Hussain Khan, *Seir Mutaqherin* (English Translation), Vol. III, Calcutta, pp. 178-79.
3. *See* Edward Thomas, The *Chronicles of the Pathan Kings of Delhi,* London, 1871, pp. 431-32.
4. G.W. Forrest, *Selections from the State Papers of the Governor-General, Warren Hastings,* Vol. II, Oxford, 1910, ii, p. 454.
5. Clive to Court, 29 Sept., 1765, I.O. Mss. Eur. E. 12, p. 79.
6. *Ibid.,* pp. 76-77.
7. *See* H. Verelst, *View of the Rise, Progress and Present State of the English Government in Bengal,* London, 1772, appx. pp. 227-39.
8. *See* 3rd Report from the Committee of Secrecy (1773), Parl. Branch Coll 7, p. 61; *also* B.B. Misra, *Central Administration of the East India Company,* 1773-1834, Manchester, 1959, p. 178.
9. I.O. Home Misc. 351, p. 15 (7 April, 1773).
10. *See* 7th Rep. Committee of Secrecy (1773), p. 346a.
11. I.O. Bengal Rev. Cons., 18 May, 1785, p. 400.
12. I.O. Bengal Rev. Cons., 18 May, 1785, pp. 393-94.

13. *Minute of the Marquis of Hastings*, 2 Oct., 1815, para 96.
14. I.O. Bengal Rev. Cons. 1 Aug. 1822, No. 64, para 20.
15. *See* SS. 11-18, Reg. VII, 1822.
16. Pare Papers, House of Lords, No. 445 of 1853, p. 136, paras. 6-7.
17. *Ibid.*, p. 137, para 9.
18. *Ibid.*, p. 135, para 3.
19. The office of Magistrate was first transferred to Collector in 1823 in three of the frontier districts of Rangpur, Ramgarh and Jangal Mahals (*See* I.O. Home Misc. 530, pp. 771-74). The arrangement extended to several other districts in 1831 (*See* Judicial letter from Bengal, 6 Sept., 1831, v, pp. 130-31).
20. *See, Report of the Bengal Police Committee*, 18 Aug. 1838 (Legislative Proceedings, 1 July, 1842, No. 5).
21. Legislative Letter from the Court of Directors, No. 20, 21 Aug., 1844.
22. Home (Judicial) Progs. 15 Feb., 1845, Nos. 9-11.
23. *See* Home (Pub.) Cons., March 28, 1868, No. 49, p. 87.
24. See Campbell's proposals on administrative reforms. Home (Public) Cons. 28 March, 1868, No. 149.
25. *Selections from the Records of the Government of India*, I.O. Records Dept. No. 10001 (89), pp. 29-30.
26. *See, Report of the Indian Famine Commission*, 1880, chap. ii, pp. 101-4.
27. *See, Reports of Local Government on the Working of the Reformed Constitution*, 1924. I.O. Cmd. 2361 of 1925, p. 187, paras 26-27.
28. Chief Secretary, Bombay, to Government of India, No. 4206.C, of 19 July, 1927. *See, Views of Local Governments on the Working of the Reforms* (1927), p. 117. *See* also Par. Papers, Cmd. 2361 and 2362 of 1925.
29. Para. 65. Sir Archibald Rowlands was the Chairman of the Committee.
30. *Ibid.*, para 70.
31. *Ibid.*, para 69.
32. *Ibid.*, para 91.

10

Politico-Administrative Base of Indian Field Administration

HARIDWAR RAI

PATTERNS OF FIELD ADMINISTRATION

The District Officer system is a form of field administration possessing those attributes which are the hallmark of what is called the prefectoral system.[1] It has been regarded as a species of the prefectoral genus, involving transfer of authority to regional agents empowering them to exercise overall responsibility for most or all governmental functions in their areas on behalf of the central executive. As the authority is *deconcentrated*, the regional officials have no powers of their own and the regional administration has no separate existence. It is simply a mechanism whereby the central authority does things *locally* through general representatives instead of doing everything at headquarters or doing it in the field through a host of public functionaries, all directly controlled from headquarters. In practice, of course, a certain amount of discretion may be given to these general regional agents, but they are liable to orders and direction from above and are responsible to their superiors for everything they do. This form of field administration is integrated in that the regional representative of the central executive is also charged with overseeing the activities of almost all public officials working in the area and is, therefore, contrasted with what is called the functional form of field administration. In the latter, public officials of the central executive stationed in the area belong to separate functional hierarchies entrusted with different aspects of government policy. There is no single general representative of government in the field, the lines of command run directly from the ministries to the field agents, the latter being responsible to their departmental heads at headquarters.[2]

The District Officer system makes for and emphasizes the concentration of government powers in the regional representative, making him the coordinator and supervisor in the field and the main channel of communication between technical field officials and headquarters. In the functional system, on the other hand, the control of the central executive tends to be more dispersed and less stringent and technical services tend to choose differing sets of areas rather than a common area for almost all governmental operations. The questions which merit our attention in this article are: What political motivations and imperial considerations were at work which actuated the British to establish the District Officer system? How could it ultimately crystallize, after a protracted ideological debate, into the key unit of field administration even in Bengal in the years following the upheavals of 1857? What administrative ideology and circumstances accounted for the variations, in the first-half of the nineteenth century, in the pattern of district administration–a three-fold typology, as it were,–the Bengal-Cornwallis pattern, the Madras-Munro-Elphinstone pattern, and the Punjab-Lawrence-non-regulation pattern? Such questions, as the following, which come up in the course of discussion also deserve attention and evoke intellectual curiosity: Was this system in keeping with the cultural background and the administrative-governmental traditions of this country? Or, was it only a contrivance for consolidating and reinforcing the British domination over a colonized country, inhabited by a people antipathetic and even hostile to the regime? Though the main theme of our discussion comes to an end with the adoption in Bengal of a variant of the Munro pattern in the wake of the 'Mutiny', the article makes a passing reference to later developments also.

FIRST EXPERIMENTS IN FIELD ADMINISTRATION: INHERITANCE VERSUS INNOVATION

Bengal was the first nursery of British colonial bureaucracy in India, inasmuch as it was here that the setting of British administrative policy was laid at the foundations of the British dominion. In the early years of their territorial acquisitions, the dilemma that faced them was how to rule without revealing that the British had neither the capacity nor the manpower to operate an administration. But having 'stood forth' as diwan in 1772, they discovered that the 'dual system' of government and the policy of expediency must give way to a definite government decision on the form and nature of government-administrative organization to be adopted in respect of Indian territories. Another dilemma which confronted them now was: To what extent the government organization should be anglicized? Should the British behave as inheritors or innovators? Warren Hastings, who had a big hand in shaping the foundations of British Government and administration in India, was not in favour of outright anglicization. He tended to draw, in his ventures of state-building, upon the British experience in some areas of Bengal and to combine the same with the traditions of the Mughal Government in the past. He sought "to reconcile native prejudices and custom with the exercise of alien domination"[3] and yet insisted that the organization and structure of administration must be intended to achieve the following imperial objects:

(1) "To implant the authority of the Company and the sovereignty of Great Britain in the constitution of the country."
(2) "To abolish all secret influences and make the Government itself responsible for all measures by making them all pass by its avowed authority."
(3) "To remove all impediments which prevented the complaints of the people from reaching the ears of the Supreme Administration or established an independent despotism in its agents."[4]

In consonance with these objects, as also in view of his "emotional prejudice" in favour of "Preserving Indian Society", "collectors of revenue" were appointed in 1772 to assume responsibility to direct collection of revenue. Henceforth, the District Collector became the fundamental feature of the Indian field administration, symbolizing "the transformation of the company into a regular administrative organization.".[5] The District Collector was soon invested with civil and judicial jurisdictions and police powers and the district became a geographical entity under the control and supervision of the collector on political and administrative grounds, which were embodied in the celebrated minute of John Shore. He said:

> "It is the part of a wise government to provide against all contingencies. We ought not therefore to rely upon the peaceable disposition of the native...but *establish such a control in all parts of the country* that in case of a foreign invasion...or in the event of a *rebellion* in any of our provinces, the *payment of our revenues* may not be suspended, illicit correspondence or dangerous confederacies may be checked and the contagion of rebellion stifled."[6]

Besides these weighty considerations, Shore had little confidence in the efficiency and honesty of the *indigenous agency* through which the accounts of revenue had to pass in several districts. These views were shared by another able administrator of the Company, Stuart, who questioned the desirability of centralization of revenue administration at headquarters and recommended that a covenanted servant vested with revenue and judicial powers be appointed to every district with full powers to manage its revenue.[7] The home authorities, too, in Britain realized that the firmness and vigour of the 'European character' would be helpful not only in the collection of the revenue in the most economical way, but also in *strengthening the executive,* facilitating the access to justice, keeping a watchful eye on the principal landholders, *guarding against the intrigues* of *foreigners* and *supporting the sovereignty of the Company*. The home authorities further instructed that the offices of revenue and justice be combined in the person of the collector, as the union would be compatible with "*the subsisting manners* and usages of the people". This they believed "will tend more to *simplicity, energy, justice* and economy."[8]

In pursuance of these instructions, the administration of revenue, civil justice and magistracy was united in the District Collector in 1787. It was a step towards deconcentration, leading to the definite establishment of district as a field unit of revenue and judicial administration and making the collector head of administration in his area, or the District Officer, as he subsequently came to be styled. Ever since, the district, as a territorial unit of administration with the collector representing the unified and integrated local executive and responsible for efficient administration of his charge to government, had remained the basis of Indian administration.[9] This system is based on the belief that "the real work of the revenue must be carried out by trusted officers on the spot".[10]

The duties enjoined upon the District Officer were many and varied and the powers conferred upon him were extensive.[11] He collected the revenue, administered civil justice and supervised the police and the jails. He sent several reports to government on "such varied matters as the state of crops, the quantity of grain likely to be available for export, the prices of different kinds of grain, the number of soldiers confined to hospital and their complaints, the number of people killed by tigers and the number eaten by alligators, the state of roads, bunds and bridges, the number of European inhabitants, their families..."[12] He had to draw up elaborate balance sheets of revenue and expenditure and maintain accounts for the purchase of candle, medicine, ink, pen, etc. In the words of Aspinall:

> "The District Officers had to see to the widespread publication of government publicationzs; to pay out rewards for killing tigers; to undertake extensive tours, to facilitate the dispatch of mails...and in time of war to supervise the movements of all European foreigners. Every morning he had to listen to the petitions of innumerable suitors and to make a written record of his decisions; a business which might take three hours. He solemnized European marriages and officiated at funerals, since hardly any district headquarters possessed a clergyman."[13]

The District Officer was an immensely powerful local functionary, acting on behalf of and representing the entire executive machinery in the district. All threads of control in the district passed through his hands, and he was virtually uncontrolled on account of vast distances between the seat of government and the district. Indeed, he was a 'semi-absolute monarch', ruling over a territory as extensive in area and population as Wales or Scotland and, in the name of restoring the Mughal tradition of absolutism, he was made solely responsible for the general well-being of the hundred of thousands of people in his charge. This was what the British regarded as the 'native model', quite in tune with what they believed were administrative and governmental traditions of this country.[14] This system of field administration was also comparable to the system of intendant of the 18th century France. The intendant was an official appointed by and responsible to the Central Government and was absolute in his own area.[15] Aspinall has observed:

> "In the time of Cornwallis, the District Officer enjoyed greater authority than the collector today, for until 1793 his powers were very inadequately limited by Government Regulations; there were no telegraphs nor railways to bring him effectively under the control of the Central Executive; the specialization of function which came to be so important a feature of British Administration had not begun; and local self-government through the agency of municipal councils and District Boards which had limited the Collector's responsibility and weakened his authority were then unknown."[16]

THE BENGAL PATTERN: THE UNINTEGRATED DISTRICT OFFICER SYSTEM

But the system of integrated district administration which enjoined upon and enabled the local executive official to play so large and impressive a part, was not favoured by a school of administrative reformers pioneered by Cornwallis: Cornwallis was a Whig and was, on principle, opposed to the concentration of executive and judicial powers in the hands of the District Officer.[17] He was, therefore, against the integrated system as it implied a perpetuation of what he regarded as the personal, authoritarian tradition of 'oriental' government. One of the essential bases of his system was on the contrary, that the executive should be separated from the judiciary and that the executive should itself be subjected to the rule of law. This looked like a 'revolutionary', modernistic measure and implied transplantation of English political concepts into the soil of India. To quote Eric Stokes:

> "He saw in the Company's adoption of Asian despotism the source of every ill. To him the essence of the problem was to limit governmental power and so prevent its abuse. Thus while he confirmed and extended the English administration, taking over criminal justice from the control of the Nawab and firmly

establishing the system of district administration, he was all the time concerned to limit its power."[18]

This became the *anglicized* version of the Indian field administration and came to be dignified by the name of the "Cornwallis system" or the "Bengal system" of district administration in contrast with the integrated system of district administration which was evolved in territories and provinces subsequently acquired by the British in the first two decades of the nineteenth century.[19] Nevertheless, in a way, the Bengal pattern remained the model and the 'parent' of the rival patterns that were adopted in different parts of India, for the district staff, the collector and his assistants—by whatever other titles they may be locally known—existed on the model, and with many of the characteristics, of the original instituion.[20]

With the promulgation of the Bengal Code of 1793, the District Officer and, for the matter of that, all executive officers were not only divested of judicial power but were also made amenable to the courts of judicature for their acts. The revenue and judicial functions were separated and placed in different hands. The former was assigned to the collector, and general administration, police and civil and criminal (judicial) administration were vested in the judge-magistrate. The collector ceased to be an all-powerful discretionary official, and became a mere collector of fixed public dues, being reduced to what his name implied, namely, a mere fiscal agent. He was given no political or magisterial authority; the great figure in the district became the district judge-magistrate.[21]

Thus, the unitary character of district administration was demolished. No single representative of government was left in the field endowed with sufficient authority and power who would not only wait for the people to make complaints but would go to their villages to seek for complaints and grievances and redress them on the spot, as far as possible. As has been said:

> "Above all it destroyed the simple intelligibility of the Indian political tradition in which the *hakim* or ruler invariably bore the sword of justice in his person. By taking from the collector all judicial and police powers, the one visible representative of government was left powerless to punish crime and redress

wrong and by confiding the sole administration of justice to distant courts."[22]

The passive, dispersed and 'unintegrated' system of district administration, to use the category of Fried,[23] obviated the necessity of employing 'native' officials on a large scale even in subordinate grades. It was also incompatible with an extensive 'Indianization' of the revenue service and did not require that knowledge of the vernaculars and that intimate acquaintance with the habits and customs of the people which more direct and more periodic systems of revenue assessment did.[24] For instance, Regulation of 1787 in Madras required every collector to complete, exclusive of the official records, an account of the different parganas, noting the state of the population, cultivation, the conduct of the zamindars towards their tenants, the customs and usages and to transmit these accounts periodically to headquarters.[25] But under the Cornwallis system, revenue was to be paid diet into the district treasury; there was no attempt to register either the tenures and holdings of cultivators or changes in the ownership of lands. No motive remained, therefore, to induce the collector to study minutely rural tenures and conditions. *Kanungos*—the hereditary custodians of knowledge concerning the land—were abolished; and *Patwaris*—the village accountants—were declared to be merely private servants of the zamindars. *Tahsildars*—the time-honoured revenue officials—were similarly done away with in 1802. And, in this way the collector under the Bengal system of field administration was deprived of that infrastructure which Smith calls "eyes and ears".[26] All orders from headquarters to outlying parts of the district were transmitted through the corrupt and the oppressive police.[27]

THE MUNRO PATTERN: THE INTEGRATED DISTRICT OFFICER SYSTEM

The Bengal system of "cold and passive" district administration had established itself as "the orthodox pattern" by the first decade of the nineteenth century and had become "loaded with the dead weight of a tradition".[28] Meanwhile, other patterns of district administration based on different systems of land revenue administration with different conception of the role of the collector and other revenue functionaries and as a rival to and perhaps a reaction against the Bengal system were emerging. Among these, the Munro system also known as the Madras system of district administration grounded in the *ryotwari* system of land revenue was the first and also the most important to pose as alternative to the Bengal system.[29] It sought to challenge the 'innovation' and 'anglicization' characteristics of the Bengal system.[30] Even the Select Committee of the House of Commons in its fifth report, on the authority of Munro, questioned publicly the principle of the permanent assessment of the revenues and favoured the *ryotwari* system and it was ultimately decided in 1814 that Munro's view of governing India must be put into effect.[31]

As a pragmatist in politics and administration, Munro was opposed to what he called 'fanciful theories' and was against 'disturbing' the ancient customs, as they appeared to him to prevail under the rule of the 'Moghul dynasty'. "Under the Moghul rule", he observed, "the officer to whom was committed the charge of administering the revenue in every district was...vested, throughout the district, with extensive judicial authority." It was the business of that officer, as Munro understood it, to hear and to determine all disputes arising out of the land-tax and to defend the *ryots* against the tyranny of his own officers. He was equally impressed by 'regularly constituted municipalities' (Panchayats) in Indian villages, which administered both their revenue and police matters, and exercised, to a considerable extent, magisterial and judicial authority in all matters, private as well as public. He further saw that at the head of every village "in the provinces subject to the presidency of Fort St. George, were the *potail* and the *curnum*, the former being to his own village at once a magistrate and a collector, the latter a sort of notary or public accountant. Under them, again, the *talliars* or village police, consisting of a body of hereditary watchmen...And, similar to this was the organization of large tracts of country embracing forty or hundred villages. At the head of each...was a zamindar or *poligar*, *tehsidar* or *amildar*, who received the revenue from the *potails*, exercised an authority over them, and was to his district, in almost every respect, what the *potail* was to his village".[32]

Whereas the Bengal pattern of district administration was characterized by an absence of native rural officials and village institutions, Munro sought to authorize the village panchayats "to hear and determine disputes". He decided to empower the *patel* or head of the village, to do "the function of the commissioner within his village" with limited powers in petty civil and criminal cases, appoint new grades of Indian "native judges" with largely extended jurisdiction, and limit the right of appeal from the lower courts. "We should give the natives", he said, "village and district courts suited rather to the present state of society...than to our ideas of what such courts ought to be..." and emphasized that "the natives themselves are the best judges of what is suited to their condition".[33]

The collector was the centre of the Munro system of field administration and the custodial of all intelligence for use of the government, because it was from him "chiefly that the government must derive its own information".[34] In his view, experience was the only real training for the collector; day-to-day work among the Indians was worth more than "the study of all the Regulations and Codes of Calcutta and Madras together."[35] He bitterly complained that "no exertion" was required from the Bengal collector, which made him indolent. The collector, to him, was the only channel through which government could obtain any tolerably correct information on the resources of the district and it was chiefly from his opinions that their own opinion might be formed. He sincerely deplored:

> "...if the affairs of the district fall into confusion, he cannot put them right, because, as he has not made himself acquainted with the revenue details and local usages and he has no practical experience, he is ignorant of the cause of disorder, and of the means by which it is to be remedied."[36]

He advocated a completely unified system of district administration: "there must be one authority in a district; the authority to be efficient must be single, and the collector will best uphold his own by maintaining that of his Tahsildars."[37] And this system of integrated administration could be built up only when the office of the "Zilla Magistrate", "the superintendence of the village and Zilla Police", and the power to decide cases of disputed boundaries, were transferred to the collector.[38] He suggested "the transfer of the police and magisterial duties from the Zilla judge to the Collector", because all the rest were subordinate to and dependent upon this.

The superiority of the Madras collector over his Bengal counterpart emanated not only from the fact of union of executive and criminal judicial powers in his hands, but also from the fact of the bigger size of the Madras district, which was large enough to be split into sub-divisions (taluks) under sub-collectors. Besides, the organization of the Madras district was "personal" and "semi-military" in character and stood in contrast to the "impersonal administrative system of Bengal". And, above all, "the Madras collector was answerable directly to the Board of Revenue at the seat of government, while in Bengal three provincial Boards of Revenue interposed, exercising an impersonal control by correspondence rather than relying on personal inspection and direct command." [39]

THE DECCAN PATTERN: THE PROTOTYPE AND EXTENSION OF THE MUNRO SYSTEM

A prototype of the Munro system of integrated direct administration was fostered and developed by Mountstuart Elphinstone in the Bombay Presidency. By the beginning of the nineteenth century, the territorial possessions of the Bombay Government had expanded considerably. The final downfall of the Peshawa in 1818 gave the Company an enormous addition of territory, which included certain parts of Gujarat, the whole of the Deccan except the small kingdom reserved for the Raja of Satara, the whole of Khandesh, and the district of Dharwar, including Belgaum, Ratnagiri and Kolaba. The same year, Elphinstone received his appointment as Commissioner for the settlement of the Deccan. The pattern of administration he devised in the Deccan is known as the 'Deccan System'.[40]

In his formative years, Elphinstone had been influenced by Munro and his ideas of field administration, and had, therefore, imbibed an unfavourable opinion of the Bengal system.[41] He not only sought Munro's advice "in day-to-day problems of administration, but also studied his published writings with attention".[42] With such a background of intellectual association with the integrationistic school of administration coupled with his own pragmatism and his preference for being "taught by time",

Elphinstone thought it his first duty to preserve as much as possible of the existing system of administration, not of course as being the ideally best, but as the best under all the circumstances and for the time.[43] He, like Munro, sought to steer clear of "innovations" and "regulations". "My employment", he wrote to a friend, "is very humble. It is to learn which system is in force and to preserve it unimpaired...I shall think I have done a great service to this country if I can prevent people making laws for it until they see whether it want them."[44]

In devising his system of field administration, he was cautious lest the effects of the new order of things should be upsetting. He was aware that some changes were likely to take place in spite of all efforts to prevent them. But he wanted them to be cushioned and went so far as to block the efforts of the Governor of Bombay to assume the administration of the Deccan and to introduce a programme of innovations.[45] Though conscious that the village community was probably not compatible with a good form of government, he instructed his subordinates to utilize existing village institutions, as fully as possible, and, accordingly, tried to preserve Maratha judicial institutions, especially village panchayats. Though not particularly enamoured of the *ryotwari* system of revenue, he insisted on the maintenance of existing peasant rights in land. Thus, the problem before him was how to reconcile the two sets of ideas—*the ideas of paternalism* and those of *utilitarianism*—in his administrative system.[46]

His main object, so far as the revenue system was concerned, was to preserve, as far as possible, unimpaired the practice of the Maratha Government in the Deccan, subject, however, to the abolition of farming the revenue, the levy of assessment according to the area actually cultivated, and the imposition of new taxes. The country which, in the days of the Peshawa, had been divided among many *mamlatdars* and *kamavisadars*, whose powers and territorial jurisdiction varied greatly in extent, was now placed under the five principal British regional officers, namely, the collectors of Poona, Khandesh, Ahmednagar, and the Carnatic and the political agent at Satara. He relied almost entirely on Munro's example for the administrative organization of the territories annexed to Bombay, adopting the *ryotwari* system of land settlement and the corresponding administrative structure which united the offices of magistrate and the revenue officer. He found that the maintenance of law and order, the collection of revenue and the administration of justice were closely interwoven into the fabric of Indian village life and, therefore, concluded that "any change in them might not merely change its texture but even tear it apart."[47]

He followed his own maxim: he relied "more upon the men whom he had chosen to be collectors than upon any comprehensive or detailed measures of policy." His conception of the collector was identical with "the classic idea of the collector of the Munro school...the man with wide discretionary powers, constantly travelling about his district, unhampered by forms and ceremonies, always and everywhere accessible to anyone with a complaint or petition."[48] All powers, except of capital punishment were vested in the collector, who was also magistrate, judge and head of the police. Every sentence of death had to be referred to the Deccan commissioner for confirmation before it was carried out. His instructions of July 1818 gave very wide powers to the collector in all judicial matters, authorizing the collector to modify the existing methods and institutions of justice as he saw it expedient to do so. The general aim always was to maintain the Maratha system where it was not repugnant to reason and equity. In practice, this implied that the collector could change without difficulty, the existing system as he deemed fit.[49] This system of field administration was unitary in character and the head of the district was the unquestioned representative of government in his area.

THE DELHI PATTERN: THE PRECURSOR OF THE NON-REGULATION SYSTEM

Yet another deviation from the Bengal system was the Delhi system, which like the Munro and the Deccan system allowed of no separation of powers and became, in a way, the precursor of the paternalistic non-regulation system.[50] Charles Metcalfe, as Resident of the Delhi territory from 1811 to 1819, built up his own system of revenue and judicial administration, though it was as Vice-President of Bentinck's Council that he "brought the gospel of paternalism to bear upon the administrative organization of the Bengal territories".[51]

Metcalfe's Delhi system is characterized as an "outcome of a chance and a discovery–the chance that exempted Delhi from the

Bengal Regulations, and his own discovery of the autonomous village system. The chance made it possible for him to exploit the discovery".[52] Its main principle lay in maintaining the old undisturbed, which virtually implied having no system as such. Like Munro and Elphinstone, he believed in strengthening old customs and institutions which, to him, were basic. Modifications in the old were to be matters of detail. He treated the whole Delhi territory as a *Suba,* of which he was the *Subedar*, the Governor. All his assistants were his *naibs*, and were assigned no definite territorial jurisdiction. Below the Resident and his assistants, authority came down straight to the *amil* or officer-in-charge of a *pargana* or sub-district. In British usage, the *pargana* became a tahsil and the *amil* a tahsildar.[53]

As regards the administration of justice, two courts–one each for criminal and civil justice—were established under the presidency of the Resident himself and his assistants. The assistant in-charge of the city criminal court was also superintendent of the city police. The question of civil justice in villages was largely concerned with disputes about land and, secondarily, about debts. Here, Metcalfe relied upon existing village panchayats. He did not establish district courts. The only innovation he made was an appeal to Delhi or to a touring magistrate. He detested "the Regulation judicial system and he and his school prevented its spread so far as they could".[54] The judicial scheme of the Delhi system was based:

> "...partly on the principle of a jury and partly on that of a panchayat: that is to say, the members were generally chosen on the nomination of the parties; but they were required to decide without delay; the matter in dispute was brought to a distinct issue and the whole proceedings were regularly recorded by a government clerk who was deputed for the purpose, with instructions to follow a prescribed course. The disputes were generally between communities of yeomen cultivating their own fields, for the possession of land generally of little value, but very easily contested by the people. The headmen of the contending villages, acting for and in the presence of the whole body, were require to nominate six on each side, making in the whole twelve. The right to challenge was freely allowed; and the jury (so to term it) was required to be unanimous."[55]

In Metcalfe's time, his assistants were not stationed in any one district, there being no smaller division of the Delhi territory, which he treated as one administrative unit—a district. The tours of the assistants of the country provided only spasmodic opportunities of appeal to the dissatisfied villager. These, however, were intended to act as correctives rather than as substitutes for village justice. This system, thus, became a precursor of the non-regulation system subsequently perfected in territories inhabited by wild or tribal people; its most important feature being:

> "He would have none of the Cornwallis' division of judicial from executive, he would have no one glued to his chair in court or office. The man who collected the revenue was also responsible for order, he was policeman, magistrate and judge."[56]

Metcalfe always favoured the union of executive and judicial functions in the hands of local officials. Even as a senior member of the Governor-General's Council, he deplored "the continued separation of the office of judge, magistrate and collector" and observed in a Minute:

> "...I should recommend, as...best suited to the character of our native subjects and best calculated to promote their happiness, the division of the country into small districts, in each of which an European officer should be superintendent, uniting all authorities in his own person and having under him native officers for the administration of the district in all its branches..."[57]

He believed that the best form of government, in the interest of the people was that which was "most simple and most free from artificial institutions". He also affirmed that the best form of government, in the interest of preserving British dominion, was that which was "most conducive to union of powers, and most free from the elements of collision and counteraction". The pattern of field administration he devised was military in form and personal in orientation; his vision of administration being that of a paternalist of a benevolent sort. He regarded Munro as his mentor and preceptor and sought to follow Munro's ideal of a society of farmers enjoying a freehold property right under the paternal care of the collector.

The collector was to embody and perpetuate in his person "the Indian tradition of personal government", and provide a focus for the ordinary instincts of loyalty. He was to be a kindly autocrat living among the people, acting from personal observation and experience and linked into a personal chain of command.

Munro, Elphinstone and Metcalfe were the three principal representatives of what may be called the patriarchal, unitary system of administration. They regarded the Cornwallis system as "a system of abstract principles inapplicable to India, as an impersonal bureaucracy instead of a personal, human and tangible form of government. Government conducted from the office rather than from the tent and the saddle, necessarily preceded by forms and precedents; and when its functions were kept confined to the operation of courts of justice and to the mere realization of the revenue its criterion on success was similarly limited to superficialities."[58] In contrast to this, the protagonists of the integrationistic school advocated an easily intelligible form of government and law, a government closest to the life of the people and most sympathetic to their indigenous institutions. Their view of government in the field has been thus summed up:

> "To the ryot, government must be represented simply; not by a multiplicity of officers and a multiplicity of written forms, but by a single officer, who had powers to enquire, to judge and to punish, without the delay and intricacies of the Western legal process. This officer was not to be a distant and awful figure, presiding in his cutchery like a deity in his temple, but a familiar lord, visiting and speaking with them of their quarrels and their crops, and looked up to as *ma-bap*, father and mother. In practical terms, this meant a union of powers, at least at the district level."[59]

THE BENGAL SYSTEM UNDER PRESSURE: A CONTINUING DEBATE ON THE FORM OF FIELD ADMINISTRATION

The Cornwallis system did not remain unaffected for long by the arguments and circumstances which accounted for the establishment of the integrated system of field administration. It was discovered by the authorities that, in the post-Cornwallis era, the district judge in a Bengal district had to bear a desperate judicial burden in view of the strict separation of judicial and executive functions. It was, therefore, decided that something positive should be done to relieve the district judge by empowering him to refer to the collector those cases of rent and revenue which involved any accounts.[60] This measure was the first intent into the citadel of the Cornwallis system and was an index to the commencement of a retransfer to the collector of judicial powers. In 1812, the powers of the collector were considerably increased in respect of suits and actions arising from the management of land revenue and the judge was obligated to refer all such cases to the collector for enquiry and report. Besides, by another measure passed in 1810, the government was empowered to appoint persons other that judges as magistrates. Meanwhile, the publication of the Fifth Report of the Select Committee in 1812, exposed the defects of the Bengal system and emphasized the desirability of a radical change. The argument in essence being:

> "The pressure on the civil courts dictated a resumption by the collector of his powers in civil justice: the difficulties found in administering criminal justice and in the regulation of the police demanded that the collector should once more have magisterial powers, and be responsible for the superintendence of the police. With the same object of improving the administration of justice, additional powers were to be given to Indian agents..."[61]

Thus, the mood and thinking of the home authorities ran counter to the spirit of the Cornwallis Code and seemed to be expressions of the general approbation of the Munro system of district administration. On the top of this, there occurred change of far-reaching importance in 1812, which considerably modified the plan of Cornwallis. The Governor-General in Council was empowered by a Regulation to invest the collectors of revenue with the powers of magistrates, and to entrust the magistrates with the power of collecting revenue.[62] The idea was to strengthen the hands of the collectors so that they might be able to collect the arrears of revenue expeditiously. The 'weaknesses' of the Bengal system were further exposed in view of the emergence of new ideas, such as liberalism, utilitarianism and humanism, which called for "a new view of the functions of government".[63] Meanwhile, a general belief was gaining ground that since serious breaches of the peace were mostly connected with land disputes, the combination of magisterial and revenue functions in the person of the collector would be most desirable, besides being in consonance with "the contemporary philosophy of liberalism which advocated functionalism on the one hand and centralism on the other."[64]

In the last years of the twenties of the nineteenth century, judicial and revenue administration in the districts of the Bengal Presidency was found to be in a bad way. There was a vast distance between the collectors in the districts and the Board of Revenue at the Presidency, which obstructed the flow of business and resulted in big accumulation of correspondence on matters of details. There was clearly no effective control over the district revenue administration, nor was there a coordinating authority, in the form of commissioner, to oversee the working of the judicial and revenue system as a whole. This situation called for a controlling authority resident in the vicinity[65] as also a unity of purpose and action in district administration. The rigid separation of judicial and revenue branches under the Cornwallis system, leaving no authority short of the supreme Government itself to coordinate their operations and supervise the system as a whole appeared to Bentinck, the Governor-General, and some important members[66] of his Council, to be a serious mistake in a *colonial* possession. Bentinck felt that the District Officer must combine the offices of the magistrate and the collector, so that he could have an authority in the district superior to all others. He was so much impressed by the Munro system of district administration that he urged upon the Company to "confirm and persevere in the system long since recommended by them to the Madras Government, upon the authority of Sir Thomas Munro, of uniting the appointment of collector and magistrate, of destroying the independence of each other of every officer employed in the same district, of making Collector's great office, consisting of deputy collectors and joint magistrates and assistants subordinate to one head, and acting upon the same system".[67]

During this period, the question of how to organize the district administration hinged on the issue of whether to separate or integrate the offices of collector and magistrate. The administrative reforms of 1829-31 signified the triumph of the tradition of the

Munro School of district administration over that of the Cornwallis School. The Regulation VIII of 1931 deprived the judges of all jurisdiction over summary suits relating to rent, and transferred them to the exclusive cognizance of the collector, whose decisions were to be final, subject to a regular suit which was to be brought in the civil courts. The authority of the collector became pre-eminent in the district. "Exercising the office and dignity of magistrate, with command of police functions and with summary jurisdiction in rent cases, the collector was now more properly termed as District Officer. The double institution of the divisional commissioner and District Officer permanently modified the Cornwallis structure and *supplied the orthodox model for future British colonial* administration."[68]

But this arrangement was soon questioned and there followed an interesting debate on which of the two systems of district administration—the integrated or the unintegrated, the Munro or the Cornwallis—would be the more suitable for the Indian situation. Although the home authorities had advocated the Munro system in 1814, the lapse of time and changes in the composition of the home authorities raised the Cornwallis system in the estimation of the India House, and now they were prepared to approve the union of powers in the collector only in special cases.[69] But what further accelerated the trend in favour of the Cornwallis system was the arrival of Macaulay in India, as law member, in June 1834. Individualist in his political persuasion, he had "no sympathy for that authoritarian element which had lent its support to the strengthening of the executive and closer union of powers in India".[70] He was averse to the administrative traditions of the Munro school and could not perceive the slightest connection between the police duties and the administration of justice. His responsiveness to liberal and humanitarian ideas compounded with his political conviction tended to avert the threat to the Cornwallis' judicial and revenue administrative system.[71] The tide turned in favour of the weak local executive in the traditions of the Cornwallis school, for Macaulay advocated reduction of the powers and duties of the executive by divesting it completely of judicial functions and by making the collector firmly subordinate to the judiciary.[72] He even favoured the abolition of the post of commissioner and declared that "our system" would improve if "the functionaries engaged in the collection of revenue" were divested of "all their judicial functions".[73] To quote him:

> "It is a bad sign for a state when the machinery which is provided for the administration of justice is contemptibly weak while the machinery which screws revenue out of the people is irresistibly strong. It is a bad sign of a state when the judge can be defied with impunity unless he calls in the aid of the tax gatherer."[74]

Thus, within five years of the formal introduction of the administrative measure of 1831, Bentinck's conception of the integrated District Officer system was already being assailed in the Governor-General's Council. H. Shakespeare, another member of the Council, was equally emphatic in his opposition to the union of the offices of collector and magistrate and characterized this arrangement as "destructive of the efficiency of both departments, and almost always to one".[75] Though a complete reversal of the unitary characters of the local executive as conceived by Bentinck was out of the question, in practice, some serious modifications were in the offing, and Auckland, the Governor-General, got the home authorities to agree in 1837 to confer upon his Government discretionary authority to separate the offices of collector and magistrate in Bengal whenever the pressure of business made this necessary.[76] The discretionary power was extensively used, and by 1845 the separation in all the districts of Bengal was completed except in three districts of Orissa. This attack upon the administrative reforms of Bentinck was reinforced by the deprivation of the commissioner of his police functions and the revival of the office of the superintendent of police.

But a more interesting debate occurred in the wake of the submission of Auckland's Police Committee Report in 1838.[77] The members of the committee were divided on the issue of the union executive and judicial functions in the district executive. The majority favoured separation on the ground that the union of revenue and magisterial functions resulted in neglect of police and magisterial duties to the detriment of revenue work. But an ideological note was struck by an influential member of the committee, Frederick Halliday, who urged separation in the name of the principle of jurisprudence, justifying it as a necessary element in good government. No magistrate, he felt, should have a previous knowledge of the case on which he was to pronounce his verdict as a judge. He observed in his famous Minute:

> "The union of Magistrate with collector has been stigmatized as incompatible, but the union of thief catcher with judge is surely more anomalous in theory and more mischievous in practice. So long as it lasts, the public confidence in our criminal tribunals must always be liable to injury, and the authority of justice itself must often be abused and misapplied."[78]

THE PATERNALIST-NON-REGULATION SYSTEM AND THE TRIUMPH OF INTEGRATIONISTS

In spite of this powerful plea supporting the separation of executive and judicial functions at the district level and the perpetuation of the Cornwallis traditions in Bengal field administration, the current of thinking in the official circles moved swiftly in favour of the strong, monocratic local executive. This was somewhat understandable, because the end of the 1830s marked the end of a period of reforms and the beginning of the forties synchronized with the launching of a resurgent aggressive imperialism under Ellenborough, the Governor-General.[79] Dalhousie, his famous successor, followed the policy of imperial expansion and consolidation with still greater vigour and, under both of them, the system of field administration was bound to be affected by their general approach to problems of administration. For instance, Ellenborough was opposed to the division of power among the Company, the Board of Control, and the local authorities in India, treating this as a sign of grave imperial weakness. He liked soldiers as much as he disliked civilians and during his administration, he substituted army officers for the covenanted civil service wherever it was possible for him to do so.[80]

On the annexation of Sind and Punjab, in particular, the integrated unitary pattern of field administration was introduced in its purest form. It was a non-regulation, paternalist form of administration and was characterized by "simple and more direct modes of procedure and by the greater accessibility of officials to the people; but chiefly by the union of all powers, executive, magisterial and judicial, in the hands of the District Officer... subject, however, to the appellate and supervisional jurisdiction of the Commissioner of the division in all branches of work."[81] Being paternal rather than formally legal, this system of administration depended for its successful operation, in large measure, upon the personal qualities of character, initiative and vigour.[82] The administrative staff in these areas consisted partly of civil servants drawn from the regulation areas by the prospects of more rapid promotion, partly of military officers withdrawn from their regiments and to some small extent of officials promoted from subordinate positions. However, the elements of administration in such areas were predominantly military, with the civilian part occupying a secondary position. Military officers were at the same time required to conform to the 'principles and spirit' of the Regulations and to act according to justice, equity and good conscience in cases not covered by laws and rules.[83] The ideology of the paternalist, non-regulation system was thus characterized by three features:

(1) The concentration of authority and responsibility in the District Officer (called deputy commissioner in such areas), the union in one person of the administration of civil justice and of revenue being thought to be essential for the preservation of the indigenous system of land tenures.
(2) The districts must not be so large as to make the undivided responsibility impossible, they must be small enough for the District Officer to get a complete knowledge of them and the people.
(3) The administration was grounded on a set of simple laws and rules, which were not intended to upset or 'anglicize the Indian institutions.[84]

This integrated pattern of field administration was being increasingly appreciated by British administrators and statesmen on *administrative* and *political* considerations. An influential section of the key civilians in Bengal had been convinced that the separation of the judicial and executive functions of the District Officer was the chief cause of the weakness of the Bengal district administration.[85] The collection of land revenue, because of the operation of the permanent settlement, had become a matter of routine and did not, therefore, bring the District Officer into close touch with the people. His main duties were supervisory and light on account of the revenue being paid directly into the government treasuries with the interposition of local officers, such as *tahsildars* and *kanungos*. The collector, however, because of his duties and position, possessed personal and official influence with the zamindars, and it was being felt in Bengal official circles that this power might be used to further the cause of law and order and ultimately of political consolidation, whereas under the existing system, it either remained barren and passive or was actually used to thwart the work of the magistrate.

It was at this psychological moment that Cecil Beadon, Secretary to the Government of Bengal, enunciated, in a Minute, his celebrated theory of "oriental government" in which he described the union of powers in the local executive as being consistent with indigenous custom and institutions. He proposed that at the head of each district, there should be a chief executive officer called collector or magistrate, who should represent in his area the totality of the powers of the Government. He should be assisted by an adequate staff of assistants and should be responsible to the commissioner, who should, in turn, exercise authority over every executive department in the division—revenue, minor justice, police, registration, public works, education and jails. In one or more districts, he suggested, there should be a European judge, in-charge of the civil and criminal justice, but always liable to have his executive arrangements and his supervision over lower judges controlled by the commissioner.[86] His scheme was reminiscent of the system of field administration forged by such paternalists as Munro, Elphinstone and others, and like them, he also observed that "the true theory of Indian Government...is the entire subjection of every civil officer in a division to the commissioner as the head of it, and the entire subjection of every officer in a district to its executive chief".[87] He argued that since the main duties of covenanted English officers in India were those of superintendence and control, they could be best and most effectively performed for the common weal when they were centred in one authority within a given tract of country. His scheme envisaged a well-knit chain of authority from the Governor down to the deputy magistrate and collector, each in complete charge of his territorial jurisdiction and subordinate to his superior.[88]

These views found favour with Dalhousie, the Governor-General, who believed with Beadon that the separation was a big error, for it disrupted the unity in local administration and resulted in the neglect of magisterial work.[89] Though John Peter Grant, another influential member of the Governor-General's Executive Council, sough to refute their views and supported the Cornwallis pattern of dispersed and unintegrated field administration (for he held a low opinion of the duties of the collector and a high opinion of those of the 'great office' of judge).[90] Canning who succeeded Dalhousie, approved of the theory of paternal, oriental government, himself suggesting that the division of authority was to be avoided rather than sought. He believed that this form of government was more congenial to and best understood by the Indian people under the prevailing conditions, and held that the concentration of all responsibility upon one officer cannot fail to keep his attention alive, and to stimulate his energy in the department to the utmost, whilst it will preclude the growth of those obstructions to good government which are apt to spring up where two co-ordinate officers divide the authority.[91]

The upheavals of 1857 lent considerable weight to the arguments of the integrationists and increased the respectability of the Madras-paternalist system of district administration. The Government appeared to be convinced of the need of its interpreter and supreme representative in every Bengal district who could keep himself in touch with the moods and feelings of the people so that the Government were never taken unawares. The Punjab which had been settled in a *direct* and *personal* manner had remained loyal to the empire and had even helped "in stemming and hurling back the tide of revolt".[92] This seemed "to argue for it an intrinsic superiority" over the Cornwallis pattern of field administration, leading inevitably "to a reaction in favour of the patriarchal system".[93] Consequently, after the calm was restored and elements hostile to the regime were suppressed, Stanley, the Secretary of State for India, in his despatch of the 14th April, 1859, directed that "the offices of Magistrate and Collector where now disunited in Bengal should be combined in the same person".[94] "The magistrate-and-collector" or "the District Officer once again became the undisputed representative of government in a Bengal district.[95] Thus, "during the hundred years between Plassey and Mutiny, the wheel had turned full circle and the Company had come back to the old Mughal view that executive power must be concentrated in the hands of the local representative of Government...Paternal and authoritarian rule had been restored."[96]

LATER DEVELOPMENTS

The politico-administrative decision of 1859 tended finally to bring the Bengal pattern of district administration in line with the Munro-paternalist system, exalting the Bengal District Officer, like his counterpart in other parts of the country, to clear supremacy over other government officials in his district. The arrangement emphasized the monocratic as opposed to collegial form of administrative responsibility. Thus, an important effect of the 'Mutiny' was to convince the British that the office of the District Officer must be so strengthened as to make him the symbol of imperial rule, the mainstay of British dominion and the instrument of centralized political control and stability in an 'oriental' society inhabiting a people of diverse religio-cultural backgrounds, of widely differing social and economic status and of doubtful loyalties to the Empire.

During the decade following the 'Mutiny', an impressive political-administrative structure was forged in India whose essence laying a series of one-man authorities, one subordinate to another, each responsible for the administration of the area in his charge. The District Officer was the most important level of hierarchy in the structure; he served as a channel of communication, upward and downward, from the Governor-General down to the people, represented total executive power of government, achieved coordination of all its field activities and acted as 'the administrative-maid-of-all-work' being responsible for everything pertaining to the life of the people in his charge. Indeed, until the paternalistic elements in the structure of field administration declined by the beginning of the second decade of the present century, the District Officer was the *government* to the simple village people of his district, and it was this belief more than anything else, which made them look upon him as a giver of all favours and dispenser of justice. If the Viceroy was the symbol of the Crown in India, it was the District Officer who was the seat of authority so far as the mass of the people were concerned. The position of the District Officer, until far-reaching changes were effected by the Montagu-Chelmsford reforms of 1919 in district administration, had been picturesquely described in these words:

> "He is the great sahib whose nod is to be obeyed…before whom all the great people of the village…bow. He is the mighty one to whom the most flowery languages and ornate titles apply. He or those who obey him orders the life of the people of India, and, next to the Creator and the laws of nature, he comes in the hierarchy of arbitrary powers. Those above him are too remote from the life of the people to be anything but indefinite gleams, those below him are outwardly and visibly his servants."[97]

The District Officer system of the nineteenth century and of the early years of the twentieth century became considerably modified under the impact of political and technical challenges of the past 50 years and tended increasingly to approximate to the unintegrated prefectoral pattern of field administration. But there still is a major, valid justification for the District Officer system as a mechanism for area coordination of a large number of specialized services at the local level in newly independent countries of Asia and Africa. Indeed, the strength and unity and variety and richness of administrative experience which characterize the office of the District Officer are particularly called for to meet the requirements of development and modernization.[98] That the European counterparts of the District Officer system can be recommended for adoption in a country like Britain, the classic land of local Government, is a tribute to its staying-power and its ability to create "a pool of really general administrators of which the British have no equivalent, with the possible exception of town clerks".[99] Even the contention that this system of field administration is both the product and the mainstay of colonial and absolutist regimes is rebutted on grounds that carry conviction. "It would…be a mistake", says Smith, "to associate the prefectoral system too closely with any one ideology or system of government".[100] Chapman goes so far as to refute the charge, on the basis of his acquaintance with continental bureaucracies, that the system is in any manner destructive of local autonomy.[101] Fried, on the strength of his study of the Italian administrative politics, maintains that "a prefectoral system is basically a neutral device which can be made to serve a wide range of purpose".[102] In fact, according to him, it may as well be used "to defend a democratic regime, to bolster democratic forces, to provide a sense of security and order, and to dissolve or alleviate the tensions that might undermine a democracy".[103]

CONCLUSION

The District Officer system was something more than a legacy of the British State-building since it also incorporated elements of indigenous administrative traditions and government organization. The British felt that its approximation, at any rate in form, to what they called the "native model" would impart legitimacy to the colonial political order and would be emotionally satisfying to the Indian people. The system, nevertheless, was primarily designed to achieve one subsuming political object of consolidation and pacification of the conquered Indian territories so that the collection of land revenue could become a matter of administrative routine and the employment of violence could become a monopoly of the colonial polity. The system sought to lend strength, stability, efficiency and unity of purpose to the administrative machine and keep under firm imperial control, through a dependable bureaucratic arm, the hostile and dissatisfied sections of the 'native' population disposed or otherwise adversely affected in the process of conquest and pacification of Indian territories. Since the District Officer was the man-on-the-spot at a governmentally convenient level, he became the authoritative channel of communication between the people and the government and upon his ability, resourcefulness and responsiveness depended, in very large measure, the peace, stability and general happiness in the Empire.

The variations in the patterns of the District Officer system were occasioned as much by local circumstances, such as the state of social, cultural and political developments of the people of the areas concerned as the politico-administrative ideology of the administrators placed in their charge. The 'Mutiny' decisively tilted the balance in favour of the Munro-paternalist pattern, leading to the cessation of the debate on the suitability or otherwise of the integrated District Officer system at the policy level, at any rate, till the closing years of the nineteenth century. This became the 'British model' of field administration, reflecting, at the same time, the British conservative yearning for an ordered, hierarchical polity in their colonial possessions. This system of field administration tended, however, with the passage of time, to be modified by the growing functionalization of government activities.

REFERENCES

1. Some of the major traits of the prefectoral system are: (*i*) division of national territory into administrative areas variously called 'provinces', 'departments', 'districts', 'prefectures', etc.; (*ii*) appointment of a generalist public functionary, representative of and responsible to the Central Government in each area; and (*iii*) charging him with the functions of social and political representation, maintenance of law and order, supervision of most or all government operations and overall coordination in the area. *Cf.* R.C. Fried, *The Italian Prefects*, New Haven, Yale University, 1963; B.C. Smith, *Field Administration*, London, Routledge and Kegan Paul, 1967; B. Chapman, *The Prefects and Provincial* France, London, George Allen & Unwin, 1955; B.Chapman, *The Profession of Government*, London, George Allen & Unwin, 1959; F.Ridley and J.Blondel, *Public Administration in France*, London, Routledge and Kegan Paul, 1964; and Haridwar Rai, "The Institution of the District Collector", *The Indian Journal of Public Administration*, Vol.XI, No. 3 (July-Sept.), 1965.
2. For details, *see* R.C. Fried, *Op. cit.*, B.C. Smith, *Op. cit.* and Herbert Jacob, *German Administration since Bismarck*, New Haven, Yale University Press, 1963.
3. Sophia Wietzman, *Warren Hastings and Philip Francis*, Manchester, Manchester University Press, 1929, p. 50.
4. See Hastings' letter of 21st March, 1776, to Sulivan in G.R. Gleig, *Memoirs of the Life of the Right Hon. Warren Hastings*, London, Richard Bentley, 1841, Vol.II, p. 30.
5. *See* A.K. Ghosal, *Civil Service in India under the East India Company*, Calcutta, University of Calcutta, 1944, p. 142.
6. Bengal Revenue Consultations, 18th May, 1785 (emphasis added).
7. *Ibid.*, 10th May, 1785.
8. For this instruction of the Home authorities (Court of Directors), dated 12th of April, 1786, *see* the *Second Report from the Select Committee of the House of Commons on the Affairs of the East India Company*, App. 12 (emphasis added).

9. F.D. Ascoli, *Early Revenue History of Bengal and the Fifth Report,* 1812, Oxford, Clarendon Press, 1917, p. 39.
10. R.B. Ramsbotham, "The Revenue Administration of Bengal, 1765-1786", H.H. Dodwell, *The Cambridge History of India,* Delhi, S.Chand, 1958 (First Indian Reprint), Vol. V, p. 431.
11. The District Officer of this period has been likened to "a sort of proconsul whose irregularities were exempt from the jurisdiction of the ordinary tribunals, and who was accountable only to the Executive which he served". *See* W.S. Seton-Karr, *The Marquess Cornwallis,* Oxford, Clarendon Press, 1890, p. 90.
12. A. Aspinall, *Cornwallis in Bengal,* Manchester University Press, 1931, p. 86. *See also* Cornwallis' Minute of the 11th February, 1793, in the *Second Report of the Select Committee of the House of Commons on the Affairs of the East India Company,*1819, App. I (A).
13. *Ibid.*, pp. 153-54.
14. For a detailed discussion on this point, *see* Haridwar Rai, "The Institution of the District Collector", *The Indian Journal of Public Administration, Op. cit.*
15. *See* A. Aspinall, *Op. cit.*, p. 138. See also Haridwar Rai, *Ibid.*, for evolution of the institution of the French intendant and its likely impact on the institution of the District Officer.
16. A. Aspinall, *Op. cit.*, p. 133.
17. "...the traditional Indian system of government, in which the executive official played so large a part was wholly unfamiliar to him. He was accustomed to a mode of government under which the law was administered by a series of courts, and the duties of executive officials were reduced to a minimum. This was, in his eyes, the best method and the one which he resolved to set up." *See* J. Allan, T.W. Haig and H.H.Dodwell, *The Cambridge History of India, Op. cit.*, p. 496.
18. Eric Stokes, *The English Utilitarians and India,* Oxford, Clarendon Press, 1959, p. 4. He maintains that the Permanent Settlement of Bengal (1973) was a frank attempt to apply the English Whig philosophy of Government "having as its central belief that political power is essentially corruption and inevitably abused; that power to be exercised with safety must be reduced to minimum, and then kept divided and counter-balanced."
19. *Ibid.*, pp. 140-168. *See also* D. Bearce, *British Attitude Towards India* (1784-1858), London, Oxford University Press, 1961.
20. B.H.Baden-Powell, *The Land-Systems of British,* Oxford, Clarendon Press, 1892, Vol. I, p. 389.
21. Aspinall has observed: "The steady elaboration of codes of instruction and procedure drawn up with the object of promoting

efficiency, uniformity and a high standard of administration, tended to set bounds to the collector's power, whilst the judicial code of 1793 made him answerable before the ordinary courts of justice for unlawful acts done in his official capacity. The combined effect of these changes was to weaken the tradition or arbitrary power and to abolish the idea that the District Officer was above the law and irresponsible for his conduct except to the Executive." *Op. cit.*, p. 155.

22. Eric Stokes, *Op. cit.*, p. 144.
23. R.C. Fried, *Op. cit.*, p. 155. Chap,VI.
24. Cornwallis introduced a permanent settlement of revenue in Bengal because it divested the executive of all discretionary authority and eliminated the dread of 'periodical assessment as a disturbing factor in economic life.' It was intended to realize the ideals of 'simplicity and certainty in government' and to secure the confidence of the Zamindars in the Company's administration. *See* S. Gopal, *The Permanent Settlement in Bengal and its Results*, London, George Allen & Unwin, 1949, pp. 16-18. *See also* M.N. Gupta, *Land System of Bengal*, Calcutta University, 1940, p. 144.
25. *See* M. Ruthnaswamy, *Some Influences that Made the British Administrative System in India*, London, Lucaz, 1939, p. 245.
26. V.A. Smith, *The Oxford History of India*, Oxford, Clarendon Press, 1923, p. 596.
27. Even much later, it was only in the *Khas Mahals* or government owned estates that the collector in the provinces of Bengal and Bihar could come into frequent and intimate contact with the people. "The great extent" remarks Gopal, "to which the rulers of Bengal lost touch with their subjects was perhaps one of the most pernicious results of the measures of 1793." *See* S.Gopal, *Op. cit.*, p. 27. *See also* R.Carstairs, *The Little World of an Indian District Officer*, London, Macmillan, 1912, p. 19.
28. Eric Stokes, *Op. cit.*, p. 15.
29. *See* Haridwar Rai, "The Changing Role of the District Officer (1860-1960)". *The Indian Journal of Public Administration*, Vol.IX, No. 2 (April-June), 1963, pp. 238-240, and *District Administration in West Pakistan*, Inayatullah (ed.), Peshawar, Pakistan Academy for Rural Development, 1964.
30. *See* G.R. Gleig, *The Life of Major-General Sir Thomas Munro*, London, Henry Colburn & Richard Bentley, 1851, Vol.II, p. 170.
31. *See Parliamentary Papers*, 1819, Vol.XIII, p. 518, *See also* K.N.V. Sastri (ed.), *The Munro System of British Statesmanship*, Mysore, Mysore University, 1939, App. B.
32. For his conception of the 'native' form of government, *see* Munro 'On the State of the Country and the condition of the people" ,

G.R. Gleig, *Op. cit.*, Vol.II, pp. 124-170. *See also* the broad outline of his scheme of revenue and judicial administration in his letter to the Chief Secretary, Government of Madras, dated 12th December, 1814, *Ibid.*, Vol. I, pp. 425-57.

33. For Fort St. George Judicial Consultations of 19th August, 1815, see K.N.V. Sastri, *Op. cit.*, App. B.(4).
34. G.R.Gleig, *Op. cit.*, Vol. II, p. 354. *See also* K.N.V. Sastri, *Op. cit.*, p. XXX. Munro stressed the role of the collector as the sole representative of government in the district and as its most trusted supplier of information about the state of the district. This was possible only when he had the entire resources of the government in the district at his beck and call.
35. T.H. Beaglehole, *Thomson Munro & the Development of Administrative Policy in Madras 1792-1818,* Cambridge University Press, 1966, p. 128.
36. G.R. Gleig, *Op. cit.*, p. 158.
37. Revenue Minute of Munro, dated 9th of January, 1821. *See* K.N.V. Sastri, *Op. cit.*, p. XXX-XXXI.
38. Munro's letter to the Chief Secretary, Government of Madras, dated 24th December, 1814. See G.R.Gleig, *Op. cit.*, Vol. I, p. 456-57.
39. *See* Eric Stokes, *Op. cit.*, p. 144. *See also* T.H.Beaglehole, *Op. cit.*, p. 138.
40. *See* Kenneth Ballhatchet, *Social Policy and Social Change in Western India* (1817-1830), London, Oxford University Press, 1957, Chapters III, VI, VII & IX.
41. J.S. Cotton, *Mountstuart Elphinstrone*, Oxford, Clarendon Press, 1892, p. 123.
42. Kenneth Ballhatchet, *Op. cit.*, p. 32.
43. J.S.Cotton, *Op. cit.*, p. 124.
44. His letter to Erskine, dated the 4th of August, 1818. *See* T.E.Colebrooke, *Life of the Honourable Mountstuart Elphinst one*, London, R. Bentley, 1884, Vol.II, p. 46. In his letter to Strachey, dated the 21st April, 1821, he observed: "As to regulations, I think they should be introduced by degrees; I doubt whether anybody could tell me what was good for the Marathas." *Ibid.*, p. 124.
45. "There seems no ground for fearing", he wrote to the Governor-General in 1818, "that we shall remiss in introducing our own system, and it is better that it should gradually encroach on the institutions of the country than that it should overwhelm them at once..." See Kenneth Ballhatchet, *Op. cit.*, p. 31.
46. *See* Eric Stokes, *Op. cit.*, p. 149; and Kenneth Ballhatchet, *Op cit.*, p. 36.
47. Since these was the sole functions of government those days, he felt that they should be administered as an integral whole. *See* Kenneth Ballhatchet, *Op. cit.*, p. 104.
48. *Ibid.*, p. 105.

49. *Ibid.*, pp. 105-06.
50. The regulation system was in force in the older provinces governed by the laws made under the Charter Acts, which were called 'Regulations' until 1834, when the more modern designation of 'Acts' was adopted. The non-regulation system was employed in less advanced areas acquired at a later time and inhabited by 'wild' martial or less 'civilized' people. For a discussion on the evolution of the ideology of paternalism, see Haridwar Rai, "Paternalism in Indian Administration": The Non-Regulation System of Field Administration under the British", *The Indian Journal of Public Administration*,Vol.XV, No. 2, April-June, 1969, pp. 193-211.
51. Eric Stokes, *Op. cit.*, p. 144.
52. Perceival Spear, *Twilight of the Moghuls: Studies in Late Moghul Delhi*, Cambridge, Cambridge University Press, 1951, p. 88.
53. *Ibid.*, p. 88.
54. "In his civil capacity as Commissioner in the purely British territory, the Resident had to keep order, to administer justice, to superintend the appointment and collection of the revenue and to develop, as far as practicable, the resources of a very imperfectly developed country." As to the assistants of the Resident, they combined "the functions of magistrate, collector and judge". *See* R. Bosworth Smith, *Life of Lord Lawrence*, London, Smith Elder, 1883, Vol.I, pp. 43-44.
55. Evidence of Holt Mackenzie, Parliamentary Papers, 1832, Vol. IV, p. 24.
56. *See* P. Woodruff, *The Men who Ruled India*, London, J. Cape, 1954, Vol. I, p. 271. It has also been remarked that "Justice" in the Delhi district, "a non-regulation province, was administered not so much by hard and fast regulations, as on principles of natural equity". *See* R. Bosworth Smith, *Op. cit.*, p. 44.
57. *Parliamentary Papers*, Vol. XIII, 1831-32, pp. 407-08.
58. Eric Stokes, *Op. cit.*, p. 20.
59. *Ibid.*, p. 21.
60. See J.W.Kaye, *The Administration of East India Company*, London, Richard Bentley, 1853, pp. 340-44. For the views of Henry Strachey on the evil effects of the union of judicial and magisterial business in the hands of the district judge, *see also* W.K.Firminger (ed.), *The Fifth Report from the House of Commons on the Affairs of the East India Company, 1812*, Calcutta, R.Cambray, 1917, Vol. II, pp. 565-66.
61. L.M. Penson, "The Bengal Administrative System, 1786-1818", H.H. Dodwell, *The Cambridge History of India, Op. cit.*, Vol. V, p. 458.
62. *See* Regulation IV of 1821.

63. R.Muir, *The Making of British India*, Manchester, University Press, 1923, p. 216.
64. B.B. Misra, *The Central Administration of East India Company*, Manchester, Manchester University Press, 1959, p. 289.
65. *Parliamentary Papers*, 1831-32, Vol. XII, p. 386.
66. Holt Mackenzie, a member of the Governor-General's Council, suggested in his report that the new method of control and supervision over field administration should be individual and personal, and opined that the collective and deliberative boards representing the collegial system of administration had failed. See *Parliamentary Papers*, 1831-32, Vol. XII, pp. 385-89. Another member of the Council, Butterworth Bayley, made similar suggestion. *Ibid.*, pp. 404-05. The view of Charles Metcalfe, another influential member of the Council, were even more paternalistic. He stood for a complete union of powers in local administration. Districts were to be grouped into divisions, with each division under a commissioner, who was to exercise the "highest powers in all branches of the administration". *Ibid.*, pp. 407-08.
67. *See Parliamentary Papers*, 1831-32, Vol.IX, App. M. The views of Holt Mackenzie, embodied in a Minute dated the 31st of October, 1830, are also worth quoting: "In a word", he observed, "to disjoin the several parts of Government in a country which is not self-governed, is like placing the different members of the body in-charge of different physicians, severally acting with their respective limbs according to individual theory without treatment of other parts, and each holding in his hand the power of destroying life but helpless to save from the blunder of his brethren. It is to animate the lifeless frame with a plurality of souls". *Ibid.*, Vol. VIII, pp. 135-160.
68. *See* Eric Stokes, *Op cit.*, p. 138 (emphasis added). The system of field administration evolved in India was adopted by the British for the administration of their colonies in Africa. "The chain of command", to quote an expert on African Administration, "was precise, clear and simple. District Commissioners or officers were responsible for the peace, welfare and good order of their districts or divisions, and supervised and co-ordinated the functions and activities of all local departmental officers including the police and the Treasury...District Commissioners or officers were answerable to their Provincial Commissioners had general responsibility for and supervision over all government and local government activities in their provinces. The chain of command stretched upwards through Chief Commissioners or Regional Governors to the Governor and Commander-in-Chief at the apex. The Governor himself was answerable to the colonial Secretary."

See A.L. Adu, *The Civil Service in New African States*, London, George Allen & Unwin, 1915, pp. 14-15.

69. *See* letter from Court to Bengal, dated on the 1st of February, 1832, in App.I, *Parliamentary Papers*, Vol. XII, 1831-32.
70. *See* Lord Macaulay's Legislative Minute, No. 16, dated the 25th June, 1835, in C.D. Dharker (ed.), *Lord Macaulay's Legislative Minutes*, Madras, Oxford University Press, 1948, pp. 225-26.
71. G.D.Bearce, *Op. cit.*, p. 135. *et. seq.*
72. "The tide", to quote Strokes, "which had reached full flood with the establishment of the Commissioner system and the union of magistrate and collector, was turned aside by Macaulay to cleanse and widen the old channels rather than carve out new." *See* Eric Stokes, *Op. cit.*, p. 193.
73. C.D. Dharker, *Op. cit.*, p. 209.
74. *See* Macaulay's Legislative Minute, No. 31, dated the 7th March, 1836., *Op. cit.*, p. 235.
75. Eric Stokes, *Op. cit.*, p. 237.
76. L.S.S.O.'Malley, *The Indian Civil Service*, 1601-1930, London, John Murray, 1931, p. 67.
77. The Police Committee was set-up by Auckland under the chairmanship of Robert Bird in 1837 to investigate into several complaints of landowners and indigo-planters regarding unsatisfactory condition of the police system in Bengal. The committee submitted its report in 1838.
78. See *Report of the Police Committee*, Calcutta, 1838, App.I, pp.XX, *et.seq.*
79. G.D. Bearce, *Op. cit.*, p. 185.
80. *See* Richard Temple, *Men and Events of My Times in India*, London, John Murray, 1882, pp. 24-25. *See also* L.S.S.O.' Malley, *Op. cit.*, pp. 51-52.
81. Patrick Fagan "District Administration in the United Provinces, Central Provinces, and the Punjab, 1818-57", H.H.Dodwell, *The Cambridge History of India*, *Op. cit.*, Vol.VI, p. 87.
82. Most of the British civilians in India believed with John Strachey that "when the people had never been accustomed to anything but personal rule of the roughest sort, it was often necessary, on the introduction of our government, to concentrate executive and judicial authority in the same hands. Government by regular course of law cannot be substituted in a moment for a Government of irresponsible power. *See* John Strachey, *India: Its Administration and Progress*, London, Macmillan, 1903, p. 93.
83. *See* J.Thomas Prichard, *The Administration of India, 1859-68*, London Macmillan, 1869, p. 157. *See also* George Chisney, *The Indian Polity*, London, Longmans, Green, 1894, pp. 187-88.

84. For details *see* Haridwar Rai, "Paternalism in Indian Administration: The Non-Regulation System of Field Administration Under the British", *Op. cit.*
85. *See* George Campbell, *India As It May Be: An Outline of a Proposed Government and Policy,* London, John Murray, 1853, p. 215.
86. For a detailed account of the weaknesses of the Bengal district executive in the two decades preceding the Indian 'Mutiny', *see* the Minute dated the 3rd of December, 1853, of Cecil Beadon, Secretary to the Government of Bengal, in *Parliamentary Papers,* 1857, Vol. LIX, pp. 298, *et. seq.*
87. *Ibid.*
88. He observed that "the principle which holds good of a local Governor in the presidency which he governs, holds equally good of a commissioner within his division, and of a Magistrate and Collector (or, as he would more properly be called, a Deputy Commissioner) within his district, and the principle is more capable of further advantageous extensions to local sub-divisions as convenient extent".
89. *See* Government of Bihar and Orissa, *Report of the Committee Appointed to Formulate a Scheme for a Separation of Judicial and Executive Functions in Bihar and Orissa,* Patna, Government Printing Press, 1922, Vol. I, p. 4.
90. For the Minute of John Peter Grant, dated 23rd November, 1854, *see Parliamentary Papers,* 1857, Vol. LIX, p. 307, *et. seq.*
91. C.E. Buckland, *Bengal Under the Lieutenant-Governors,* Calcutta, S.K.Lahiri, 1901, Vol. I, pp. 24-25.
92. *See* Eric Stokes, *Op. cit.*, p. 268.
93. *Ibid.*, Percival Griffiths has stated that the Mutiny revealed the "weakness of the previous organization". See *The British Impact in India,* London, Macdonald, 1952, p. 163. E.Thompson & G.T. Garrat have remarked that "the suddenness of the outbreak of the Mutiny suggested that British officials were out of touch with the people, and that Indian officials could not be trusted". See *Rise and Fulfilment of British Rule in India,* Allahabad, Central Book Depot, 1954 (Indian Reprint), p. 425.
94. *See* Government of Bihar and Orissa, *First Decennial Review of the Administration and Development of the Province,* 1912-22, Patna, Superintendent, Government Printing Press, 1923, p. 55.
95. H.V.Lovett, "District Administration in Bengal, 1858-1918", H.H. Dodwell, *The Cambridge History of India, Op. cit.*, Vol.VI, p. 245.
96. Percival Griffiths, *Op. cit.*, p. 165.
97. Ramsay Macdonald, *The Government of India,* London, Swarthemore Press, N.D., p. 97.

98. A United Nations study on development reveals that the integrated District Officer system of field administration is more conducive to the proper coordination of the functions of specialized departments within a particular administrative area and concludes that "the task of coordination at the community level is likely to be most difficult in countries which did not have administrative districts, i.e., in which national departments maintain direct administrative control over their field activities". *See* The United Nations, United Nations Technical Assistance Programme, *Public Administration Aspects of Community Development Programme*, New York, 1959, p. 18. *See also* Haridwar Rai, "Coordination of development Programme at the District Level with Special Reference to the Role of the District Officer in Bihar", *The Indian Journal of Public Administration*, Vol.XII, No. 1 (January-March), 1966. For a discussion of the role of the District Officer as chief executive of the Government, *see* Haridwar Rai, "The District Officer in India Today", *Journal of Administration Overseas*, Vol.VI, No.I, January, 1967. For attacks on the District Officer system from specialized departments, *see* Haridwar Rai, "District Magistrate and Police Superintendent in India: The Controversy of Dual Control", *Journal of Administration Overseas*, Vol.VI, No. 3, July, 1967.

99. Brian Chapman deplores that "Britain knows nothing of the system of 'general' administrator resident in the provinces acting as the principal link between local authorities and Central Government...what is important in this context is that the French and Italian prefects, the Belgian provincial governor, the Dutch Commissioner of the Queen, are men with real experience covering the whole field of public administration. Their daily duties involve them in questions of planning, economic expansion, education, police, transport and highways, government finance, and so on. This means that European countries have a reservoir of men to call upon who have a wide experience of administration in all its aspects...Compared to them senor British Civil Servants are sheltered spinsters." *See* Brian Chapman, *British Government Observed*, London, George Allen & Unwin, 1963, p. 24.

100. B.C. Smith, *Op. cit.*, p. 64.

101. "...anyone who has examined the work of the Swedish governors or the Dutch commissioners is unlikely to be greatly impressed by the view that these officers are harmful to local self-government". *See* Brian Chapman, *The Profession of Government, Op. cit.*, p. 73.

102. Robert C.Fried, *Op. cit.*, pp. 313-314.

103. *Ibid.*, p. 313.

11

Changing Role of the District Magistrate

ASOK MUKHOPADHYAY

EVOLUTION OF DISTRICT MAGISTRATE

During the 50 years of independence, many institutions of Indian administration have undergone changes—some minor and others quite radical. The institution of the District Officer—variously called as District Collector, District Magistrate and Deputy Commissioner in different parts of India since the British days—has undergone quite a big change over the last five decades.

East India Company Days

The office of the Collector was first created on May 14, 1772 when a Regulation prescribed: "The Company having determined to stand forth as the Dewan, the Supervisors should now be designated Collectors." The 'district' was made the basis of Indian administration in 1786 when the office of the District Collector was made permanent. In 1790, East India Company took over administration of criminal justice from the Nawab of Bengal and District Collector was vested with the responsibility of 'magistracy', that is, law and order. Lord Cornwallis, in 1793, withdrew judicial powers from the Magistrate-Collector and gave them to the Judge-Magistrate of the district. In 1831, the powers of the District Magistrate were again increased to enable him not only to collect the revenue and maintain law and order but also to decide lower criminal cases. In 1836, the powers of the District Magistrate were again curtailed. In 1839, there were three top officers in the district, viz., District Magistrate for law and order, the District Collector for revenue collection, and District Judge for civil and higher criminal cases. In 20 years of this trifurcation of responsibility for district administration, the oriental theory of governance was in the ascendance under the inspiration of Sir Cecil Beadon, Sir Frederick Halliday, Sir James Fitzjames Stephen and others. As a result, the office of the District Magistrate became a centre of tremendous concentration of powers. This position continued for over a century till the judicial powers were taken away from the District Magistrate and given to District Judge in early 1970s. Meanwhile, since independence, a number of autonomous departments and directorates have been established at the State-level and the role of skilled specialist administrator has been recognized. But the District Magistrate continued to function as the representative of the Union and the State Governments in the district. The posting, transfer and promotion of District Magistrate are now decided by the State Chief Secretary with the approval of the Chief Minister.

Imperial Times

In the older days, the District Collector was the imperial government to the people. Ramsay McDonald once described the District Magistrate as "the tortoise which supports the elephant upon which rests the Government of India". The mofussil was then a self-contained little community with certain distinctive features—physical as well as social–that set it apart from the metropolis. District administration headed by the District Magistrate was marked by paternalistic approach and discretionary authority and–what is, perhaps, most important–a direct bridge between town and country. The intrepid civilian used to tour throughout his area on food, bicycle or horseback to have an intimate idea of the state of affairs in the district. The institution of Collectorate did not confine its role to only collection of land rents. Much of what is known about the countryside–history, geography, castes, customs, traditional beliefs, crop patterns or trade and commerce–is due to exhaustive field work of long-dead civilians, such as Elphinston, Colebrook, Grierson, Campbell, O'malley, Hunter, B.C.Allen, Ranvenshaw, R.C.Dutt and others. But circumstances in the post-independence India did not encourage the District Collector-Magistrates to devote as much time and energy to scholarly work and establish a rapport with their charges. However, the District Magistrate, in the early years of independence, continued to play an important role in the affairs of the States. As late as the early sixties, a retired ICS officer described the District Magistrate as "the coping stone, the vital wedge-like piece, that both divides and joins."

PHASE OF DECLINE SINCE LATE 60

The system's skeleton scurvies but not sustaining spirit. Of late, the role of the District Magistrate, in practice, is declining. The country too is succumbing to the insistent demands of urban and democratic culture. Since the late sixties, the power of money, the weight of political patronage and the pressure of influence have brought a significant change in the role of the District Magistrate. His crucial role in administration is lost like the sprawling garden in his bungalow.

"The erosion of an ethos", wrote a leading Indian journalist in the mid-seventies, "is most evident in physical decay". The old motif of sprawling bungalows for the Collector, police superintendent, and civil surgeon has been replaced by lesser quarters. Kutcherry and Circuit House or Dak Bungalow with those long arm-chair with sliding leg-rests are now discarded as unfashionable. And, of course, the station club with its monthly dance, formal as well as pot luck dinners, bridge, billiards and tennis was designed upon a clearly defined pattern dictated by administrative needs which, in turn, shaped social behaviour. In the late 19th century, the Collector-Magistrate used to have his regiment of *chaprassies*. Through this refractory medium, the people of India saw their rulers. The *chaprassie* painted his master in colour drawn from his black heart. Every lie he told, every insinuation he threw out, every demand he made was endorsed with his master's name. But the post-independence IAS officers as District Magistrates are strangers to the power game, without either the authority or the equipment to cope with the multitudinous complex forces that now swamp the mofussil life. It is now something of an exaggeration to claim any longer that a little community of microscopials, doctors, engineers, inspectors of schools, and assistant magistrates look up to him as a magnet. Symbolic of the changing times, today's VIP visitors to the district prefer the air-conditioned luxury of the guest houses maintained by the irrigation and power departments to the classical grace and dusty decrepitude of circuit houses.

Political Interference

The complaint of interference in the work of the Collector by the VIP's is not new. In the late 1870s, a civil servant in the district protested that these 'distinguished visitors' from Britain were becoming a frightful nuisance; they though that Collectors and Judges had nothing to do but to act as their guides, and that Indian officials had so little work and suffered so much from ennui that even ordinary thanks for hospitality were unnecessary; they took it all as their right. He was fulminating against the annual winter influx from Britain of MPs, reformers, industrialists and journalists. Today's 'distinguished visitors' are not less disturbing, demanding or burdensome because they appear to have a direct stake in the district. It is only in their daily functioning that enterprising and resourceful young officers have to make *ad hoc* adjustments to accommodate reality. Meanwhile, authorities have multiplied, power structures overlap, crucial distinctions are blurred, the chain of command is confused and there is scope for endless controversy.

Obsession with Prestige and Indifference to Public Welfare

A frequent complaint is that District Magistrates are appointed too soon and do not remain long enough in their parishes. They mostly operate from their sanctum of offices, receiving petitions, granting audience, transacting business on the telephone, moving out only in honour of VIP's or for ceremonial occasions and always keeping a close watch on the ladder of promotion. Their obsession with prestige and indifference to public welfare must be altered if the IAS is to survive usefully in an age that attaches greater importance to scientists and technologists. In this age, the responsibilities of governance have become infinitely more sophisticated than before independence.

Today, social graces are less important. The officer must win the confidence of villagers, knowledgeably discuss roads and fertilizers with panchayat leaders and work in harmony with MPs and MLAs. The Indian bureaucracy is still one of the many dense and refractive mediums through which the Government of India looks upon India. Today, the IAS, the successor service of the steel-framed ICS, has become the handmaid of politicians not respected by the public it serves and not trusted by other all-India services.

Deteriorating Law and Order and DM's Authority

The experience of the last two decades or so has shown that both law and order and general district administration have steadily deteriorated. The high incidence of communal tension, case feuds increasing poverty at the lower strata of society, lack of respect for law, ever-increasing terrorism, and the rivalry between the magistracy and the police are manifestations of this deterioration. Lacking the moral strength and stature to resist political pressures, District Magistrates are manipulated to serve individual and sectarian interests, as opposed to the welfare of the majority of the district. The biggest accusation against the District Magistrates today is their total lack of comprehension of the concept of 'service'.

District Magistrates are not to be blamed fully for the state of deterioration in district administration. In early 1995, the gruesome lynching of the DM of Gopalgunj in Bihar was symbolic of the decline of the authority of the District Magistrate. The British rulers considered the 'district' as the pivot of the Indian administration and the District Magistrate was looked upon as the local representative of the Government. He was not only the head of the revenue and law and order administration but the general administration of the district as a whole. He was expected to mobilize the district administration in disasters and calamities like outbreak of epidemic or flood, and to coordinate the work of other departments at the district level. He was the *primus inter pares* among the district level officers, including the Superintendents of Police and this arrangement made the position of the District Magistrate one of authority.

Radical Changes in DM's Role

After independence, in the wake of acceptance of the ideology of the "welfare state" and the technique of planned development, the District Magistrate became the District Development Commissioner. He was saddled with multifarious responsibilities for implementation of variety of laws and programmes in land reforms community development and social extension, co-operation, public distribution, poverty alleviation, and removal of social disabilities. But the scenario began changing in the late sixties. By sheer experience throughout the developing world, the lesson was learnt that development must come through people's participation in policy-design as well as project implementation.

In States like West Bengal, the rejuvenation of political panchayats since late seventies has been the District Magistrates as the Chief Executive Officer of the Zilla Parishad. He has to serve the *Sabhadhipati* (chairman) of the Zilla Parishad, a political figure in the full sense of the term, and overseas the development administration in the district. In other States like Maharashtra, Gujarat and Tamil Nadu, the District Magistrate has been given no direct responsibility for development administration but still he is responsible for achieving coordination between district administration and State administration. He is mostly responsible for removal of administrative difficulties, waste and interdepartmental frictions at the district level for the sake of smooth execution of development schemes.

The District Magistrate today has some other important responsibilities to perform. He is in-charge of the census operations in the district and acts as the Returning Officer for parliamentary elections. Moreover, he functions, in practice, as the chief public relations officer for the government in the district. He is in-charge of liaison with the military authorities in the district. The functional responsibility of different departments of the government is discharged by their respective district-level officers but the District Magistrate's role still remains symbolic of the unity of the Government as an organization so far as the district is concerned.

Inverse Relationship between Responsibilities and Authority

Though the District Magistrate's responsibilities have increased, his authority has declined since independence. In the late-sixties, his relation with local politicians started radically shifting in favour of the latter. The local MLA started looking upon himself not only as a representative of the people but also as a super local administrator with authority to direct local officers, not excluding the District Magistrate. Local politicians not only started acting as ventilators of popular grievances and articulators of the people's needs but also pressurized local administration for a particular decision in a particular case or for posting a particular officer in a particular place or for preventing a particular employee from being transferred to new place. This kind of political interference in administration increasingly became the order of the day making a mockery of the rule of law. By subverting the fundamental principle of democratic administration and introducing political bias in administration, this manner of political interference subverted democratic governance itself. The entire district administration was thus subjected to party-political influence. This trend has gained in strength during the last three decades. A new phenomenon called 'criminalization of politics' began vitiating district administration totally. The influence of criminals grew so much that since late eighties criminals themselves have come to the forefront of politics and managed to sit in various elective bodies of decision-making.

In another respect, the authority and image of the District Magistrate suffered adversely. The work of the police is technical in nature. It cannot be supervised by non-technical administrative authority. Hence, the senior police officers, like DIG and SP, started resenting the authority of the DM in law and order matters. Subsequently, the functionaries of other technical services also asserted their autonomy and resented the authority of the DM over the technical service people in the district. After the autonomy of the police in the district was accepted by the government, the subordinate staff in the police force started taking advantage of the politician-criminal nexus and challenged, in practice, the authority of their own superiors.

Corruption and Criminalization of Politics

Corruption of various kinds entails criminalization of politics. Every political party wants to derive maximum benefit from administrative services which by seventies largely lost their commitment to any value system. The decline of the values and behaviour pattern of the District Magistrates, as in the case of other administrators elsewhere in the services, is responsible for the decline of professions and institutions in the district. The real culprit is the acquisitive spirit dominating all strata in the present Indian society (Perhaps this is a global phenomenon today). Everybody wants to exploit everybody for purely personal advancement and gain. Rightly or wrongly, the popular impression about the ICS officers was one of erudition, integrity, objectivity and unquestioned competence. Most of the professional administrators today do not enjoy any public esteem as India's experience in the nineties typically shows. The decline in the authority and prestige of the District Magistrate is not an isolated phenomenon but is part of an all-round decline of institutions and professions caused by the steady erosion of the value system.

FUTURE OF DISTRICT MAGISTRATE

Considering the changed role of the District Magistrate in India today, some fresh thinking is called for. The original imperialist idea of administering a vast colony, like India, was to have an all-powerful generalist administrator who was made squarely responsible for maintaining peace and tranquillity and managing other affairs in the basic units of administration. This idea of the British imperialist administration was taken up by Napoleon for good governance in France. The role of the French Prefect as a generalist administrator, presiding over the affairs of the prefecture, was mainly designed after the model of the District Officer in India. After serving the nation well for nearly two centuries, the France Prefect has recently given way to a new system of local and regional administration in France because of the new demands of the political forces and the new role of technology in planning and development.

Need to Redefine His Role and Responsibilities

At the turn of the century, India also may think seriously if the system of direct administration, especially in the context of the 73rd and 74th Constitutional Amendments, needs substantial change and reorientation. But so long as Rule of Law as the basic principle of democratic governance cannot be ensured, the role and responsibilities of the District Magistrate must not be diluted. At least, the politico-administrative experiences in Punjab, Bihar, North-East and elsewhere during the last two decades have amply shown that the district administration headed by the District Magistrate needs to be strengthened by re-defining the powers and responsibilities of the DM in his favour, otherwise political chaos and administrative mismanagement are sure to negate India's advance in other fields of nation-building.

The existing system of posting young IAS officers at the helm of district administration and that too for a brief period is not conducive to promoting quality of governance in the districts where bulk of the population lives and the majority of development projects are implemented. Senior officers having adequate exposure in the secretariat should be considered for posting as District Magistrate because the new role envisaged for such an officer in the changed context of democratic decentralization should be intrinsically different from that of a junior officer always looking for a berth in the secretariat or something higher up in course of career advancement. A mature officer, sufficiently senior in comparison with the mandarins in the secretariat, would be in a better position to serve the nation well by his administrative knack and capability of resisting unhealthy local political pressure and tendering well-informed advice in a dignified manner to the elected leaders in-charge of district administration and development activities. The politician and the administrator on the spot can still evolve not rivalry but good partnership. The political and administrative systems should succour each other as they survive in uneasy coexistence.

SUMMING UP

The District Magistrate today has an image of the jeep-borne, VIP-chasing, generalist officer of the Indian Administrative Service. Thanks to democratic decentralization and Panchayati Raj, decision-making, even in administrative matters, has shifted from administrators to elected politicians. In India, today, there is a lamentable lack of professionalism among the administrators. The rise of 'political bureaucracy' is an important post-independence phenomenon. The typical District Magistrate and, for that matter, the typical administrator in India, today, is regarded as narcissistic, self-glorifying breed. Even when not personally corrupt, he is a rule-of-thumb mumbo-jumbo, who is anti-intellectual, anti-knowledge and anti-theory. This temperamental characteristic is the heart of the civil service crisis in India's current milieu of opportunism and demoralization.

12

Decentralizing Administrative Machinery for Development Needs: A Case Study of Andhra Pradesh

Y. VENUGOPAL REDDY

Many developing countries have been attempting decentralized approach to development (with varying degrees of purposiveness and success). There are a number of dimensions to the attempts, such as altering the structures, redefining powers of functionaries at different levels, differentiating between developmental and regulatory activities, integrating administrative structures with local self-government and devising measures for popular participation. In the process of policy application, these dimensions tend to get merged into a set of actions. Existing literature covers theoretical aspects as well as policy applications in this broad field.[1] However, one important element of these policy changes relates to the redefining administrative boundaries of spatial units and locating headquarters of such units from which functionaries administer (or serve the developmental needs) the areas, and population inhabiting the areas. This element (which may be called spatial dimension) would thus involve analyzing links between central place and hinterland with reference to locally appropriate transport network and locational aspects of public services. At a policy level, special analysis of this nature cannot ignore either history or political compulsions. This article seeks to narrate somewhat unique experience of State (province) of Andhra

Pradesh (area of 275 thousand sq.kms. and population of about 60 million and divided into over 20 districts) in attempting decentralization of administrative machinery with an underpinning of spatial analysis.

It is necessary at the outset to indicate that the scope of this article is limited to the need for and the process of redefining administrative boundaries. The constitutionally defined units, viz., the zones (i.e., a group of states which constitute the federation in India) and the states are excluded from the scope of this article. Hence, it will cover the boundaries of districts and in fact focus on the administrative boundaries of units below the district. Further certain issues, such as the relationship between the regulatory and development agencies, the nature of administrative machinery, the extent of democratic decentralization, etc., are not discussed here.

BASIS OF EXISTING UNITS IN INDIA

In India, the administrative units are identified as nation, state, division (group of districts, district, sub-division, taluk, firka, or circle and village).[2] The levels up to and above the state were defined almost entirely on political and linguistic and related considerations and incorporated in the Constitution of India or subsequent legislation. The division is basically an intermediate tier between state and district and exists only in some larger states.

The really operative basic unit in Indian administration has been the district. It will be noticed that the districts, as inherited by independent India, came into existence entirely due to historical accident.[3] However, district continues to be a pivot of the structure of administration in India and is also treated as unit-area for a number of developmental purposes both by the Union Government and by the State Governments. A number of district-level autonomous bodies have also been formed in which both the Union Government and the State Government participate. However, the size of district varies considerably both in terms of area and population. The Planning Commission, even during the first Five Year Plan period, indicated the need for early review of the size of districts by the State Governments among others, from the point of view of the facility of implementing developmental programmes.[4] Consequent on reorganization of the states in 1956 and subsequent creation of some new states, adjustments and creation of new district boundaries have no doubt taken place. Over a period, a number of states did change the boundaries of certain districts. There has, however, been no large scale attempt to redefine the boundaries of the districts in each state on rational basis and even the desirability of defining boundaries on the basis of techniques of regional planning continues to be a major issue of debate.[5] In fact, a major study for readjustment of district boundaries has been done only for the erstwhile Mysore State (now Karnataka State) under the aegis of the Indian Statistical Institute.[6] In the State of Andhra Pradesh, three districts have been formed since 1956, viz., Prakasam (1970), Ranga Reddy (1978) and Vizianagaram (1979). These were again based on ad-hoc decisions with reference to identified local situation in terms of administrative viability or developmental needs.

The taluks, similar to that of the districts, have been brought about totally by historical accident and are basically units of regulatory administration. The boundaries of few taluks have also been changed from time-to-time on the basis of local needs. The taluks encompass both urban and rural areas. However, in the First Five Year Plan, a comprehensive scheme, known as Community Development Programme, was introduced through the establishment of what are known as development blocks. The development blocks cover areas which are not part of urban local self-government. Each district was divided into a number of blocks and each block at that time comprised about 100 villages with a population of about 60,000. Over a period, there has been efforts to make marginal adjustments in the boundaries of the blocks to make them conterminous with taluks (occasionally the boundaries of taluks had also to undergo change to help this process). It may thus be seen that the boundaries as well as the headquarters of taluks and those of the blocks have essentially been the result of historical accident and *ad hoc* decisions respectively. Thus, taluk represented basic administrative unit for regulatory administration and block for developmental administration; a typical district comprised 10 to 25 taluks/blocks. There are well over 300 districts in India.

This system continues in most parts of the country till today. Recently, changes were brought about in Karnataka and Andhra Pradesh. The experience of Andhra Pradesh is described in subsequent paragraphs. To some extent, the changes in Karnataka and Andhra Pradesh were based on need for redefining the administrative boundaries brought to the fore by the Report of the Committee on Panchayati Raj Institutions, popularly known as Asoka Mehta Committee.[7] The Committee reiterated that the districts should be the first point of decentralization, under popular supervision, below the state level. However, below the district level, the Committee suggested Mandal Panchayat covering a population of 15,000 to 20,000. The block level panchayat samitis were expected to be replaced by a Mandal Panchayat over a period though the Block level would continue as an interim measure. In effect, therefore, a new administrative unit, viz., Mandal was suggested by the Committee. In a radical departure, in terms of concept, from the old community development programme which insisted on village as the major unit of development and community life, the Committee emphasized the movement of goods and services as between a primary village and central place. The need for location of facilities at certain central place was recognized. The necessity for focal centre, it was argue, become greater with the commercialization of agriculture and dependence of the rural population on centralized inputs, marketing facilities and social facilities in some of the select settlements.

In this connection, it is interesting to note that the Report indicated that some of the states had undertaken exercises to carve out such growth centres in terms of conceptual framework of rural development. Andhra Pradesh had undertaken such exercises in the context of the Fifth Five Year Plan of Andhra Pradesh.[8] Recommendations of the Report on this aspect of decentralized set-up seems to have emanated out of its appreciation of the exercises undertaken in Andhra Pradesh.

NEED FOR REDEFINING

With this background, it may be possible to recapitulate the major reasons for suggesting redefining of the administrative boundaries in respect of the blocks which were originally conceived as ideal units for development administration and were demarcated with reference to some norms of population and number of villages. These developments are:

(*a*) The recognition that the process of development requires a linkage between the village as a primary unit and higher order settlements, such as central villages, towns, etc.

(*b*) The experience gained in terms of location of social services, such as schools, hospitals, veterinary dispensaries in different villages in the blocks in an uncoordinated manner resulting in stress on the transport and lack of viability for many villages.

(*c*) Due to growth of developmental activities, the number of functionaries in each department has multiplied. As a result, the same functional specialization of a department was represented by two to five functionaries located and working from the block headquarters. This indicated avoidable diseconomies and scope for dispersing the functionaries to other villages in the block.

(*d*) A large number of developmental programmes including family based programmes and commercialization of agriculture resulted in the need to locate some of the infrastructural facilities, like warehousing and social service facilities in a number of central villages within the block. These locations also tended to be uncoordinated. People in the rural areas were demanding services nearer to them than the Block headquarters. The utilization of these services, if they were to be restricted to the Block headquarters, was getting to be difficult for the poorer sections in view of the transport costs involved.

(*e*) Apart from the expansion of the developmental activities, the sheer increase in the growth of population over a period of 30 years necessitated redefining of the boundaries to recognize the need for centrality and reduction in geographical size to take care of the expanded population.

(*f*) Further, with greater democratization in the country, the scope for more effective popular participation could be taken advantage of by reducing the size of unit of local government.

(*g*) A more effective integration between regulatory and developmental administration was possible through a formal integration of borders of taluk and block into a single unit.

(*h*) Finally, the political compulsions (i.e., new party taking over power at the state compared to past) of creating new bases to build the party helped in giving political will for redemarcation in both Karnataka and Andhra Pradesh in early 1980s.

CONCEPTUAL FRAME ADOPTED

In defining the territorial units for administrative purposes, keeping in view the fact that these are meant to be instruments of social and economic change, three important related concepts will have to be appreciated.[9] These would be homogeneity, centrality and viability.

First, while homogeneity of unit depends very much upon the purpose of identification and the criteria used, in the specific context of identification of territorial units of micro regions, the basis will have to be population distribution, geographical area and circulation or movements of the people, goods and services. Implicitly, therefore, nature of movement of the people in connection with the provision and utilization of goods and services covering aspects of distance and mode of transport will be relevant.

Second, it is recognized that by its very nature, development does not appear everywhere and all at once. There is an inherent tendency for activities to get centralized. To avoid misallocation of resources, through over-concentration, it is necessary to select human settlements which are central to the users or beneficiaries and simultaneously disperse social and economic infrastructure. The significance and degree of centrality is determined by both the regional versus local importance and ubiquitous versus non-ubiquitous distribution of infrastructure.

Third, all infrastructural facilities cannot be located in all settlements because a certain minimum number of users is essential for effective utilization of the facilities. The distances, mode of transport, frequency of trips, population-size of relevant users, level of income of the users, and the nature of the use would all determine whether a particular settlement has the necessary viability. While in a theoretical sense we should recognize the hierarchical nature of the centres from central place in villages to a metropolitan city, for the limited purpose of redefining administrative boundaries, the link with big cities, i.e., growth centres and growth poles, is not focused in this article.

The framework of determination of territorial units should, therefore, recognize the fact that the defining of boundaries is a task which implies, in a developmental contest, simultaneous identification of the central place as well as the villages which have to be serviced by the central place. In an administrative sense, therefore, the approach will have to be demarcation of the boundaries of the new territorial unit as well as recognizing the headquarters of such a territorial unit. In identifying the territorial unit, the major factors will be area and population. These have to be linked to the levels of population and area that are appropriate to the functions to be performed by a central place. While this conceptual frame provides an approach; history, politics, resources available, legal framework, data availability and timeliness in providing inputs for decisions, would need search for second best solutions but with underpinning of rationality. The succeeding sections explain the case of application of such rationality.

Improvisation

In the State of Andhra Pradesh, the conceptual frame indicated above had guided the locational decisions of individual services or facilities.[10] This facilitated the adoption of the frame to suit the more demanding task of redefining the boundaries. The features of improvisation of concepts are as follows:

- (*a*) The conceptual frame had to be converted into criteria.
- (*b*) The criteria had to be sufficiently simple for the people, leaders and administrators to understand.
- (*c*) The criteria had to capture simultaneously the relevant parameters, viz., area and population for a unit, functions relevant to a centre to be headquarters, and the weights or importance for different functions.
- (*d*) The criteria had to go in for simple aggregation of different types of services at a central place as headquarters since economies of central location had to be captured. In other words, sector-activity-specific criteria of population or area coverage had to be redone to match the criteria.
- (*e*) Finally, criteria and processes had to be sufficiently flexible to allow interaction with people and elected representatives. Flexibility gives scope for changes in the proposals when

warranted by justifiable circumstances. However, all these arrangements should stand the test of judicial scrutiny.

Hence improvisation of the concepts was the first task which was carried out in a series of meetings resulting in a White Paper. The Paper explains the objectives of decentralization and makes clear that mandals are expected to be roughly one-third to one-fourth the size of the existing taluks in area and population. Thus, a mandal would have a population between 35,000 and 55,000 depending on population density of the taluk concerned. For this purpose, population according to the 1981 census was being adopted. The article also mentions that, as a general rule, the present taluk and samithi headquarters, municipalities and municipal corporations will be retained as headquarters of the revenue mandals; except for specific reasons. In the choice of headquarters for the rest, it was explained that due to weightage would be given to the facilities, like banks, bus stand or railway station, primary health centre, sub-centre or dispensary, veterinary dispensary, police station, post office, telephone exchange, high school, market yard, agricultural godown, the fact that a village is already the headquarters of a firka or revenue circle, and other special features, like availability of accommodation for offices and residence of staff. Most important, the article announces that the principal criterion for inclusion of villages in a revenue mandal would be that the mandal headquarters most accessible to all the included villages resulting in greater convenience to the public.[11]

The Chief Minister, N.T. Rama Rao in a pragmatic justification of the set-up[12] said, "At present the headquarters of the Samithi, market yard revenue office are located at different places. Poor ryots facing hardship are forced to go from place to place to mortgage their property in order to get loans for purchase of manure, fertilizers, etc. This difficulty could be avoided if all the offices are located at one place, i.e., at mandal headquarters."

Methodology

The task for bureaucracy, which also contributed in evolution of these ideas, was to come up with appropriate tools of analysis and procedures, which are described hereunder the broad heading of methodology.

The methodology of redefining administrative units has to be within the framework of white paper that has already been described.

First, weight is given to population and area by defining different ranges of population coverage per territorial unit taking into account the density of population. In other words, less the density, lesser should be population coverage per administrative unit to take account of physical access. *Secondly*, the methodology gives importance to the location of the central place first and identification of the villages which could be linked to such central place in which the central functions or services would be available. *Thirdly*, the fact that there are number of developed villages in which socio-economic infrastuctural facilities have already been created, should be taken both from the point of view of economies and respecting the existing linkages taken as a starting point for identification of central place. *Fourthly*, in terms of administrative convenience, some of the villages which have already been recognized as headquarters of taluks or blocks should be given weightage. *Fifthly*, if there are competing central places, preference has to be given to accessibility to the neighbouring villages. Sixthly, the most important facilities that have to be provided by the government, broadly termed as policy functions appropriate to the territorial unit under consideration, are given importance.

These elements have been codified through a set of detailed guidelines. In order to enable the proposals to be formulated on the basis of a clearly understood analysis, information was gathered about the population and existence of different functions in each of the villages.

The relevant ranges of density and population were centrally worked out. For instance mandals in taluks with density above 300 per sq. km. and density below 200 would have population of 55,000 and 30,000 respectively.

To determine the eligibility for being considered as headquarters, scores were assigned to the facilities (or policy functions). In assigning the scores, the existence of the facility and the level of facility were simultaneously taken into account. Assigning of scores was based on the appreciation of the requirements and the relative importance of the different levels of facilities. Thus, for instance, score of one each is given to village if it has a post office, telegraph office, rest-house, veterinary dispensary; a score of two each for higher medical facility (hospital) market Yard, telephone, police outpost, railway station; and a score of three each for banking facility, high school, bus station, and police station.

It is necessary to recognize that there are non-policy functions, i.e., activities provided by the private sector, but it is difficult to get data. In order to give weightage to these functions for determining the total score, it was considered that the size of the population of a settlement can be taken as a proxy. In other words, a village with larger population can be expected to have more non-policy functions located in the village. A correlation was, therefore, established between the population size of a village and the non-policy functions being performed. As a result, scores were added if the village had a population of more than 1000 adding two for every 1000 but with a ceiling of score of ten to avoid distortions.

Thus, through this method of scoring, the importance of different settlements in terms of their claim for a central place was identified. This process resulted in location of a number of candidate-central places for being considered as mandal headquarters. Having identified a series of candidate-headquarters, an exercise was undertaken to mark on them to maps. These were opened up for discussion at the local level to identify the linkages between the villages and the candidate-central place.

The candidate-central places which are considered eligible to be mandal headquarters were listed in the order of their importance on the basis of the scoring. The hinterland for each one of these candidate-centres was also identified on the map. The area and policy threshold requirements were then introduced in respect of each candidate-central place. Through an interactive process, it was possible to identify the list of headquarters and their hinterland satisfying the area and population threshold criteria.

Procedures

Four district elements in terms of procedures can be identified in the processes of redefining the territorial units, viz.,

First, the analytical input to identify the territorial units;

Second, formulation of legal provisions to bring these territorial units into existence;

Third, ensuring the views of the public particularly political representatives, on the proposals to ensure wide acceptability of the proposals;

Fourth, the necessary follow-up action in terms of redeploying the existing administrative personnel and formulation of a plan of action for locating the services as required in different central places.

The initial step, therefore, was the formulation of proposals on systematic basis keeping in view the methodology indicated. This was done through a process of analytical frame of candidate-centres and areas being provided to the district collectors who are the representatives of the State Government in each district. The district collectors responded to the spatial framework provided by the Planning Department on the basis of the technical exercises. Detailed guidance was given to the collectors to help them come out with specific proposals.

Proposals received on the basis of technical exercises and the assessment of the local conditions by the collector, were examined by a Cabinet Sub-Committee which held a series of discussions in the districts with the elected representatives and in this light made some modifications to the proposals of district collectors. These were notified to public through wide publicity and objections to the intentions of the government invited within a stipulated time. After considering the objections of the public, marginal modifications were made to the notified proposals.

It may be noted that legal framework had already been in existence in terms of an Act enabling the formation of district or sub-district units. The government had issued that notification under this Act. As per the provisions, objections were invited from the public and after detailed legal consideration of the objections, a final notification was issued bringing into effect the new administrative units, viz., revenue mandals.

It was possible to redeploy the existing staff of the revenue administration easily since the administrative set-up was already under the control of the State Government and appropriate personnel with sufficient experience were already available. Related facilities had to be planned simultaneously. However, till the related facilities were fully brought into existence, some of the facilities at one headquarter had to be shared by more than one mandal. At the same time, a survey had been undertaken to identify the locational gaps in the availability of services that ought to be provided in each mandal headquarters.

On the basis of such survey, provisions have been made in the development plans of each sector to locate these facilities. For instance, the primary health centres, the veterinary hospitals, etc., are proposed to be started on this basis by introducing them as integrated parts of the plans of individual sectors. In respect of facilities like banks, the State Government has taken up with the Reserve Bank of India the need to set up banks in these headquarters. Simultaneously, the Director of Town and Country Planning has been asked to identify land in each of the mandal headquarters where these facilities can be located in an integrated fashion. The building plans are also being finalized accordingly. Further, to avoid land grabbing and land speculation, the government had issued orders banning assignment of government lands in a specified radius in these headquarters. Common facilities, including shared computer facilities, are proposed to be established in each one of these mandal headquarters during the Seventh Five Year Plan[13] linking them with state headquarters through the districts.

Separate action was also required to bring about the necessary changes in the local self-government. Thus, panchayat samithis which were mostly co-terminus with the erstwhile taluks got abolished after the expiry of their tenure of June 1986. They are now replaced by units co-terminus with revenue mandals. Elected bodies for each of the mandals have been brought in subsequently.

CONCLUSION

While macro-economic policies have gained importance in the context of development planning, spatial dimension, as applied to decentralizing administrative machinery, had been a relatively neglected area though it affects rural poor very intimately. Part of the reason is lack of analytical tools capable of policy application. The case study of Andhra Pradesh (India) illustrates a possible set of analytical tools.

REFERENCES

1. D.A. Rondinelli, *Decentralization in Developing Countries: A Review of Recent Experience*, World Bank Staff Working papers, Washington, DC, 1983; and Diana Conyers, "Decentralization and Development:

A Review of the Literature", *Public Administration and Development*, Vol. 4, 1984, pp. 187-97, Charles Downs, "Regionalization, Administrative Reform and Democratization: Nacaragua 1979-84" *Public Administration and Development*, Vol. 7, 1987, pp. 383-97.

2. Y. Venugopal Reddy, *Multilevel Planning in India*, New Delhi, Vikas, 1979.
3. V.L.S. Prakasa Rao, *Spatial Framework for Development Administration and Planning*, Hyderabad, Centre for Economic and Social Studies, 1985.
4. India, Planning Commission, *The First Five Year Plan*, New Delhi, Manager of Publications, Government of India, 1952.
5. Y. Venugopal Reddy, *Op. cit.*
6. V.L.S. Prakasa Rao and L.S. Bhat, *Regional Studies No. 1, Planning Regions in the Mysore State: The Need for Readjustment of District Boundaries*, Calcutta Indian Statistical Institute, 1960.
7. India, Ministry of Agriculture, *Report of the Committee on Panchayat Raj Institutions*, New Delhi, Manager of Publication, Government of India, 1978.
8. Government of Andhra Pradesh, *Fifth Five Year Plan, Technical Papers III, Area Planning Approach*, Hyderabad, Government of Andhra Pradesh, 1975.
9. V.L.S. Prakasa Rao, *Op. cit.*
10. Government of Andhra Pradesh, *Technical Paper III, Op. cit.*
11. Government of Andhra Pradesh, *White Paper on Creation of Revenue Mandals*, Hyderabad, Legislative Assembly, Government of Andhra Pradesh, 1985.
12. N.T. Rama Rao, *Mandal Set-up of Administration*, Hyderabad, Director of Information and Publicity, Government of Andhra Pradesh, 1985.
13. Government of Andhra Pradesh, *Seventh Five Year Plan*, Hyderabad, Government of Andhra Pradesh, 1986.

13

District Collector and Decentralised Health Planning

B.B.L. SHARMA AND A.D. TRIPATHI

Seventh Five Year Plan document of Government of India records: that the nation is committed to attain the goal of health for all by 2000 AD. To achieve this, primary health care has been accepted as main instrument of action. Again, the plan document states clearly that family welfare occupies an important position in the socio-economic development plans. Health and family welfare planning plays a crucial role in human resource development and in improving the quality of life of the people. Besides, Maternal and Child Health (MCH) is intimately related to family welfare. So, the thrust of all developmental plans of the Government for the betterment of people is an improvement in the quality of life of the people. This concern is reflected all through the various plans seeking better health care and population stabilisation in the country. However, this thrust had become more explicit in the current plan:

(*i*) To achieve the goal of health for all by 2000 AD and precisely for that hardly 11 years are left to attain that target; and

(*ii*) To achieve the population stabilisation at the replacement level for India by 2000 AD.

In the area of population stabilisation, some success is there, but that is less than desired due mainly to:

(*i*) Less than optimal use of available resources;
(*ii*) Lack of infrastructure facilities, which hamper the quality of programmes;
(*iii*) High levels of maternal, infant and child mortality;
(*iv*) Political, social, economic, cultural factors; and
(*v*) Lack of desired effective administration, coordination and integration of programme efforts.

Although, the demographic situation in India is a matter of grave concern and poses challenge for development, Government is confident on the basis of its national experience and also through the documentation of international experiences that the goals for demographic stabilisation, better MCH care and improved health can be achieved.

Now, it has been very well-understood that population stabilisation, improvement in MCH and general health care requires a multi-dimensional and multi-involvement approach. This is more relevant in the light of the recent focus on decentralised micro-planning. This, in fact, means revitalisation of planning process at district level and below. Though, the Planning Commission issued guidelines to the states for initiating district planning as far back as in 1969, yet it remained un-operational. This, at least, is more true for the health and family welfare sector.

IDEAL ADMINISTRATIVE AND ORGANISATIONAL LEVEL

In the context mentioned above, it is envisaged that the most ideal administrative and organisational level will be that of a district to make efforts for initiating the district level planning to solve the population and health problems. This could be achieved through multi-dimensional approach or multi-pronged strategy to be evolved at district level to resolve the problem. This is becoming more pertinent in the light of the considered thinking about decentralised planning, right from the grassroot level, for which district will be a suitable nodal and intermediate point for developmental efforts.

When it becomes an agreed preposition, then the functionary to be the 'kingpin' of such efforts is the District Collector or Deputy.

Commissioner as it is called in some states. Before indicating what role District Collector can play more effectively, it will be better to see what position and role the District Collector has which can be more effectively utilised for giving boost to family welfare, MCH, and health programmes in the district.

Position of District Collector in India

The First Year Plan document points out that the structure of the administration developed during the past century was based on the district as principal unit with District Collector as the government's principal representative in touch with the people.

Besides, being in control of the administration of law and order and revenue in the district, the District Collector held a coordination responsibility for the activities of all departmental agencies within the district. In the hierarchy of administration, he enjoyed status and power which gave him considerable influence over the local population.

The district is still the most important single unit of administration and District Collector is the intermediary between the State Government executives and people.

Changing Role of District Collector

Since independence (1947) and particularly from the advent of planning (1952), the primary emphasis in district administration is on the implementation of development programme in close cooperation and with the active support of people. This envisages integration of various development departments in the district and linking up in relation to all development work. This also requires coordination and supervision of district development programme by District Collector.

In this context, it is also recognised that it is at the district level that attention in implementation of programme is focused and it is at the district level again that the relationship of administration and citizen assumes significance. Not only district administration provides principal points of contact between the citizen and the process of government, but in it is also found a structure and organisation for influencing the policy decisions at the district as well as state levels. It is because the Collector is the principal representative of State Government in the districts in India. District Collector through its agencies in the field give him a position of prominence not only for informing himself and the government but also coordinating and integrating the developmental activities of government with the aspirations of the people.

As Coordinator and Facilitator

This is because of the fact that Collector in the district is the captain of the team of officers of all departments and is responsible for securing the necessary coordination and cooperation in the perpetuation and execution of the district plans in the community development. The position may vary from state to state but District Collector invariably is the Chairman of District Development Council/Zilla Parishad, and in some States Collector is also the Chairman of the Standing Committee of Zilla Parishad.

After having identified the position and authority of District Collector, let us try to illustrate:

(*i*) How his position of authority and importance is most suited for health and family welfare programmes; and

(*ii*) The backdrop of information, knowledge, and skills required by him for administering, gearing up, and coordinating the programmes related to population stabilisation and health care.

AUGMENTATION AND ENERGISING THE HEALTH INFRASTRUCTURE

Strategy document of Government of India (1986-1990) towards population stabilisation indicates, on the basis of documented studies, that the reach and utilisation of family welfare, MCH and health care services is low and not very much satisfactory quality-wise. This prevailing condition of low reach and utilisation of services by the people is one of the big bottlenecks in solving the problem of population stabilisation and better health care. Many factors are responsible for this. One of the most important factors is the 'inertia' of the functionaries delivering the health and family welfare services to rural areas and urban slums. Others relate to non-filling of the positions, uneven distribution of staff and the problems connected with logistics and supply of medicines, drugs, equipment and other items falling in the category of infrastructure.

MODEL ORGANISATIONAL SET-UP

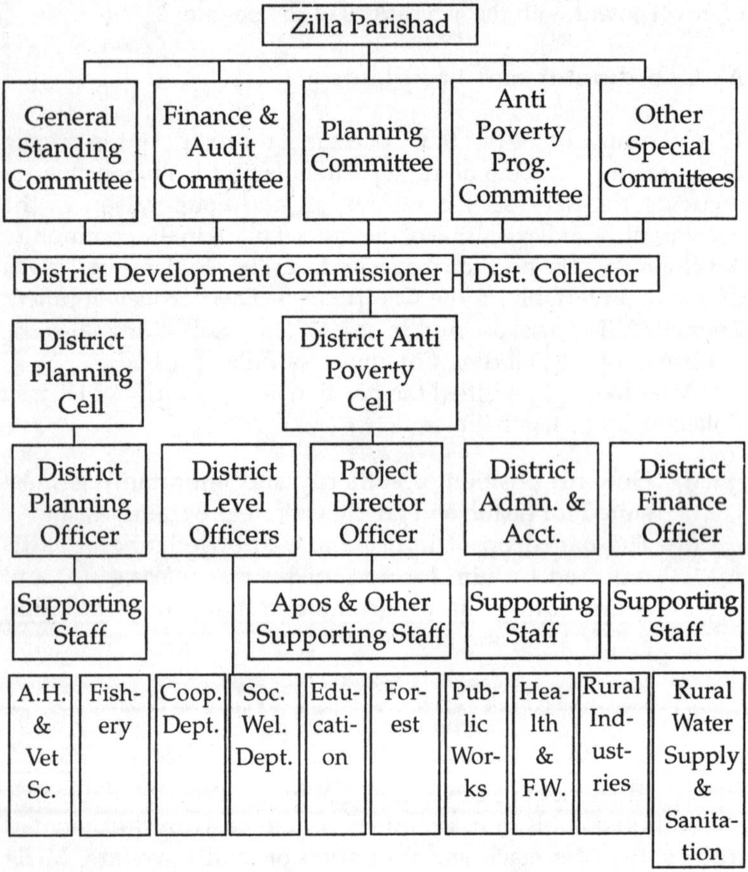

Source: *Report of the Committee to Review the Existing Administrative Arrangements for Rural Development and Poverty Alleviation Programmes*, Department of Rural Development, Ministry of Agriculture, December 1985.

What District Collector can do in the context of the district planning process for augmentation and energising of the infrastructure, particularly in rural areas, using his position and authority, has to be seen. District Collector can go systematically to find out all possible reasons prevailing precisely and mainly for the low reach of services and 'inertia' amongst the concerned staff. For example, on the part of health functionaries, the efforts may be lacking because of lack of basic facilities to them, like that of construction and allotment of residential accommodation, lack of transport, etc.

District Collector, first of all, may get a quick snap-shot observation-survey conducted to find out the precise and detailed reason for the low outreach of health and family welfare services in his district. For this District Collector can get prepared a map of the whole district, its blocks, villages and those pockets where outreach and utilisation of family welfare and health services remained: (*i*) low althrough, (*ii*) low only currently, and (*iii*) have never reached. This will give him the idea of his whole district for and with reference to health and family welfare planning. Thereafter, District Collector can call for or seek from the workers, their supervisors and also with the help of district intelligence machinery, the reasons for non-achievement of family welfare and MCH targets and low utilisation of health and family welfare services in the various pockets of the district. Getting this systematic exercise done will facilitate sorting out the problems in minute details, whether these are related to augmentation and energising existing infrastructure for 'inertia' or otherwise due to some other considerations.

When the quick analysis reveals that low performance is due to dormancy of the health and family welfare staff or inadequacy of personnel to man the positions, he can further probe, with district health authorities, the reasons for this sort of position and the efforts done by district level health authorities to overcome the prevailing situation. Here, he can play direct and indirect roles or he can provide direct and indirect support to the system to energise the infrastructure. District Collector can write a special note and report to the State Health Authorities to help improve the situation, particularly with reference to filling the positions, and improving the logistics so that health functionaries may be able to work more effectively. The direct role which he can play, exercising the position of his authority and leadership is as follows:

(*i*) Getting clearly delineated the job responsibility of all categories of employees;

(*ii*) Providing residential accommodation to all health functionaries right from peripheral level (village level) to district level;
(*iii*) Sanctioning advances for purchase of transport to all health functionaries;
(*iv*) Getting the existing and available infrastructure facilities evenly distributed all the regions of a district;
(*v*) Developing a special constant monitoring mechanism in the collector's office; and
(*vi*) Making a cell to redress grievances of the health and family welfare functionaries.

Augmentation and Energising Other Departments

It is now well-recognised that family welfare, MCH and health care is not the exclusive or sole responsibility of the functionaries belonging to health and family welfare departments. This is more true in the context of quick promotion and implementation of these programmes at the district level. Here merely reducing or mitigating the inertia amongst health and family welfare staff may not pay full dividends. But the full and quick success of the programmes are related to moderation of fertility, reducing the mortality and improvement in the utilisation of health care services. This can happen when all other developmental departments join hands and work in a composite manner to the success of these programmes. In this context, District Collector can play a major role being captain at the district level. He can bring all the departments at one platform to contribute towards the goal of reaching health for all and population stabilisation levels in the district in due course. His directions in this regard are prone to show desired results. He can show how these programmes of health and family welfare will be helpful to their respective departments and their activities and how in turn these departments can extend help for health and family welfare activities while doing their own work. The real effort of a District Collector lies in the intersectoral coordination. For example, a District Collector may use his position to further energise and involve the department of education (the teachers) for improving school health programmes. He can get created a chain of school health clubs in all village schools for spreading education about immunisation, nutrition, health care and informing them about advantages of small family norms. District Collector can make use of his being head of District Development Committee in his district and utilise departments of agriculture, forest and social welfare in the efforts for improving the nutritional aspects of the programmes. Projects like that of 'Poshak Ahar' can vigorously be run with District Collector as a leader and monitor of such efforts in which even community financing can also be generated by him besides energising other departments. District Collector can use the mechanism of meetings with the staff of other departments and picking and choosing enthusiastic workers to assigning tasks and rewarding their efforts. Main role on the part of District Collector can be to convince other departments at District level about the importance of their contribution in social programmes like family welfare, MCH and health care.

Formation and Activising of Committees

Unless some formal official structure is not developed at (*a*) the District, (*b*) Municipal/Corporation levels, (*c*) Block and Panchayat levels, and (*d*) Village level from amongst the functionaries of other departments operative at district level, the real, continuous and full involvement of various departments at these levels will not be possible. Without devising an organisational structure for the project, multi-sectoral involvement and action towards small family norm, increasing programme performance for health, family welfare and MCH will not be a workable preposition. After due orientation and sensitising various developmental departments about their prospective role and importance for contributing towards health and family welfare work, it will be in the fitness of the working that District Collector gives direction about formation of District/Block/Village level committees which would have in these committees functionaries from all developmental departments at these levels. These committees will have representatives from Department of Health and Family Welfare also and suitable action plans can be got drawn for implementation in the specified area in the specified time limit. Technical support can come from Department of Health and Family Welfare and these Committees would function under overall control and direction of District Collector as head of apex committee at the district level.

Through these committees, small activities can be got initiated which will have integrated bearing on the improvement of health and family welfare programmes.

Orientation and Sensitisation

District Collector can take a special administrative responsibility in the orientation and sensitisation of the district level and block level officers belonging to various departments regarding the importance and gravity of problem of family planning and MCH and health care. District Collector can also have dialogue and informal meeting with District Officers to elicit what role they can play in augmenting the programmes for health and family welfare. This orientation and sensitising may be possible by holding: (*i*) initial contact meeting, and (*ii*) arranging symposia inviting population scientists from State or the Centre. During orientation, the District Officers from various departments can be briefed about the demographic, health and socio-economic profile of the district *vis-à-vis,* the State and the country as also that about possible solutions available or sought elsewhere. An outcome of these meetings, seminars, workshops, conferences could be that interaction will generate in other departments and may lead to develop a concrete thinking and action plans, to contribute towards health and family planning efforts at the district level through their respective machinery.

Coordination with Voluntary Organisations

Strategy paper towards population stabilisation (1986-90) indicates that voluntary organisation will be associated more closely and actively with the programme in order to fully exploit their potential for innovation and dedication to the cause, proximity to and credibility with the people. In this context, District Collector's role can be vital as he is the Government's representative in the district, directly in touch with people as well as people's organisation involved in welfare activities. District Collector's role becomes more crucial in the light of the suggestions made in the Action Plan strategy of Government of India towards the priority programme of population stabilisation in the country. In the coming years, efforts should be made so that every district will have at least three voluntary organisations working for the health and family welfare programme. One of them may be designated as the lead voluntary organisation.

The efforts can be initiated at the district level by the District Collector for identifying suitable voluntary agencies operating in the district or adjoining area. District Collector's role is not limited only to identifying and recommending suitable voluntary organisation but also nominating a support committee for voluntary efforts in health and family planning. In this committee, people can be drawn from different walks of life including those from various voluntary organisations. This broad based committee, with District Collector as its chairperson, can guide, direct, consolidate the efforts being done by voluntary and other agencies in the area of family welfare and health care. This committee at the district level can have committees at block level for monitoring the efforts. District Collector can make financial assistance available through district funds as well as by approaching state authorities and foundations/enterprises operating in the district.

Generating Community Participation

The basis of primary health care depends on the effective role of the community. The community can play its role more effectively when it is induced for involvement, interaction, initiation and planning for participation towards health and family welfare efforts for their betterment. To start with, this is difficult. Hence, patience and perseverence are needed for generation of community participation, as a support mechanism to boost up programme component of primary health care, *viz.*, family welfare, MCH, etc. In this effort, role of District Collector as a chief catalytic agent at the district level is the most important. Through his position and authority, District Collector can induce and facilitate the efforts of mobilising the community. More than this, through his available administrative apparatus and set-up which functionally penetrates up to grassroot community level, District Collector can act as a manager of whole administrative set up to steer towards participatory efforts. He has multiple developmental activities to cater to the community, directly and indirectly and through these activities, District Collector can generate, manage and monitor participatory processes in the community. His position can enable him to combat the hindrances which come in the way of community participation. His administrative contacts and the administrative network of intelligence at his disposal makes his position unique to understand and control such factors.

Formation of Popular Committees

As a main instrument of generating positive and continuous community response from the community groups to promote family welfare, MCH and health care programme, official or departmental/governmental committees may not be able to do full justice to solve the demographic and health situations or problems at district level and below. Full implementation of policies and programme strategies devised at the official level is possible through formation and active participation of popular committees at different levels and developing their corresponding links with each other at all levels. The structure of such popular committees at all levels, *i.e.* district/block/village, should be such that it should have members from all sections of the society at large and those specifically of different communities. For example, District Collector can workout a plan for formation of these committees to help the F.W.-MCH-Health programme efforts consisting of:

1. Elected representatives of people—MP/MLA/MLC/Member of Zilla Parishad;
2. Members of different political parties;
3. People belonging to professional groups, like lawyer, doctors, engineers and teachers;
4. Members from cultural groups;
5. Religious leaders;
6. Media related people;
7. Members of voluntary organisations in the area;
8. Members from weaker sections, S.C/S.Ts.; and
9. People belonging to artisans groups.

Involvement of Special Groups

For generation and management of community participation as an adjunct to the official efforts to push the family welfare, MCH and Health Care Programmes at the periphery levels, involvement of special groups by District Collector is necessary. Such special population or community groups may be too many to enumerate. However, few important ones will be women's groups or Mothers Health Clubs, Student Groups or School Health Clubs, Youth Clubs, Farmers Group, etc. Not necessary that such groups would be already existing in the villages. Wherever these are not there in existence, these are required to be got created by District Collector utilising his district extension functionaries of health and other departments. The village extension, block extension and district extension staff may be given the special task of inducing the participation of such groups and this work should be started with the formation or creation of groups like village women's health clubs, village school health clubs, etc. However, wherever such groups are already formed in whatever scanty and semi-organised manner. District Collector should direct, through meetings and circulars, his extension force in the district departments to further strengthen and activise such existing groups. This is possible through making these women, children and youth groups more broad-based and multi-functional. These Mother's Health and F.W. Clubs and youth groups can simultaneously be oriented through inputs like: (*a*) small training and demonstration courses, and (*b*) financial help for many diverse but interrelated activities of applied nutrition programmes, child care immunisation, family welfare and environmental sanitation.

Special involvement of students community is possible when District Collector takes it up with education department. This involvement can be started with his direction in initiating formation of school health clubs where students and teachers can participate at all levels, i.e., village, block and district. Through his direction, such special group of school health clubs can be utilised by him to augment various programmes at all levels, viz., school health programmes, etc. He can utilise the force of student community through his district extension machinery to activise immunisation and other programmes as school children are the potential health educators and change agents and women (mothers) are considered first and best provider of health care.

Involvement of Private Medical Practitioners

Intersectoral coordination for promotion of health and family welfare work envisages three types of coordination: (*i*) within the official health system, (*ii*) within the overall health system, including non-official health resources (manpower, etc.), and (*iii*) outside the health system. The District Collector is in position to take advantage of all the three tiers of intersectoral coordination. But his most potential resource will be the involvement of private medical practitioners for the promotion of health and family welfare efforts in his district. The specific reason for this resource being most important is that private medical practitioners penetrate deep in the community life up to the grassroot level. Not only these practitioners—whether Aurvedic, Allopathic, or indigenous traditional health healers—are available at the doorsteps or in village corridors to the people but they have also earned faith and reputation of the people over the period of time. Such a medical manpower, howsoever inadequately qualified it may appear in terms of qualified medical standards, is definitely a force to reckon with.

District Collector can mobilise this potential medical manpower arranging orientation and sensitising camps for them. Private medical officers can be involved through calling them in workshops, meetings and informal dialogues initiated by District Collector from time to time at various levels and on various occasions, both formal and informal. He can generate feeling through his 'managerial leadership', so that the private medical practitioners, particularly in rural areas may start feeling concerned about national programmes for the people. A blueprint of action plans for private medical practitioners can be got developed at district level and District Collector can act as a 'monitor' of such action plans which may have some reward and appreciation mechanism for sustaining private medical practitioner's interest in the programme.

SOME THRUST AREAS

For contributing towards solutions of problems related to population stabilisation and MCH care, etc., District Collector has lot of scope, authority, and managerial and administrative opportunities. He can energise and electrify the whole situation directly through the programmes within the purview of health services as well as via special developmental measures which are beyond family planning. Many thrust areas for District Collector's direct and immediate concern can be identified and listed. Few thrust areas are discussed here which may have some bearing and relevance to the programme efforts and in which he can play a major and important role:

1. Child survival and immunisation;
2. Increasing age of marriage; and
3. Implementing differential strategy.

A stage has come in India's demographic scene where its future fertility goals will be difficult to achieve unless these goals are intimately and deliberately linked with some developmental variables. Developmental variables are to be taken in broader sense. For realising and sustaining one such goal of development is the reduction in infant and child mortality. Universally low infant mortality has been found to be linked with decline in fertility. Keeping this contention in view, District Collector may start special drives with the help of district health authorities and also utilising infrastructural support from Agriculture, Veterinary, Tribal and Social Welfare and other allied departments and developing 'institutional linkages' for nutrition-cum-immunisation and child care programme. District Collector's working in this perspective, particularly for weaker sections not only would bring forth more chances of tackling various developmental problems but he will also be able to provide and develop a 'motivational base' for pushing the programmes for family welfare, MCH and health care in his district.

Action Plans for Special Thrust Area Programmes

District Collector can have specific role in bringing the concerned department and agencies, particularly for two special programme drives: (*i*) successful implementation of universal immunisation at District/Block/Village level; and (*ii*) Oral Rehydration Therapy programmes. District Collector may use his good offices in getting detailed action plans developed for these important strategies of child survival and through his specially appointed committees, in which Village Health Guide and Trained Dai should be a member at village level. At Block level, District Collector can get organised special *Bal Swasthya Melas* where demonstration for ORS and child nutrition benefits of immunisation, etc., should be demonstrated to people. Initiation of such efforts by District Collector will give boost to family welfare and MCH efforts at the district and lower levels.

Raising Mean Age of Marriage

In our country, although legal age of marriage is 18 years for girls yet in practice seven per cent females get married in the age group of 10-14 years and about 44 per cent married females are between 15-19 years of ages. Nearly three million estimated marriages (of 4 million total) annually take place in the age group of 15-19 years. This situation is worst in some states. Similarly, there are many districts in India where this situation further gets aggravated.

This dimension of low female age of marriage results in many complex problems of ill health, too early pregnancy and mortality of children and high fertility. What District Collector as an administrator can do in this regard depends on his innovative approaches and thinking. With his efforts, he may counteract this problem which is mainly confined to villages and more so in particular classes and communities.

Mere administrative authority of sending circulars/letters/ wireless messages may not be sufficient for implementation of this social legislation regarding restraining the child marriages. More than its legality or legal consequences, the health, social and economic benefits to the individual and family, particularly belonging to weaker sections, are required to be highlighted through extension efforts organised at his level. District Collector can constitute a committee, which can be called Social Consciousness Committee, drawing people from all departments and all walks of life who have been social activists to promote social change programmes like that of shifting the attitude of the people towards increase in age at marriage. His efforts as monitor-manager and coordinator of social change for increasing age of marriage will rest not much in negative manner of emphasising deterrent punishment for breach of law relating to minimum age at marriage. Rather, as the highest administrative representative for managing social change, District Collector would be able to do a lot in this direction as discussed below:

(*i*) Forming 'Social Consciousness Committees' at village/block/district level for (*a*) creating awareness about the legal age at marriage, and (*b*) transmitting benefits, particularly health and social benefits, to family.

(*ii*) Involving voluntary organisations to create social climate for raising marriagable age for females.

(*iii*) Promoting female education facilities through incentives to those families of weaker sections who educate and marry of their daughters beyond prescribed legal age of marriage. Since this measure requires multisectoral support, District Collector through his control and authority may make use of district education set-up for augmenting female education.

(*iv*) District Collector may get generated funds and resources from the public and other private establishments to arrange mass simple and dowryless marriages for the daughters of weaker sections, who participate in programmes of upholding legal age of marriage and having small family.

(*v*) District Collector, as manager of the social affairs in the district, can workout various schemes of giving incentives through IDRP funds, and funds from wasteland development schemes to the newly married women who not only confirmed to the minimum legal age at marriage but also properly spaced their children after marrying above the legal age of marriage, and got their child immunized.

(*vi*) As a multi-sectoral departmental move, District Collector may involve women welfare agencies, human resource department functionaries, students, teachers and media infrastructure at the district level for propagation, in village and urban slums, efforts for raising marriageable age of females and its positive benefits to family, women and children in particular.

Throughout the district, all the time and over the years, same or uniformed and identical strategy of functioning, coordinating and integrating of family welfare, MCH and health care may not be viable and very effective. Wide differences exist not only in Blocks and Tehsils in a district but also within Blocks area and cluster of villages where the performance and acceptance of family welfare, MCH and health care services are either very low or very high. District Collector can take special cognisance of such situations prevailing in the area District Collector may evolve, with the help of his associates at the district, different and corresponding strategies workable in different blocks/ pockets and regions within the district. His approach in solving such problems may generate out of his 'fact finding' and analytical style to go into the details about the minute reasons of prevailing situation. In some pockets of the district, the reason for lesser success may be unapproachable all whether road, non-deployment of staff or political resistance. At some other places, the better success in certain blocks and pockets may be due to commitment of functionaries working in the area, active interest of voluntary organisations better logistics, etc. District Collector can derive suitable insights from factors associated with low or high performance, i.e., factors which either push or block the programmes. His managerial skills and authority can help mitigating or lessening the blocking factors and further pushing the positive ones. So, his strategy will be a blending of many aspects of efforts, including involvement of few social scientists from the district institutions in the social council and that of some social workers to work for the programmes, in order to help correct the inhibiting factors.

Revitalising the Mass Media

For meeting or reaching and contacting more people, a multipronged strategy of revamping the media activities and the whole communication programme is required. In this context, the special role of District Collector will be with reference to energise the media efforts already going on and also developing more interest in the development of the folk media in the district. High technology based medium for propagations of messages about health and family welfare, MCH, etc., may have higher reach in terms of their respective wavelength, etc., or physical recording. However, the reality now is that the impact of traditional and folk art is greater and deeper in this regard.

The special campaigns, utilising appropriate technology and local talents, particularly in the rural areas, for popularising the preventive and promotive aspects of health care along with the importance of small family norm, advantages of well spaced children, maternal-child health care, etc., are required to be got developed using Collector's good office and powers at the district level. Special efforts in this campaign could be on immunisation and de-emphasising the preference for male children. In this social venture, District Collector's meeting with the Village Groups and Village Associations will be of great advantage. These meetings can both be formal and informal and such meetings could also be tagged with other developmental meetings.

Informal Meetings with Village People

District Collector as communicator or in the role of a communicator can make an effective dent on the thinking of people with the informal dialogue mechanism than merely issuing the leaflets, circulars, appeals or orders, etc. Mere his presence in the meetings, particularly with rural folk, may build a strong bridge between family welfare, MCH and health programmes and people than through any formal and sophisticated communication mechanism. By virtue of his being a strong link between people and Government, District Collector knows the language of the people. His authority and power enables District Collector to get the programme efforts translated in reality more quickly through his day-to-day involvement in developmental efforts. Much, however depends on his style of functioning.

Role of OTC and Small Newspapers

Two more mechanisms that the District Collector can find more useful as operational strategies for revamping the whole communication programmes are: (1) strengthening and streamlining of Orientation Training Camps (OTCs), and (2) involvement of small newspapers for creating a positive atmosphere for implementing programmes related to health and family welfare and MCH. These two strategies can form a strong base for convincing the people. District Collector can encourage these organs through his liberal financial support and other mechanisms, viz., inviting the editors and writers in these small newspapers at the district level to the official meetings for discussions on health and family welfare programmes. Some financial allocation can be made for feature writing for propagation of health and family welfare themes in the press.

Decentralisation and Financial Process

ICSSR and ICMR document on *Health For All: An Alternate Strategy* indicates that the allocated budget should reach the most peripheral body that controls the health activity (*e.g.*, the Gram Panchayat for the village and sub-centre, the Panchayat Samithi for the Community Health Centre and Zilla Parishad for the District Health Centres). In this respect, the District Collector's role can be very crucial in seeing whether such delegation of administrative and financial responsibility to the local authorities—and ultimately to local communities—is taking place or not. District Collector can work for and towards decentralisation of such efforts which may contribute towards promotion of health and family welfare programmes. His efforts will be most beneficial through strengthening the whole procedure of sanctioning and simplifying the procedures for disbursement of money.

Monitoring and Review of Progress

Monitoring and evaluation of District Action Plans to boost up family welfare, MCH and health care programmes are not isolatory exercises to be operationalised in vacuum. Instead monitoring and evaluation can be linked through the intervention of District Collector with various stages and mechanisms for planning and plan implementation. No doubt, without a good monitoring system, whether it is a sophisticated Management Information System (MIS) or a simple lay reporting, the programme cannot succeed. A successful monitoring system has to pass through various stages. Few of these suggested stages/steps and mechanism for planning, implementing along with monitoring and evaluation, to be directed and administered by District Collector, are given in the chart on page 249. These are not exhaustive but tentative. District Collector may get an exercise done to redo and reshape these steps and stages that are more relevant to his district situation. This exercise should form part of the Action Research Plan at District/Block/Village Level.

Suggested Stages and Mechanism for Planning, Implementation, Monitoring and Evaluation of District Action Plan for Health, Family Welfare and MCH

Full Knowledge of National/State/District Level Objectives

STAGE-I

General identification of beneficiaries in terms of
- Demographic
- Social
- Economic
- Health & FW Data

Resourses
- Agriculture
- Rural Industry
- Health
- Education
- District Rural Development Agencies

Organisational Structure
- Officially sponsored like panchayats, women's orgns. and village health guides
- Youth clubs, schools, colleges, etc.
- Traditional religious, cultural & social
- Voluntary orgns.

STAGE-II

Client Groups for Health, FW and MCH
- Satisfied users and innovators
- Prospective Acceptors
- Non-responsive and resistors (their values and attitudes)

Formulation and Reassessment of Strategies
- Entry point i.e. education & awareness
- Incentive
- Linkages with other developmental deptts.
- Participation through various community groups
- Information, education and communication

STATE-III

Preparation of draft action plans for the district

Discussion of draft action plan with other district development deptts., voluntary organisations and community groups

Resource, Estimation and Mobilisation
- Govt. resources
- Voluntary agencies and community
- Inter and intra-sectoral coordination
- Private enterprises

STAGE-IV

Plan implementation

Assignment of time bound role and responsibilities
- Health and FW functionaries
- Other developmental deptts.
- Voluntary orgns.
- Community groups

Monitoring through Meetings, Visits and Reports
- Activity-wise
- Department-wise
- Community group-wise
- Non-govt. organisation functionary-wise

Evaluation
- Comparison with baseline information

The suggested first step–which would help overall planning, implementation, monitoring and evaluation–is having full knowledge of national objectives/goals, viz., National Health Policy, National Population Policy, National Nutrition Policy and National Education Policy. Besides this. District Collector's detail knowledge about state level objectives/goals will help him formulate District level goals/objectives, etc. This would give him thematic idea of arriving at practicals solutions about his own district while remaining in conformity with state/national goals and objectives. Thereafter stage one will include: (*i*) identification of prospective beneficiaries in terms of demographic, social, economic health and family welfare data, (*ii*) identification or listing of resources under health and family welfare, agriculture, rural industry, education, district rural development agency, (*iii*) identification of available organisational structures–official as well as non-sponsored ones like women's organisation, youth clubs, traditional, religious, cultural and social organisations, voluntary organisations, private medical practitioners, village health guides, village trained dais; and (*iv*) identification of documentation of special schemes like that of rural employment, etc.

After having identified the prospective beneficiaries and client groups, knowing their values and attitudes, the strategies so developed will be monitored from time-to-time. The plan objectives or goals set for the district has to be monitored and evaluated with a timeframe or timescale, with a quality recording scale and 'change scales' developed with the assistance of District Statistical unit and other health programme machinery at his disposal. The suggested 'entry points' can be education, incentives, communication of information, participatory efforts through groups, etc. For plan formulation and monitoring, knowledge and identification of entry points will be necessary.

Assignment of time-bound roles and responsibilities to individuals and groups of various departments, besides health resource estimation, mobilisation and allocation for the activities and their monitoring would have to be done through meetings at all levels, developing quick reporting system and getting prepared PERT charts, etc., for scheduling and Gantt charts, etc. Preparation of Gantt charts for activity monitoring would help District Collector to make needed mid-course adjustment' at the interval of three to six months for solving the problems and making the programme delivery of family welfare, MCH and health care more effective.

REFERENCES

Government of India, *Report of the Working Group on District Planning*, Vol. I, New Delhi, Planning Commission, 1984, p. 167.

Government of India, *Report of the Working Group on District Planning*, Vol. II, New Delhi, Planning Commission, 1988, p. 220.

Government of India, *Seventh Five Year Plan—1985-90*, Vol. II, New Delhi, Planning Commission, 1985, p. 421.

Government of India, *Revised Strategy for National Family Welfare Programme: A Summary*, New Delhi, Ministry of Health and Family Welfare, 1985, p. 32.

J.P. Gupta and B.B.L. Sharma, "*District and Block Level Planning for Health*", Paper presented at the *Thirteenth Annual Conference of Indian Association for the Study of Population*, 1988, p 19.

14

New Pattern of District Administration in Andhra Pradesh

RAM K. VEPA

It is commonly recognized that the administration at the district and sub-district levels forms the pivot of the entire framework of administration of the country. Increasing recognition has been accorded in recent years to the need for an effective administrative structure at these levels. The V.T. Krishnamachari report on district administration some years back and the numerous state reports on the problems of district administration testify to this fact. The Administrative Reforms Commission has also given considerable thought to the need for reorganization of district administration. With the implementation aspect of the Plan projects becoming increasingly important, it is only natural that the pattern of administration at the district level should figure prominently in all discussions of Administrative Reforms.

IMPACT OF PANCHAYATI RAJ SYSTEM

There has, however, been a significant development in the last ten years which has made a considerable impact on traditional district administration. The system of elected leadership at the village, block and district levels embodied in the Panchayati Raj pattern has made a significant impact on the effectiveness of district administration. Panchayati Raj has introduced a new element in district administration; since 1959 when Rajasthan and Andhra Pradesh first introduced the Panchayati Raj system, it has practically spread all over the country in some form or the other. Although local self-government has had a long history in India beginning with Lord Ripon, there is a significant difference between the old taluka and district boards and the newer Panchayat Samithis and Zilla Parishads set up under the Panchayati Raj pattern. While the former institutions were largely meant to train local leadership who operated in a narrow framework, the newer institutions, such as the Panchayat Samithis and Zilla Parishads are conceived as integral parts of development administration.

Basically the Panchayati Raj pattern is similar in almost all the States: at the village level there is an elected body known as Panchayat which is presided over by a Sarpanch who has executive powers of administration. At the block (and in some cases the taluka levels) there is another body commonly known as the Panchayat Samithi which is organically related to the Panchayat by the Sarpanch being automatically a member of the Panchayat Samithi. The executive functions at the Samithi level are handled by Block Development Officer (drawn mostly from the revenue department) and a team of officials who are to implement the resolutions of the Panchayat Samithi. At the district level there is a Zilla Parishad consisting of all the presidents of the Panchayat Samithis as well as the Members of the Legislature presided over by a non-official elected chairman. The Secretary of the Zilla Parishad who is from the permanent official cadre, supervises the implementation of the resolutions passed by the Zilla Parishads.

ROLE OF THE DISTRICT COLLECTOR

Although there are minor variations in the Panchayati Raj pattern at the block and village levels, the most significant difference in the pattern is at the District level and particularly with regard to the role of the District Collector (or the Deputy Commissioner as he is called in some States). In fact, the role of the Collector in the Panchayati Raj pattern has been a hardy annual at all meetings of the Development Commissioners year after year. One might particularly note the role allotted to the Collector in three significant variations of the pattern. In Madras, the District Development Council (as the Zilla Parishad is called in that State) is purely an advisory body and is presided over by the Collector as, in fact, was originally envisaged in the Balwant Rai Mehta report on democratic decentralization which initiated the Panchayati Raj system. In Andhra Pradesh, the Collector is a member of the Zilla Parishad and is also the chairman of all the standing committees where executive decisions are to be taken. In Maharashtra, on the other hand, there has recently been a trend to keep the Collector completely out of the Zilla Parishad and to function merely as an observer at the district level. An equal ranking officer from the Indian Administrative Service has, however, been provided to the Zilla Parishads to function as its chief executive officer and to supervise the implementation of the development plans at the district level. It is significant that while in Andhra Pradesh a few executive functions, such as secondary education, major communications, etc., have been allotted to the Zilla Parishad, the Zilla Parishads in Maharashtra have been made responsible for the entire spectrum of development effort.

Although not enough time has lapsed to evaluate the performance of varying patterns of the Panchayati Raj system at the district level, it is apparent that each of these suffers from some defect or other. In Madras, for instance, the complete absence of executive functions to the District Development Council reduces that body to ineffectiveness and makes the Collector more or less independent of its decisions. While this may contribute to speed and even efficiency, it is to be recognized that the democratic element which is sought to be introduced through Panchayati Raj is significantly absent in such an arrangement. If local leadership is to be developed, the Madras pattern does not provide any method by which this could be done. On the other hand, in the Maharashtra pattern the role of the Collector is completely reduced and one wonders whether in course of time the institution of the Collector itself will wither away. With a de-emphasis on the revenue and agricultural functions at the district level (except in sporadic cases of disturbances) the role of the Collector as a representative of the government is likely to be more ceremonial than functional. The chief executive officer of the Zilla Parishad would in effect operate as the development head of the district; whether this system of two functionaries of equal rank at the district level is desirable or not is somewhat debatable. A cardinal principle of the traditional system introduced two centuries ago at the district level is the unity of command and much of the success of that pattern can be attributed to this principle. It is, therefore, doubtful whether the Maharashtra system of having two functionaries at the district level would in practice work smoothly, particularly in the case of emergency, as is arising more often in recent years. The Andhra Pradesh system has worked reasonably well although the relative roles of the Collector and Zilla Parishad Chairman are somewhat delicately balanced. There have been instances where friction has developed between these two in some districts, but much depends upon the personal adjustments each would make towards the other.

RAJU COMMITTEE REPORT

In view of the considerable dissatisfaction amongst the public as to the implementation of the Plan schemes, the Government of Andhra Pradesh appointed in April 1967, a Committee with Shri M. T. Raju, then first member, Board of Revenue (and currently, Chief Secretary to Government of Andhra Pradesh) as chairman to devise methods by which the implementation of plan schemes could be more effectively done at the district level. The committee, in almost record time, submitted a report to the government outlining completely a new pattern of district administration, which was discussed at various conferences both of the collectors and chairmen, Zilla Parishads as well of the leading officials and non-officials at the state level. After a considerable debate, the Government of Andhra Pradesh have recently decided (in November, 1967) to accept the recommendations of the Raju Committee Report and are proposing to implement them shortly. In view of the considerable significance that is attached to the recommendations made in this report, it is proposed to outline them briefly and to discuss them in the rest of the article. It is somewhat significant that at a recent seminar held at Hyderabad by the Andhra Pradesh Regional Branch of the Indian Institute of Public Administration and attended to by the Regional Branches of Madras, Mysore, Kerala and Maharashtra, the recommendations of this report evoked keen interest and considerable discussion.

The relevant extracts of the government order embodying the recommendations of the Raju Report are given in the Appendix (p. 261). The main features of the report, however, are the formation of a Zilla Development Board for each district, which shall consist of the District Collector as Chairman and the Chairman, Zilla Parishad as a member. For the present, the Secretary, Zilla Parishad (who is a Revenue Officer of the rank of a Deputy Collector) will function as Secretary of the Board. The Zilla Development Board will be responsible for the overall economic growth of the district and will formulate as well as implement the programmes designed to secure such growth and in particular programmes connected with agricultural and industrial production. At the beginning of each year the Board will prepare a draft district plan incorporating agricultural and industrial production programme for the year based on the allotments made available to it by the various state heads of departments. The Board has also been given power to re-allocate the budgetary provisions under the same head, exercising the powers of the head of the department.

The district plan shall broadly consist of an estimate of the additional production of agricultural and industrial products, time schedule for their execution, and the period within the additional anticipated production is likely to materialize. The plan is to be placed before the Zilla Parishads and after its approval will be implemented by the various departments at the district level. The Board is expected to meet at least once in a month (and oftener as may be necessary) to review the progress of implementation of the district plans in the light of the inspection reports submitted by the District Officers and the revenue divisional officers.

The implementation of some of the schemes would continue to be undertaken by the Zilla Parishads and Panchayat Samithis in such fields as education, communications, health and social welfare. Schemes relating to agricultural production and industrial growth which at present lie normally outside these bodies have, however, been brought under the purview of the Zilla Development Board. The Board has, therefore, a co-ordinated view of the entire development plan of the district which is now fragmented between the Zilla Parishads, Panchayat Samithis as well as the various departments at the district levels.

To ensure effective implementation of the integrated district plans, the agriculture, irrigation, co-operation, Panchayati Raj, and industries departments have been placed directly under the Collector at the district level. Suitable financial and administrative powers now being exercised by the heads of departments are being delegated to the Collectors, to whom the present District Officers of these departments will function as Personal Assistants.

To relieve the Collector of revenue, civil supplies and other matters which at present take up a considerable portion of his time, posts of District Revenue Officers have been created to be manned by IAS officers working under the administrative control of the Collector. At the sub-divisional level the Revenue Divisional Officer has been placed directly in the picture for the effective implementation of the district plans in respect of the blocks within his jurisdiction. He shall attend meetings of the Panchayat Samitis and shall send frequent reports to the Zilla Development Board on the implementation of the various plans in his sub-division.

At the state level, a State-level Development Board has been constituted with the Chief Secretary (who is also the Development Commissioner) as Chairman, Members of the Board of Revenue, Secretaries to Government in the P.W.D., Agriculture, Panchayati Raj, Industries and Finance as well as heads of departments connected with the plan schemes as Members. It is the State Development Board that will be responsible for supervision of the implementation of the district plans. The members of the Development Board are expected to tour the districts extensively and inspect as many works as possible. The Board also would meet at different district headquarters so as to obtain a first-hand knowledge of the implementation of these schemes.

DISCUSSION

It is interesting to highlight some of the important points of difference in the framework of district administration envisaged in the Raju Committee Report as compared to what is existing at present.

1. For the first time, the Raju Committee Report breaks new ground in formally assigning a key role to the Collector in the development administration. In recent years, there has been considerable speculation as to whether the post of Collector was still necessary and in some states like Maharashtra the Collector has been reduced to a complete non-entity as far as development work is concerned. The Raju Report brings back the Collector right into the centre

of the picture and makes him in fact a key functionary in the entire pattern of development administration.

2. The Report harmonizes the traditional pattern of administration at the district level which has operated for two centuries with the new Panchayati Raj pattern. It is significant that the Chairman of the Zilla Parishad is the only other member of the Zilla Development Board where his views would naturally carry greater weight in the decisions of the Board. It is also significant that no powers at present being exercised by the Zilla Parishad or the Panchayat Samitis have been taken away from them, and that a new institution has been created to supplement their efforts in the district.

3. The emphasis in the Raju Report is on *implementation* of plans since it has been recognized (and widely accepted) that a basic weakness of the present system is poor implementation rather than formulation. It is, therefore, significant that a much greater responsibility has been placed on the Collector and the team of officials on the proper implementation of the plans once a broad approval of the plan has been given by the Zilla Parishad. The frequent review of the implementation by the District Development Board and the State-level Board would serve to pin-point any administrative weaknesses which could be remedied immediately. In this respect the Andhra Pradesh scheme corresponds closely to the pattern of community development administration which is being practised with much success in Malaysia where each district headquarter has a complete statistics of the plans and target of achievements in the district which are reviewed by the minister concerned through frequent visits to the headquarters. It is, therefore, considered that the recommendations of the Raju Committee Report would certainly focus greater attention on the need for better implementation of the existing plans.

At the recent seminar at Hyderabad (to which a reference has been made earlier) some doubts were expressed on the framework conceived in the Raju Committee Report. It was suggested whether it would not be desirable to leave the powers of the Collector somewhat vague and indefinite as at present and let him work out through conventions a role for himself in the development administration rather than lay down any formal scheme of control. While there may be some validity in this approach, it was recognized that in view of the important tasks to be done in the near future, it would be undesirable to leave them merely to conventions which would largely depend upon the personality of the Collector. In view of the need for a rapid economic growth at the district level, it was felt that a more formal framework should be established in which the Collector and his team of officers are given greater powers and their performance assessed in the light of that responsibility.

Another apprehension which was expressed was whether the Collector could function as a head of the department at the district level and if so, whether he would be a subordinate to the head of the department. It was also felt that the heads of departments themselves might feel less committed to the implementation of the plans in view of the greater role being allotted to the Collector at the district level. It was, however, explained that there was no inherent conflict in the role of head of department and that of Collector. In fact, if an *ex-officio* status were accorded to the Head of the Department as is being contemplated in most of the states, there would be nothing anomalous in the work of the Collector being assessed by the Head of the Department who is normally expected to be senior to the Collector in service. In any case, the Head of the Department operates at the state level making provision of funds and keeping an overall perspective of the working of the department at the state level while the Collector's work would be confined to that of the district. In fact, the Collector would be a supplemental agency of the Head of the Department in achieving the targets allotted to each department of the state.

A third doubt was expressed whether the Panchayati Raj institutions would reconcile themselves to the setting up of a new institution at the district level, which might take away something of their prestige. As has been mentioned earlier, no power now being exercised by the Zilla Parishads and Panchayat Samithis has been taken away from them. The constitution of a Zilla Development Board which is purely an executive committee was merely to bring a measure of co-ordination with the entire development plans which is at present lacking since some of them are implemented through the Panchayati Raj institutions and others through government departments. The membership of the Chairman, Zilla Parishad in the Development Board would, in fact, enhance the prestige of the Zilla Parishad as a whole and it was felt that a more effective implementation of the plans would, in the ultimate analysis, bring credit to the Panchayati Raj institutions. In fact, much of the criticism now being made against the Panchayati Raj bodies would perhaps diminish if there were a more effective implementation of the development plans and to that extent it was felt the success of the Panchayati Raj pattern was likely to be enhanced rather than affected by a more effective framework being provided at the district level.

CONCLUSION

The consensus at the Hyderabad seminar was that the new system of administration envisaged in the Raju Committee Report marked a radical departure from recent trends and was more in tune with the pattern of administration that had existed so long. However, it may be watched and assessed after some time after which it could well be adopted by many other states. It was also felt that a success of such a system would depend largely upon the personnel concerned and particularly on the type of Collectors posted to the districts. It was felt that these should be of sufficient maturity in age and seniority in service to be able to lead the team of officials at the district level. It was suggested that at least a ten-year seniority might normally be considered for a District Collector who should bring to his office not merely sympathy with popular aspirations, but also administrative efficiency and an enthusiasm to get the work done. It was also considered that a person once posted should be retained for at least three years to be able to function with some effectiveness. With the right type of personnel manning these posts, it was felt that there was no reason why a scheme of administration envisaged in the Raju Committee Report should not succeed. In the last analysis it is administration at the district and sub-district levels that is closest to the people, and any success achieved at these levels in better administration would ensure better returns on the considerable expenditure being incurred on development effort and consequently generate greater public enthusiasm for the plans.

APPENDIX

Reorganized Pattern of District Administration

There shall be a Zilla Development Board for each district which shall be constituted as follows:

1. District Collector *Chairman*
2. Chairman, Zilla Parishad

For the present, the Secretary, Zilla Parishad shall serve as Secretary of the Board.

The Zilla Development Board shall be responsible for the economic growth of the district. It will be the task of the Board to formulate and implement programmes designed to secure the economic growth of the district and in particular programmes connected with agricultural and industrial production. These programmes will include irrigation, power, animal husbandry, fisheries, co-operation and marketing.

FORMULATION OF THE DISTRICT PLAN

The state heads of departments concerned with schemes relating to agricultural and industrial production including irrigation, minor irrigation and rural electrification shall, within 15 days of the budget allotments being made for them, furnish to the Collector of each district a list of schemes, both plan and non-plan, intended to be taken up in that district during the year. The district heads of departments will simultaneously furnish to the Collector their proposals for utilization of the growth potential available within the district for which no budgetary provision as such is necessary. The Panchayat Samithis shall also simultaneously furnish to the Collector plans pertaining to agricultural and industrial production which are to be financed from their own funds. The Collector shall convene a meeting of the Zilla Development Board to which the district heads of departments concerned shall also be invited. The Board will examine the production potentialities of each of these schemes and fix targets of production which are to be achieved under these schemes during the year. The Board will thus prepare a draft Integrated Agricultural and Industrial Production Plan for the year calculated to secure maximum production with the available resources (referred to as the District Plan hereafter). For this purpose, the Board shall have powers to re-allocate the budgetary provisions under the same head exercising the powers of a Head of Department.

The draft District Plan so prepared shall be placed before the Zilla Parishad for its approval.

Any new scheme related to economic growth formulated hereafter by any department shall contain an estimate of:

1. Additional production of agricultural and industrial products as the case may be;
2. Time schedule for the execution of the scheme; and
3. The period within which the anticipated additional production will materialize.

Every such scheme shall be referred to the Zilla Development Board which will examine the estimate aforesaid of the additional production envisaged and the anticipated period of its materialization. Only in the light of the commitment that the Board will undertake in regard to the prospects of additional production will the accord of sanction for such schemes be considered.

Implementation

It shall be the responsibility of the Zilla Development Board to implement the district plan and achieve the targets envisaged tinder it. The Board shall meet once a month and as oftener as may be necessary to review the progress of implementation of the district plan in the light of the inspection reports submitted by the District Officers and revenue divisional officers. The Board will report to the State Board of Development, proposed to be constituted, every quarter the progress of the execution of the plan, marking copies of relevant extracts to the concerned heads of department. This progress report will also be laid before the Zilla Parishad. At the end of the year the Zilla Development Board shall submit a report to the State Board indicating the economic growth achieved and explaining the short-falls, if any, and the reasons therefor. The State Board will submit an annual report to government reviewing the economic growth achieved in each of the district.

Parishad and Samithi Level

Of the various fields of activity undertaken by the Zilla Parishad and the Panchayat Samithis, those relating to education, communications and amenities programmes like health and social welfare account for most of their budget provisions. These subjects fall outside the purview of the Zilla Development Board. The only schemes which fall within the purview of the district plan will be schemes relating to agricultural and industrial production. Even these will continue to be administered by them in the same manner as hithertofore. The Zilla Development Board will be concerned with these schemes only for the purpose of securing their integration in the district plan and for their implementation according to the time schedule. The Zilla Parishads and the Panchayat Samithis will be responsible for implementation of the schemes included in the district plan falling within their purview.

Administrative Changes

In order to ensure efficient implementation of the integrated district plans, the following departments will be brought within the purview of these orders at the district level: (1) agriculture, (2) irrigation, (3) co-operation, (4) Panchayati Raj, and (5) industries. The Collector shall be the head of each of these departments in the district, except irrigation. In order to enable the Collector to discharge his duties effectively in the reorganized set-up, the Committee has given its recommendations in its report on May 20, 1967 about: (1) the financial and other powers to be delegated to the Collectors; and (2) the reorganized set-up of the departments at the district level.

The recommendations of the Committee on both these aspects have been accepted by the government. Formal orders delegating the powers to the Collectors in accordance with (1) above will be issued by the concerned departments of the Secretariat.

The following shall be the administrative set-up at the district level in respect of the departments mentioned above:

1. *Co-operative Department*: One additional post of Special Category Deputy Registrar in the scale of Rs. 600-50-1,000 is sanctioned for each district. The Special Category Deputy Registrar of Co-operative Societies will work under the administrative control of the Collector and will function as P.A. to Collector. The posts of Regional Joint Registrars will be abolished with effect from the date the Special Category Deputy Registrars of Cooperative Societies are appointed.
2. *Agriculture Department*: There shall be one Deputy Director of Agriculture for each district. At present there are already 11 Deputy Directors of Agriculture. Nine posts of Deputy Directors of Agriculture are, therefore, sanctioned to provide for the posting of one Deputy Director of Agriculture for each district. The Deputy Director of Agriculture will also function as P.A. to the Collector. The expenditure on this account shall be met from the savings under the I.A.A.P. and I.A.D.P. schemes.
3. *Industries Department*: The Assistant Director of Industries already existing in each district will work under the administrative control of the Collector. The Regional Offices of the Joint Directors of Industries will be abolished and the Joint Directors will be transferred to the Headquarters Directorate of Industries, and will function on a state-wide basis as subject-matter specialists.
4. *Irrigation*: In the case of irrigation, the Executive Engineer (Irrigation) shall be under the administrative control of the Collector: (*a*) in respect of the execution of sanctioned works included in the district plan; and (*b*) in respect of items which are within the competence of the Executive Engineer and for which concurrence of the Collector is required under existing orders.
5. *Other Departments*: The other district heads shall carry out such directions as may be issued by the Collector from time to time in regard to the implementation of the schemes included in the district plan.
6. *Revenue Administration in the Districts*: In order to relieve the Collector of the revenue and civil supplies work, so as

to enable him to devote himself entirely to development work, the government agree with the recommendations of the Committee and sanction one post of District Revenue Officer, in the senior time scale of the I.A.S., for each district. The District Revenue Officer will work under the administrative control of the Collector.

Formal orders regarding the posting of Special Category Deputy Registrars arid Deputy Directors of Agriculture will be issued by the Food and Agriculture Department. Separate orders will be issued by the General Administration (Special) Department regarding the posting of District Revenue Officers.

7. *Divisional Level*: The Revenue Divisional Officer will be responsible for the supervision and effective implementation of the District Plan in respect of Blocks within his jurisdiction. He shall be the reviewing and evaluating authority in respect of schemes included in the plan which fall within his division. He should make frequent field inspections, locate bottlenecks and see that action is taken for these being removed. He shall send inspection reports of the Collector so that the Zilla Development Board may be apprised of the progress of the schemes. The Revenue Divisional Officer shall attend the meetings of the Panchayat Samithis and staff meetings of the Blocks in his jurisdiction. The district heads will furnish to the Revenue Divisional Officer from time to time their notes of inspection on the work of their field staff in relation to their schemes within his Division.

State Level

There shall be a Development Board at the State level which shall be constituted as follows:

1.	Chief Secretary and Development Commissioner	Chairman
2.	Members, Board of Revenue for Irrigation and Ayacut Development.	Members
3.	Special Secretary to Government, Public Works Department	Member

4.	Special Secretary to Government, Food & Agriculture Department	Member
5.	Special Secretary to Government & Commissioner, Panchayati Raj	Member
6.	Secretary to Government, Industries Department	Member
7.	Secretary to Government, Finance Department	Member
8.	Director of Agriculture	Member
9.	Registrar of Cooperative Societies	Member
10.	Director of Industries	Member
11.	Chief Engineer (General)	Member
12.	Joint Secretary to Government, Planning Department	Member-Secretary.

The State Development Board will be responsible for supervising the proper implementation of the district plans. It will also review the progress of the various district plans. The members will tour intensively in the districts and inspect as many works as possible. The Board itself could meet in different districts by turns.

The State Development Board will be responsible not merely for the district plans but also for other Plan schemes relating to agricultural and industrial production.

15

Changing Pattern of Development Administration in the District

C.N. BHALERAO

The development administration in the district plays an important role as an instrument of socio-economic change in Indian rural society. Theoretically, the role of the administration in the Panchayati Raj programme is that of providing technical advice and guidance to Panchayati Raj institutions and executing development programmes. The fundamental approach to be followed in the execution of development programmes is that of community development which seeks to involve the village people in their own social and economic development, thereby making the village masses effective working groups in programmes of national development. It is assumed by the authors of Panchayati Raj programme that decentralization of powers and functions to Panchayati Raj institutions will result in the participation of the local community in development programmes which would enable the administration to implement the programmes more effectively. It is outside the scope of this paper to examine whether the present approach to securing popular participation in rural development programme; at the present stage of development, is sound, though this is an important question and needs a more thorough analysis than attempted hitherto.[1] An unrealistic or confused approach to this can undermine the role of the bureaucracy in the initial and important phase of the programme of rural development.

THE SUBSTANTIVE ASPECTS OF ADMINISTRATION

There have been various studies on district administration in

India.[2] While these studies have drawn attention to various weaknesses of the administrative system in the district, the reforms made in the administration so far have had little impact on its general standards and effectiveness. The failure to raise administrative competence to the desired level is largely due to a wrong approach to the question of administrative reforms. The approach followed by Government (and also in research studies by some Universities) is based on a mechanical and isolated view of administration; it conceives of administration in purely technical and formal terms, with its emphasis on organization, methods and procedures. It is true that administration is a technical process; but administration as part of the governmental process can be understood empirically only in its relation to the politics of government, the social structure and economic organization of society. Administration both influences and is influenced by social and political development. It is this process of complex interaction between administration and society which is becoming a major concern of empirical studies on administration in developing countries.

The problems of administration in developing societies arise mainly as a result of the conflict between traditional administrative practices and the need for a dynamic and modern system of administration on the one hand, and between traditional society and the administration which is being oriented towards the goals of development and popular participation, on the other. This conflict is leading to tensions and disequilibrium both within the traditional rural society and the development administration. The tensions and conflicts in the administration can be resolved only when there is a balanced form of development in which the political process is responsive to the needs and issues of society and in which the political leadership is committed to an organizational and administrative revolution.

LACK OF DYNAMIC LEADERSHIP

A fundamental feature of Indian administration is the increasing inter-play of politics and administration at all levels of government, resulting in the politicization and debureaucratization of administration. The most important field in which politics adversely affects the efficiency of governmental administration is the formation of the Cabinet and the allocation of portfolios to ministers. The Ministries of Panchayati Raj and Rural Development are generally considered unimportant and consequently, they are given under the charge of relatively less able ministers.[3] These ministries are often hampered by their conflicts with Food and Agriculture ministries with the result that practically the entire rural development programme and its organization presents a picture of confusion. In general, as a result of the considerations which influence the selection of ministers, inter-ministerial conflicts and a lack of communication between field experience and policy-making, the governmental leadership in the development programme has not been able to display a dynamic approach to the problem of rural development. This is clearly evidenced by the adoption of wrong priorities in rural planning and lack of comprehension of the substantive issues involved in development administration.

POLITICIZATION

Recent studies on development administration indicate that the officials are increasingly coming under the political control of the non-officials. The officials are afraid of the non-officials because of the latter's connections with the higher-ups in the party and the power to write annual confidential reports on the officials and to generally manage their transfers. The Block Development and Extension Officers, afraid of their political superiors, tend to conform to the dictates of the non-officials even when they are convinced that it may not be in the public interest to do so. It is observed that the non-officials also tend to interfere with the day-to-day administration of the Panchayati Raj institutions. Further, the factional groups, especially in the Panchayat Samithis, cut across the administration. Some of the officials appear to have become almost full-fledged politicians and are learning to play their "politics" skillfully enough to be free from the harassment of constant transfers or transfers to isolated and unimportant areas and to command good prospects in their jobs. The politicization of development administration is on the increase and is gradually undermining its independence and standards of efficiency and is leading to more and more frustration in the bureaucracy. It is to be noted, however, that this interaction between bureaucracy and politics is making the former less authoritarian and, to some extent responsive to the needs of the society.

THE ADMINISTRATION AND SOCIETY

A basic reason for the increasing politicization of development administration in India is the lack of effective channels of democratic political participation and inadequate communication between political leadership and society and between the administration and society. There is not a well-spread democratic infrastructure of effective voluntary organizations and interest groups in society through which the people could participate in the political decision-making process and development in the district. A large number of existing voluntary organizations at the lower level represent vested interests, are bureaucratic and are characterized by factional politics and do not permit free participation by the individual. The only way to arrest this trend is to activise and democratize the existing, and encourage the growth of new, voluntary organizations in society and build up active channels of communication between the people and administration.[4]

The test of an effective democratic and developmental administration is the extent to which it represents the needs and experience of the rural society and acts as an effective instrument of social change. Some studies indicate that many of the Village Level Workers, the Extension Officers and Social Education Organizers do not possess rural background[5] and are consequently unable to mobilize or catalyze human resources, to motivate the village people and to exercise leadership or even to provide adequate guidance to rural groups. This failure to respond to the needs and desires of the rural community is also due to inadequate technical training and knowledge of the dynamics of community development. It has been rightly emphasized that the basic cause for these shortcomings has been "insufficient understanding and use of social skills in the motivation of village people plus an inadequate understanding of the network of human relationships in villages, and the ways by which both technical assistants and administrators can effectively communicate with those whom they seek to serve".[6] The development bureaucracy cannot play much useful role in rural development unless it makes use of proper social skills and motivation techniques. This can be done only when the development bureaucracy and its leadership possess an intimate knowledge of the problems and processes of rural society and are devoted to the tasks of rural transformation.

BUREAUCRATIC CULTURE

Some change is no doubt taking place in the values, outlook and methods of working of the development bureaucracy. The bureaucracy is gradually learning to implement development programmes with the cooperation of the rural people and their representatives; it is also becoming conscious of its responsibility to the elected representative of the people. But, beyond this change, the administration does not appear to have undergone any basic changes in its *modus operandi.* Generally the administration functions in a mechanical manner, following more the quantitative criterion of performance rather than the qualitative one. The statistics in terms of tours and visits, amount and materials shown by the officials are impressive but they do not correspond to the quality of performance. Two factors have an important bearing on the mechanical mode of functioning of the administration—the qualities and motivation of the officials and the methods and procedures of the administration. Regarding the first, the State Governments do not appear to have given much thought to the qualities and background required of the development officials, especially at the lower level. It is observed that while recruiting the administrative personnel, such important qualities like initiative and aptitude for social service and social skills are not kept in view. In this connection, a strong case can be made out for the recruitment of trained and devoted social workers and persons with social science background to man important positions in development administration. Secondly, the earlier bureaucratic methods and procedures of administration and disregard for the needs and difficulties of the rural masses still continue. The development administration is generally characterized by delay, excessive formalism and paper work, attachment to precedents and rigid procedures and concentration of authority at higher levels resulting in inaction in administration and frustration among the people. The administration is also considerably frustrated owing to lack of a dynamic programme of personnel management and incentives for better performance.

Bureaucratic culture in India thus exhibits four main characteristics. Firstly, it is characterized by an impersonal way of operation, rigidly adhering to formal rules, precedents and procedures. Secondly, there is a pervasive sense of insecurity and frustration among the officials. Thirdly, there are barriers of communication between the higher and lower bureaucracy. And fourthly, the bureaucracy does not permit initiative, responsibility, innovation and challenge; in the absence of these qualities, the bureaucracy becomes an obstacle to change. As Prof. Lucian W. Pye points out in regard to Burmese administration, "paradoxically, the logical agents for change seem in many ways to be as changeless as any aspect of a transitional society can be. The very men who should be champions of innovation and initiators of action if the country is to develop are to an alarming degree the victims of immobilism".[7]

POSITION OF THE DISTRICT COLLECTOR

Panchayati Raj programme is undermining more and more the position of the District Collector as the pivot and coordinator of district administration in most of the States. On the one hand, the responsibilities of the Collector as District Development Officer have increased, making it difficult for him to effectively administer the development programme of the district along with his law and order and revenue functions. On the other hand, his effective administrative power over development administration has diminished. In short, the Collector today has responsibilities without effective powers. The Collectors are also being subjected to political pressures and influences and are becoming afraid of the politicians in the Zilla Parishad. In a democratic set-up, the Collector has no doubt to be responsible to the representatives of the people; but the point to be noted here is that the nature of political control on the Collector is such that it is undermining his independence, impartiality and effectiveness.

The Collector, like the other development officials, is in search of a new identity and a new image about his role and office. The demands made on his skills and the needed re-ordering of old values and attitudes and the development of new ones are resulting in profound contradictions in his role.

NEED FOR CO-ORDINATION

Sometimes the Block Development Officer is unable to achieve proper co-ordination of work at the Samithi level as some of his Extension Officers join hands with a factional group of the Samithi; in some cases they also oppose the B.D.O. at the level of the District Officers. The existence of factions in the Samithi and their alliance with some Extension Officers or opposition to the B.D.O. results in the loss of team spirit and unity of the Samithi administrative staff. Vertical co-ordination, *i.e.*, between the block and district administration, also appears to be considerably lacking. The main reason which accounts for the lack of vertical co-ordination is the dual control exercised on the Extension Officers by the B.D.O. and by the respective technical heads of the district departments. Similarly, the B.D.O. is subjected to a dual control—one by the Samithi and the other by the district departments. Co-ordination is not merely a technical function; it also involves harmonious relations and adjustments both between and among the officials and non-officials. Further, co-ordination at the lower level depends upon the degree of clarity and the quality of planning and organization by governmental leadership.

CORRUPTION

With the enormous growth of bureaucracy under Panchayati Raj and the multiplication of administration processes, a vast field has been opened in which the officials can misuse their power, sometimes in alliance with the non-officials. Corruption in the administration is partly due to the low salaries of the officials and partly to the prevalence of ubiquitous corruption at the political level. It is observed that corruption in rural areas tends to assume the character of an unwritten and all pervasive law of administrative functioning and operates in an organized manner at the lower levels of administration.[8]

A Study Team[9] recently reported that there are serious irregularities in the financial transactions of Panchayati Raj institutions. These irregularities include wrong postings in cash-books, purchases without calling for tenders, non-maintenance of stock-registers, bad maintenance of accounts and unauthorized expenditure. This finding indicates that a good deal of manipulation of finances takes place in Panchayati Raj institutions. It is admitted that the lack of adequate financial resources of Panchayati Raj bodies is one of the major obstacles in the effective performance of their functions. But a mere increase in the financial resources of these institutions does not ensure their utilization in public interest. An equally urgent need is to make the officials and non-officials more responsible to the people (by spreading education and enlightenment among the rural people and establishing conditions of socio-economic equality) and evolve proper standards and procedures in financial transactions.

Prof. Myron Weiner refers to the class of "expeditors" which has emerged in India both within and outside the administrative services and argues that "not all corruption is dysfunctional to the goals of economic development".[10] It is true that the expeditor in a developing society performs functions which are ordinarily performed within the administrative system of a modern society. The problem in a developing society, however, is that such a function by the "expeditor" in administration or politics proves to be extremely disadvantageous for the weaker sections and intensifies economic disparities between the "haves" and the "havenots".

STRUCTURAL WEAKNESSES

The characteristics of a sound administrative structure are that it provides for clear allocation of responsibilities, clear accountability and adequate delegation of powers at lower levels. The existing structure of development administration does not appear to possess these characteristics. Recent studies indicate that the officials generally do not fully carry out their responsibilities partly because of the persistent fear that they would be held accountable for any lapses and partly because their responsibilities are diffused. Confusion in responsibilities also arises out of the dual and, in some cases, triple control exercised over the officials. Again, it is found that there is a lack of adequate delegation of powers at the lower level of administration. The lower officials do not possess discretion and freedom to deal with the problems faced by them in the field, follow a pattern of functioning indicated at higher levels and are reluctant to "displease" their superiors by exercising their independence and initiative. Thus, the structure of development administration is one which discourages responsibility, delegation and initiative and leads to confusion and poor administrative performance.

We have examined in this paper some of the main features and substantive issues of development administration in the district. The development administration in India is marked by three features. Firstly, it is being heavily politicized and consequently it is losing its independence, impartiality and effectiveness. This, in itself, is not a dangerous trend since a democratic administration must be ultimately responsible to the elected representatives of the people. But here the danger is that the administration may lose its minimum professional autonomy and virtually become an arm of the ruling party. Second, there are no active channels of communication between the administration and rural society. And third, though the bureaucracy is undergoing some change in its values and outlook, it is basically of the old pattern and, both in terms of the qualities and background of its personnel and its methods and procedures of working, does not appear to act as a dynamic agent in social change. The utility of the existing development bureaucracy to act as an active instrument of socio-economic change in the rural society will depend upon the operative standards followed by the ruling political party and the emerging political leadership at lower levels, the calibre of government leadership, the emerging balance between professional autonomy of the bureaucracy and the political control on it, the calibre of lower bureaucracy and the quality of personnel management programme, the development of more suitable methods of community development work and the building up of active channels of communication between the administration and society at all levels in the district.

REFERENCES

1. The need for public co-operation, at the present stage of development, has been challenged by Sisir Gupta in "Indian Democracy: What Gives it Stability", *The Economic Weekly,* Special Number, June 1960. Also *see* W.H. Morris-Jones, "Democratic Decentralisation: Some Political Consequences", *The Economic Weekly,* Special Number, July 1962 and Samuel P. Huntington, "Political Development and Political Decay", *World Politics,* Vol. XVII, No. 3, April 1965. For an opposite view, *see*

Joseph La Palombara, "An Overview of Bureaucracy and Political Development" in *Bureaucracy and Political Development*, Princeton, New Jersey, 1963.

2. *India, Report on Indian and Slate Administrative Services and Problems of District Administration*, V.T. Krishnamachari, Planning Commission, New Delhi, 1962, S.S. Khera, *District Administration in India*, I.I.P.A., New Delhi 1960, and *Report of the Administrative Survey of Surat District*, N.B. Desai, Bombay, Indian Agricultural Society, 1958.
3. *See* "An Exercise without Novelty", Krishan Bhatia, *The Hindustan Times*, July 30, 1965.
4. C.N. Bhalerao, "Substantive Forces in Indian Administration", *The Economic Weekly*, October 17, 1964.
5. Taylor, Ensminger, Johnson and Joyee, *India's Roots of Democracy*, Calcutta, Orient Longman, 1965, p. 628.
6. *Ibid.*, p. 679.
7. Lucian W. Pye, *Politics, Personality and Nation-Building. Burmese Search for Identity*, New Haven and London, Yale University Press, 1964, p. 213,
8. *See* T.N. Chaturvedi, "Tensions in Panchayati Raj: Relations between Officials and Non-officials", *The Economic Weekly*, May 30, 1964.
9. *India, Report on the Audit of Accounts of Panchayati Raj Institutions*, New Delhi, Union Ministry of Community Development and Cooperation, 1965 (unpublished).
10. "India: Two Political Cultures" in *Political Culture and Political Development* Ed. Lucian W. Pye and Sydney Verba, New Jersey, Princeton University Press, 1965, pp. 221-24.

Index